中国寓言故事

Chinese Fables and Folktales

Translated by Donia Davia Zhang

Chinese Culture Publishing

While every precaution has been taken in the preparation of this book, the publisher assumes no responsibility for errors or omissions, or for damages resulting from the use of the information contained herein.

CHINESE FABLES AND FOLKTALES

First edition. August 7, 2025.

English Translation Copyright © 2025 Donia Davia Zhang.

ISBN: 978-1-7381946-8-1

Translated by Donia Davia Zhang.

Contents

A

1: 安如泰山，固若金汤 — 1
As Stable as Mount Tai, As Solid as a Metal City

2: 按兵不动 — 2
Keeping Your Troops Still

3: 暗度陈仓 — 3
Secretly Passing Through Chencang

B

4: 百闻不如一见，百见不如一干 — 5
Seeing is Believing, Doing is Believing

5: 百折不挠 — 6
Indomitable Spirit and Unyielding Faith

6: 别开生面 — 7
Breaking a New Path

7: 宾至如归 — 8
Guests Feeling at Home

8: 伯乐相马 — 9
Bole Identifying Qianlima

9: 不打不相识 — 10
No Fight, No Acquaintance

10: 不入虎穴，焉得虎子 — 11
Without Entering Tiger's Den, One Cannot Catch Tiger's Cubs

C

11: 成也萧何，败也萧何 — 12
Success and Failure Are Both Due to Xiao He

12: 城门失火，殃及池鱼 — 14
When the City Gate Caught Fire, the Fish in the Moat Were Affected

13:	乘风破浪	15
	Riding the Winds and Breaking the Waves	
14:	乘龙快婿	16
	Dragon-Riding Son-in-Law	
15:	惩一警百	17
	Punishing One to Warn Hundreds	
16:	出奇制胜	18
	Surprise Victory	
17:	初出茅庐	19
	A Newcomer from a Thatched Cottage	
18:	初生牛犊不怕虎	20
	A Newborn Calf Is Not Afraid of a Tiger	
19:	此地无银三百两	21
	There Is No Three Hundred Taels of Silver Here	

D

20:	打草惊蛇	22
	Stirring the Grass and Startling the Snake	
21:	大器晚成	23
	Great Talents Mature Late	
22:	呆若木鸡	24
	As Dumb as a Wooden Chicken	
23:	东窗事发	25
	Plot Under the East Window Has Been Exposed	
24:	东山再起	27
	Rising Again on the East Mountain	
25:	东施效颦	28
	Dong Shi Imitating Xi Shi's Frown	
26:	对牛弹琴	29
	Playing the Guqin to a Cow	

27:	多行不义必自毙	30
	Doing Evil Must Be Self-Destructive	

F

28:	奉公守法	32
	Serving the Public and Obeying the Law	

G

29:	改过自新	33
	Reforming Oneself	
30:	高山流水	35
	Lofty Mountains and Flowing Water	
31:	高瞻远瞩	36
	Standing High and Having Foresight	
32:	刮目相看	37
	Seeing in a New Light	
33:	管鲍之交	39
	Guan and Bao's Deep Friendship	
34:	国士无双	42
	Unparalleled in the Country	
35:	过河拆桥	43
	Destroying the Bridge After Crossing the River	
36:	过门不入	45
	Passing by One's Own House Without Entering	

H

37:	邯郸学步	47
	Learning to Walk by Imitating Others	
38:	好大喜功	49
	Desiring to Be Great	
39:	好善嫉恶	51
	Love Good and Hate Evil	

v

40:	后顾之忧 Worries from the Back	53
41:	囫囵吞枣 Swallowing Whole Jujubes	55
42:	狐假虎威 Fox Relying on Tiger's Might	57
43:	华而不实 Flashy but Insincere	59
44:	画饼充饥 Drawing Cakes to Relieve Hunger	61
45:	画龙点睛 Drawing Dragon's Eyes as the Finishing Points	63
46:	画蛇添足 Drawing a Snake with Feet	65
47:	黄粱一梦 A Dream Under the Yellow Beam	67

J

48:	家徒四壁 Only Four Walls Around the House	69
49:	价值连城 Its Price Worthy of Many Connected Cities	71
50:	兼听则明，偏听则暗 Listening to Both Sides Leads to Enlightenment, Listening to Only One Side Leads to Ignorance	73
51:	将欲取之，必先与之 If You Want to Take, You Must First Give	74
52:	狡兔三窟 A Cunning Rabbit Has Three Burrows	75

53:	脚踏实地	77
	Keeping Your Feet Firmly on Solid Ground	
54:	揭竿而起	79
	Raising the Pole to Uprise	
55:	捷足先登	81
	Walking Faster Can Get There First	
56:	解铃还须系铃人	83
	The One Who Tied the Bell Must Be the One Who Can Untie It	
57:	金石为开	85
	Opening the Stone	
58:	锦囊妙计	87
	Smart Strategies in Brocade Bags	
59:	惊弓之鸟	89
	A Frightened Bird	

K

60:	开天辟地	91
	Opening Heaven and Earth	
61:	坎井之蛙	93
	A Frog in the Well	
62:	刻舟求剑	95
	Marking the Boat to Look for the Sword	
63:	孔融让梨	96
	Kong Rong Giving up the Bigger Pears	
64:	口蜜腹剑	97
	Sweet in the Mouth but Bitter in the Stomach	

L

65:	滥竽充数	99
	Unskilled Yu Performer Making up the Number	

66:	狼狈不堪	100
	In Distressing and Embarrassing Situation	
67:	老当益壮	102
	Older but Should Be Stronger	
68:	老马识途	104
	The Old Horses Know the Way	
69:	乐不思蜀	106
	Being Happy in the Hostland and Forgetful of the Homeland	
70:	乐此不疲	108
	Enjoying It Without Feeling Tired	
71:	两袖清风	110
	Two Sleeves of Cool Breeze	

M

72:	毛遂自荐	112
	Self-Recommendation	
73:	盲人摸象	114
	Blind Men Touching the Elephant	
74:	名列前茅	116
	Front Thatch	

N

75:	南柯一梦	118
	A Dream Under the Southern Branch	
76:	南山可移	120
	South Mountain Can Be Moved	
77:	南辕北辙	122
	Wanting to Go to South but the Wheels Going North	
78:	弄巧成拙	124
	Overdoing Something	

O

79:	呕心沥血	126
	Making Painstaking Efforts, Shedding Heart's Blood	

P

80:	排难解纷	128
	Eliminating Dangers and Resolving Disputes	
81:	盘根错节	130
	Tangled Tree Roots and Intertwined Joints	
82:	旁若无人	132
	As If There Is No One Around	
83:	披肝沥胆	134
	Cutting Liver and Dripping Bile	
84:	匹夫有责	136
	Everyone Has a Responsibility	
85:	匹夫之勇	138
	A Commoner's Courage	
86:	破釜沉舟	140
	Breaking the Cauldrons and Sinking the Boats	
87:	破镜重圆	142
	Broken Mirror Reunited	
88:	扑朔迷离	145
	Bewildering and Confusing	

Q

89:	齐眉举案	147
	Holding the Tray up to the Eyebrows	
90:	歧路亡羊	150
	Lost Sheep at a Crossroads	
91:	旗鼓相当	153
	Equally Matched by Flags and Drums	

92:	杞人忧天	155
	A Man from Qi Feared the Sky Falling	
93:	起死回生	157
	Bringing the Dead Back to Life	
94:	千变万化	158
	Being Ever-Changing	
95:	千里送鹅毛，礼轻情意重	161
	Delivering a Goose Feather a Thousand Miles	
96:	前功尽弃	163
	All the Previous Efforts Would Have Been Wasted	
97:	黔驴技穷	166
	Guizhou Donkey Run out of Skills	
98:	请君入瓮	168
	Please Enter the Urn	
99:	罄竹难书	171
	Cannot Write Everything Down Even If Using All the Bamboo Slips	
100:	取而代之	174
	Replacing Someone	

R

101:	人死留名	176
	Leaving a Good Name Behind After Passing Away	
102:	如火如荼	178
	Look Like Red Fire and White Flowers	
103:	孺子可教	180
	A Teachable Youngster	
104:	入木三分	182
	Deeply Engraved Three-Tenths of an Inch into the Wood	

S

105: 塞翁失马 — 184
The Old Man at the Frontier Lost His Horse

106: 三令五申 — 186
Warned Repeatedly Three-to-Five Times

107: 神机妙算 — 188
Divine Intelligence and Ingenious Calculation

108: 声东击西 — 190
Making a Feint to the East and Attacking in the West

109: 失之东隅，收之桑榆 — 192
Lose at Sunrise and Gain at Sunset

110: 师出无名 — 194
No Legitimate Reason to Send Troops

111: 师旷问学 — 196
Shi Kuang's Question About Learning

112: 世外桃源 — 197
The Peach Spring Beyond This World

113: 守株待兔 — 200
Waiting for Rabbits to Hit the Tree Stump

114: 熟能生巧 — 201
Practice Makes Perfect

115: 树倒猢狲散 — 203
When the Tree Falls, the Monkeys Scatter

116: 水滴石穿 — 205
Water Dripping Continuously Can Penetrate Through Stone

117: 死灰复燃 — 207
Extinguished Ashes Rekindled

118: 四面楚歌 — 209
Besieged on All Sides

T

119: (姜)太公钓鱼，愿者上钩　　　　　　　　　　211
　　Jiang Taigong Fishing, Those Who Are Willing Will Take the Bait

120: 螳臂当车　　　　　　　　　　　　　　　　213
　　A Mantis Trying to Stop a Chariot

121: 天衣无缝　　　　　　　　　　　　　　　　215
　　Divine Garments Are Seamless

122: 铁杵磨针　　　　　　　　　　　　　　　　217
　　Grinding an Iron Pestle into a Needle

123: 挺身而出　　　　　　　　　　　　　　　　218
　　Stand Out and Step Forward

124: 铤而走险　　　　　　　　　　　　　　　　220
　　Take a Risk

125: 同甘共苦　　　　　　　　　　　　　　　　222
　　Share Joys and Sorrows

126: 同心同德　　　　　　　　　　　　　　　　224
　　One Heart One Mind

127: 投笔从戎　　　　　　　　　　　　　　　　226
　　Throw Away the Pen and Join the Army

128: 推心置腹　　　　　　　　　　　　　　　　228
　　Treat Others Sincerely

129: 退避三舍　　　　　　　　　　　　　　　　230
　　Retreat to Avoid Conflict

W

130: 完璧归赵　　　　　　　　　　　　　　　　232
　　Return the Jade Disk to Zhao

131: 万事俱备，只欠东风　　　　　　　　　　　236
　　Everything Is Ready, Only East Wind Is Missing

132:	亡羊补牢	239
	Fix the Fence After the Sheep Has Rid	
133:	望梅止渴	241
	Imagining Plums to Quench Thirst	
134:	闻鸡起舞	243
	Getting up to Practice Martial Arts at Cockcrow	
135:	瓮中捉鳖	244
	Catching Turtles in a Jar	
136:	卧薪尝胆	246
	Sleeping on Straw and Tasting Gall	
137:	乌合之众	248
	A Motley Crowd	

X

138:	下笔成章	250
	One Can Write an Article Readily and Quickly	
139:	相煎太急	252
	Too Hasty to Fight	
140:	先发制人	254
	A Preemptive Strike	
141:	项庄舞剑，意在沛公	256
	Xiang Zhuang Dances with a Sword, Aiming at Pei Gong	
142:	笑容可掬：空城计	259
	Smiling Face: The Empty Fort Strategy	
143:	挟天子以令诸侯	261
	Hold the Emperor Hostage to Order the Princes	
144:	胸有成竹	263
	Have a Carefully Considered and Formed Idea	
145:	悬梁刺股	265
	Tying from the Beam and Pricking the Thigh	

Y

146: 揠苗助长   266
Pulling up the Seedlings to Help Them Grow

147: 言过其实   267
Exaggeration

148: 掩耳盗铃   269
Covering One's Ears and Stealing the Bell

149: 偃旗息鼓   271
Lay Down the Flags and Stop the Drums

150: 杨布打狗   274
Yang Bu Hit the Dog

151: 叶公好龙   275
Duke Ye Liked Dragons

152: 夜郎自大   276
Yelang Thought Highly of Itself

153: 一不做，二不休   278
Either Don't Do It, Or Don't Give up Halfway

154: 一鼓作气   280
Finishing Work in One Go

155: 一箭双雕   282
One Arrow Hit Two Vultures

156: 一鸣惊人   284
A Loud Sound That Surprised People

157: 一诺千金   287
A Promise Is Worth One Thousand Ounces of Gold

158: 一去不复返   289
Gone Forever

159: 一衣带水   292
A River as Narrow as a Belt

160: 一字千金	295
One Word Is Worth a Thousand Gold Coins	
161: 以羊易牛	297
Use a Sheep to Replace the Ox	
162: 以逸待劳	299
Waiting for the Enemy to Tire out	
163: 异军突起	300
A New Army Suddenly Emerged	
164: 因势利导	302
Following the Trend to Guide People	
165: 游刃有余	304
Doing a Job with Skill and Ease	
166: 有志者事竟成	306
Where There Is a Will, There Is a Way	
167: 愚公移山	308
The Foolish Old Man Removes the Mountains	
168: 鱼目混珠	311
Pass off the Fisheye as Pearl	
169: 鹬蚌相争，渔翁得利	313
When the Snipe and the Clam Fight, the Fisherman Wins	
170: 约法三章	314
Agreement on the Three Rules of Law	
171: 运筹帷幄	316
Strategize in the Military Tent	

Z

172: 凿壁偷光	318
Borrowing Light from Cutting a Hole in the Wall	
173: 朝三暮四	319
Three in the Morning and Four in the Evening	

174:	郑人买履 A Zheng Man Buying Shoes	321
175:	指鹿为马 Calling a Deer a Horse	322
176:	纸上谈兵 Discussing Military Strategy on Paper	324
177:	智者千虑，必有一失 Even the Wisest Will Make Mistakes	327
178:	紫气东来 Purple Air Coming from the East	329
179:	自相矛盾 Self-Contradiction	330
180:	坐山观虎斗 Sit on the Mountain and Watch the Tigers Fight	331

安如泰山，固若金汤

Ān rú tài shān, gù ruò jīn tāng

[近义词：稳如泰山、坚如磐石、岿然不动；

反义词：岌岌可危、危在旦夕、不堪一击]

变所欲为，易于反掌，安于泰山。

–出自汉·枚乘《上书谏吴王》

边城之地，必将婴城固守，皆为金城汤池，

不可攻也。–出自东汉·班固《汉书·蒯通传》

As Stable as Mount Tai,
As Solid as a Metal City

If you can change your mind to stop the rebellion, it is as easy as flipping your palms, your position will be as stable as Mount Tai. – From "A Letter to Admonish the King of Wu" by Mei Sheng (?–140 BCE) [*Note*: Mount Tai is of historical and cultural significance in the north of Tai'an city, and is the highest point in Shandong province, China.]

If a city wall is made of metal, and a moat filled with boiling water, it will have a solid fortification that is indestructible. – From "The Book of Han: Biography of Kuai Tong" by Ban Gu (32–92)

按兵不动

Àn bīng bú dòng

出自《吕氏春秋·恃君览》

[近义词：静观其变、裹足不前；

反义词：闻风而动、雷厉风行]

赵简子将袭卫，使史默往睹之，期以一月。六月而后反，赵简子曰："何其久也？"史默曰："…其佐多贤也。"赵简子按兵而不动。

Keeping Your Troops Still

From "Master Lü's Spring and Autumn Annals: Relying on the Minister's Observation"

During the Spring and Autumn period (770–476 BCE), Zhao Jianzi (?–476 BCE) of Jin State was preparing to attack Wei State. Before deploying troops, he selected a minister named Shi Mo to spy about Wei. Zhao gave Shi a month to do this, but Shi came back six months later. Zhao asked Shi: "Why did you take so long to return?" Shi replied: "After six months of investigation, I found Duke Ling of Wei was very talented, there were many wise ministers in the state, the people supported him, and the whole state was united. If we want to use force to make Wei surrender, I'm afraid it will cost us too much!" After hearing this, Zhao thought the time to attack Wei was unripe, he immediately ordered to keep the troops still for 3 years, temporarily withdrew the plan to attack Wei State.

暗度陈仓

Àn dù chén cāng

出自西汉·司马迁《史记·高祖本纪》

[近义词：移花接木；反义词：明目张胆]

项王使卒三万人从汉王之国。楚与诸侯之慕从者数万人，从杜南入蚀中。张良送至褒中，汉王遣良归韩；良因说汉王烧绝所过栈道，以备诸侯盗兵，且示项羽无东意。……八月，汉王引兵从故道出，袭雍；雍王章邯迎击汉陈仓。

Secretly Passing Through Chencang

From "Records of the Grand Historian:
Annals of Emperor Gaozu"
by Sima Qian (145–c.86 BCE)

After the Qin dynasty (221–206 BCE) was overthrown, Xiang Yu (232–202 BCE) self-proclaimed the Ruler of Western Chu, and divided the country into 18 feudatory states. Xiang Yu worried that Liu Bang (c.256–195 BCE) would fight for the position with him, so he enthroned Liu Bang as King of Han and sent him to govern the Bashu and Han area. Although Liu Bang was dissatisfied, he had no choice but brought 30,000 soldiers, followed by tens of thousands of others and the princes from Chu, entered Hanzhong from Dunan. To guard against attacks from sentinels and to paralyze Xiang Yu, Liu Bang told Xiang Yu that the Han troops had no plan to return to the east. After entering Hanzhong, Liu Bang ordered a fire to burn the plank road. Later, Liu Bang appointed Han Xin (231–196 BCE) as a general and adopted Han Xin's strategy to openly send people to repair the plank road. Not knowing it was a trick, Xiang Yu relaxed his guard. Liu Bang took the opportunity to launch a surprise attack, detoured northward from the old road in the west, secretly passed through Chencang, and quickly entered Guanzhong from Hanzhong. Zhang Han (?–205 BCE), the Prince of Yong, hurriedly led his troops to Chencang to intercept, but was defeated by the Han army occupying the advantageous terrain. The King of Han pacified the Three Qins all at once and seized Hangu Pass and the areas to the west.

百闻不如一见
百见不如一干

Bǎi wén bù rú yí jiàn, bǎi jiàn bù rú yí gàn

[近义词：耳听为虚，眼见为实、耳闻不如目见；
反义词：道听途说、捕风捉影、风言风语]

百闻不如一见，兵难隃度，臣愿驰至金城，
图上方略。–出自东汉·班固《汉书·赵充国传》
百见不如一干。–民间俗语

Seeing is Believing
Doing is Believing

Seeing is believing. It is difficult to plan the deployment of troops from a faraway place. I want to go to Jincheng (lit. "Metal City") in person to take a look first, draw a map, formulate a strategy, and then report to the emperor. – From "The Book of Han: Biography of Zhao Chongguo" by Ban Gu (32–92)

No matter how many times you hear others say it, it is better to see it yourself.
No matter how many times you watch others do it, it is better to practice it yourself.
– Chinese Proverb

百折不挠

Bǎi zhé bù náo

出自汉·蔡邕《太尉乔玄碑》

[近义词：不屈不挠、坚强不屈；
反义词：一蹶不振、知难而退]

其性庄，疾华尚朴，有百折不挠，
临大节而不可夺之风。

Indomitable Spirit and Unyielding Faith

From "The Epitaph of Grand Commandant Qiao Xuan" by Cai Yong (133–192)

During the reign of Emperor Ling (r. 168–189) of the Eastern Han dynasty (25–220), the Grand Commandant Qiao Xuan (110–184) was an honest official who dared to fight against evil forces and was respected and praised by the people. After Qiao Xuan's death, the well-known writer of the Eastern Han dynasty, General of the Central Army, Cai Yong (133–192, father of the talented woman Cai Wenji), wrote an article to commemorate Qiao Xuan, praising his indomitable spirit and unyielding faith.

别开生面

Bié kāi shēng miàn

出自唐·杜甫《丹青引赠曹将军霸》

[近义词：别具一格、标新立异、别出心裁；
反义词：千篇一律、循规蹈矩、照本宣科]

凌烟功臣少颜色，将军下笔开生面。

Breaking a New Path

From "A Tribute to General Cao Ba for His Red Ink Paintings" by Du Fu (712–770)

The portraits of the heroes in the Lingyan Pavilion of Taiji Palace in Chang'an (today's Xi'an) city lost their former bright colors. General Cao Ba (c.704–c.770) had made them shine again. The original meaning of the phrase is to restore dim and blurred pictures; later it is used to refer to breaking a new path or creating a unique style.

宾至如归

Bīn zhì rú guī

出自春秋·左丘明《左传·襄公三十一年》

[近义词：满腔热情、无微不至；

反义词：冷若冰霜、漠不关心]

宾至如归，无宁灾患，不畏寇盗，而亦不患燥湿。

Guests Feeling at Home

From "The Zuo Tradition: The 31st Year of Duke Xiang"

by Zuo Qiuming (556–452 BCE)

Every time when guests came here, they felt like they were back home, never worrying about thieves, heat, or humidity. Making guests feel at home reflects traditional Chinese way of hospitality, as indicated in this maxim in *Confucian Analects*: "It is a great pleasure to have friends coming from afar." So, it is necessary to be warm and polite, and to provide convenience.

伯乐相马

Bólè xiàng mǎ

君亦闻骥乎？夫骥之齿至矣，服盐车而上太行。蹄申膝折，尾湛胕溃，漉汁洒地，白汗交流，中阪迁延，负辕而不能上。伯乐遇之，下车攀而哭之，解纻衣以幕之。骥于是俛而喷，仰而鸣，声达于天，若出金石声者，何也？彼见伯乐之知己也。
–出自西汉·刘向《战国策：楚策四》。

后来唐朝文学家韩愈写了一篇《马说》，赞扬伯乐慧眼识马："世有伯乐，然后有千里马。千里马常有，而伯乐不常有。"

Bole Identifying Qianlima

The Qianlima (lit. "Thousand-li Horse") was old, driving a cart loaded with salt to climb the Taihang Mountains. Its hooves were stiff, its knees were broken, its tail was soaked, its skin was ulcerated, its saliva was spilled on the ground, and sweat was pouring down its body. It was whipped to climb to the middle of the mountain road, unable to go up any further. When Bole saw the horse, he jumped off his carriage, hugged it and cried, and took off his clothes to cover it. The horse lowered its head and sighed, then raised its head and neighed, the sound reaching up to the sky, making a loud voice like the collision of metal and stone. Why? It knew that Bole was its bosom friend (From "Strategies of the Warring States: Chu Strategy 4" by Liu Xiang, 77–6 BCE). Later, the Tang-dynasty writer Han Yu (768–824) wrote an article, titled "On Horses," praising Bole for his ability to identify horses with his keen eyes: "There was Bole in the world, then there was Qianlima; Qianlima is common, but Bole is rare."

不打不相识

Bù dǎ bù xiāng shí

出自明·施耐庵《水浒传·第三十八回》

[近义词：冰释前嫌、化干戈为玉帛；

反义词：不共戴天、反目成仇]

戴宗道："你两个今番却做个至交的弟兄。

常言道：不打不成相识。"

No Fight, No Acquaintance

From "Water Margin: Chapter 38"

by Shi Nai'an (1296–1372)

Dai Zong (a fictional character in Water Margin) said: "You two are good brothers now. As the saying goes: 'You won't know each other without fighting.'" This phrase suggests that after fighting, two people can have a mutual understanding and can get along better.

不入虎穴，焉得虎子

Bú rù hǔ xué, yān dé hǔ zǐ

出自南朝·宋·范晔《后汉书·班超传》

[近义词：舍不得孩子套不住狼；

反义词：前怕狼，后怕虎、胆小如鼠]

超曰："不入虎穴，焉得虎子。当今之计，独有因夜以火攻虏，使彼不知我多少，必大震怖，可殄尽也。"

Without Entering Tiger's Den, One Cannot Catch Tiger's Cubs (No Venture, No Gain)

From "Book of the Later Han: Biography of Ban Chao" by Fan Ye (398–445)

Ban Chao (32–102) summoned his soldiers and spoke: "Without entering the tiger's den, how can we catch the tiger cubs? Our only strategy today is to attack the Xiongnu envoys with fire at night, so that they don't know how many people we have. Then they will be very shocked, and we can kill them all." The phrase now conveys that if one wants to obtain true knowledge, they must practice. It also means that it is impossible to gain true knowledge without practice. Only by bravely facing dangerous situations and undergoing difficult experiences can one get what others cannot get and accumulate extraordinary knowledge.

成也萧何，败也萧何

Chéng yě xiāo hé, bài yě xiāo hé

出自西汉·司马迁《史记·淮阴侯列传》

及项梁渡淮，信杖剑从之，居麾下，未得知名。项梁败，又属项羽，羽以为郎中。数以策干项羽，羽不用。汉王之入蜀，信亡楚归汉，未得知名，为连敖。坐法当斩，其辈十三人皆已斩，次至信，信乃仰视，适见滕公，曰："上不欲就天下乎？何为斩壮士！"滕公奇其言，壮其貌，释而不斩。与语，大说之。言于上，上拜以为治粟都尉，上未之奇也。信数与萧何语，何奇之。至南郑，诸将行道亡者数十人，信度何等已数言上，上不我用，即亡。何闻信亡，不及以闻，自追之。人有言上曰："丞相何亡。"上大怒，如失左右手。居一二日，何来谒上，上且怒且喜，骂何曰："若亡，何也？"何曰："臣不敢亡也，臣追亡者。"上曰："若所追者谁？"曰："韩信也。"上复骂曰："诸将亡者以十数，公无所追；追信，诈也。"何曰："诸将易得耳。至如信者，国士无双。王必欲长王汉中，无所事信；必欲争天下，非信无所与计事者。顾王策安所决耳。"王曰："吾亦欲东耳，安能郁郁久居此乎？"何曰："王计必欲东，能用信，信即留；不能用，信终亡耳。"王曰："吾为公以为将。"何曰："虽为将，信必不留。"王曰："以为大将。"何曰："幸甚。"于是王欲召信拜之。何曰："王素慢无礼，今拜大将如呼小儿耳，此乃信所以去也。王必欲拜之，择良日，斋戒，设坛场，具礼，乃可耳。"王许之。诸将皆喜，人人各自以为得大将。至拜大将，乃韩信也，一军皆惊。……陈豨拜为巨鹿守，辞于淮阴侯。淮阴侯挈其手，辟左右与之步于庭，仰天叹曰："子可与言乎？欲与子有言也。"豨曰："唯将军令之。"淮阴侯曰："公之所居，天下精兵处也；而公，陛下之信幸臣也。人言公之畔，陛下必不信；再至，陛下乃疑矣；三至，必怒而自将。吾为公从中起，天下可图也。"陈豨素知其能也，信之，曰："谨奉教！"

汉十年，陈豨果反。上自将而往，信病不从。阴使人至豨所，曰："弟举兵，吾从此助公。"信乃谋与家臣夜诈诏赦诸官徒奴，欲发以袭吕后、太子。部署已定，待豨报。其舍人得罪于信，信囚，欲杀之。舍人弟上变，告信欲反状于吕后。吕后欲召，恐其党不就，乃与萧相国谋，诈令人从上所来，言豨已得死，列侯群臣皆贺。相国绐信曰："虽疾，强入贺。"信入，吕后使武士缚信，斩之长乐钟室。信方斩，曰："吾悔不用蒯通之计，乃为儿女子所诈，岂非天哉！"遂夷信三族。

Success and Failure Are Both Due to Xiao He

From "Records of the Grand Historian:
Biography of the Marquis of Huaiyin"
by Sima Qian (145–c.86 BCE)

This idiom is a classic summary of the life of Han Xin (231–196 BCE), a founding hero of the Western Han dynasty (206 BCE–23 CE). "Success is due to Xiao He" means that Han Xin became a general because of Xiao He's recommendation. "Failure is also due to Xiao He" means that Han Xin was killed because of Xiao He's strategy. This phrase is used to indicate that the success or failure of a thing is caused by the same person. Han Xin's experience shows that at any time in life, one must correct their words and deeds, do not exceed the limit, and be cautious of others.

城门失火，殃及池鱼

Chéng mén shī huǒ, yāng jí chí yú

出自东汉·应劭《风俗通义》

[近义词：无妄之灾；反义词：爱屋及乌]

旧说：池仲鱼，人姓字也，居宋城门，城门失火，延及其家，仲鱼烧死。

又云：宋城门失火，人汲取池中水，以沃灌之，池中空竭，鱼悉露死。喻恶之滋，并伤良谨也。

When the City Gate Caught Fire, The Fish in the Moat Were Affected

From "Customs and Meanings" by Ying Shao (140–206)

There are two versions of this fable. In one version, Chi Zhongyu was the name of a person who lived next to the city gate of Song (a state in the Spring and Autumn period [770–476 BCE]). One day, the city gate suddenly caught fire that soon spread and burned down his house, he was also burned to death.

Another version is that one day, the city gate of Song state accidentally caught fire, people rushed to the gate to draw water from the moat to put out the fire. As a result, the moat was drying out quickly and the fish in it could not escape death.

乘风破浪

Chéng fēng pò làng

出自南北朝·沈约《宋书·宗悫传》

[近义词：披荆斩棘、高歌猛进；

反义词：裹足不前、随波逐流]

悫年少时，炳问其志，悫曰："愿乘长风破万里浪。"

Riding the Winds and Breaking the Waves
From "Song Book: Biography of Zong Que"
by Shen Yue (441–513)

When Zong Que (?–465) was young, his uncle Zong Bing (375–443) asked about his life goals, Que replied: "I want to ride the winds and break the waves" to overcome difficulties for a good cause. Because of this goal, Que obtained good martial arts skills at a young age and was later appointed as a general by the emperor and accomplished many military achievements. The phrase now means moving forward or sailing smoothly with the help of the winds. In modern Chinese, it often suggests continuing moving forward under good circumstances or based on certain achievements. Sometimes it also describes the rapid development of a career.

乘龙快婿

Chéng lóng kuài xù

出自西汉·刘向《列仙传·卷上》

[近义词：乘龙佳婿、东床姣婿、坦腹东床]

萧史者，秦穆公时人也，善吹箫，能致孔雀白鹤于庭。穆公有女字弄玉，好之。公遂以女妻焉。日教弄玉作凤鸣。居数年，吹似凤声，凤凰来止其屋。公为作凤台，夫妇止其上不下数年，一日，皆随凤凰飞去。故秦人为作凤女祠于雍宫中，时有箫声而已。

Dragon-Riding Son-in-Law

From "Biographies of Immortals: Volume 1"

by Liu Xiang (77–6 BCE)

Legend says that in the Spring and Autumn period (770–476 BCE), a young man named Xiao Shi liked playing the flute that could attract peacocks and white cranes to his courtyard. Duke Mu of Qin had a daughter who styled herself as Nongyu also enjoyed playing the flute. Duke Mu let Nongyu married to Xiao Shi. Thereafter, Xiao Shi taught Nongyu how to play the flute like the sound of phoenix. After years of practice, Nongyu's flute playing was just like the sound of a real phoenix, attracting phoenixes from the sky to land on their house. Duke Mu thus built a Phoenix Terrace for them. Xiao Shi and Nongyu lived on the terrace for many years. One day, Nongyu rode on the colorful phoenix, and Xiao Shi rode on the golden dragon, flew away together. Later, to commemorate Xiao Shi and Nongyu, a Phoenix Temple was built in the palace complex.

惩一警百

Chéng yī jǐng bǎi

出自东汉·班固《汉书·尹翁归传》

[近义词：惩一儆百]

翁归治东海明察……其有所取也，
以一警百，吏民皆服，恐惧改行自新。

Punishing One to Warn Hundreds

From "The Book of Han: Biography of Yin Wenggui"

by Ban Gu (32–92)

Yin Wenggui (?–62 BCE) governed the East China Sea area with wisdom and insight… What he had learned as an effective governing method was to punish one person to warn hundreds, so that all the officials and locals obeyed him, feared him, and changed their bad behaviors to good ones. The public security and order in the area soon became stable.

出奇制胜

Chū qí zhì shèng

出自春秋·孙武《孙子兵法·兵势篇》

[近义词：出其不意、攻其不备；

反义词：按兵不动、束手待毙]

凡战者，以正合，以奇胜。

故善出奇者，无穷如天地，不竭如江河。

Surprise Victory

From "The Art of War: Military Strategy"

by Sun Wu (c.545–c.470/496 BCE)

Generally, in a war, the regular troops were used to fight the enemy, and the surprise troops were used to win. Therefore, the tactics of a general who was good at winning by surprise were as changeable as heaven and earth, and as inexhaustible as the flow of a river.

初出茅庐

Chū chū máo lú

出自明·罗贯中《三国演义·第三十九回》

[近义词：初露头角、初露锋芒；

反义词：老成持重、老马识途]

博望相持用火攻，指挥如意笑谈中。

直须惊破曹公胆，初出茅庐第一功。

A Newcomer from a Thatched Cottage

From "Romance of the Three Kingdoms: Chapter 39"

by Luo Guanzhong (c.1330–c.1400)

In the Battle of Bowangpo, Zhuge Liang (181–234) used fire to attack Cao Cao's (155–220) troops, commanding as he would in a smile. It must have disrupted Cao Cao's courage, and it was the first military exploit of a newcomer from a thatched cottage. This idiom originally referred to Zhuge Liang in the Three Kingdoms period (220–280) who followed Liu Bei (161–223) to defeat Cao Cao. Zhuge Liang won the Battle of Bowangpo right after leaving his secluded thatched cottage.

初生牛犊不怕虎

Chū shēng niú dú bú pà hǔ

出自《庄子·知北游》

[近义词：无所畏惧、敢作敢为]

德将为汝美，道将为汝居，

汝瞳焉如新出之犊而无求其故。

A Newborn Calf Is Not Afraid of a Tiger

From "Zhuangzi: Knowledge Travelled North"

Virtue will appear beautiful for you, the Dao will reside in your heart, your round-eyed innocent look will seem like a newborn calf, and you will not seek external things. In modern Chinese, this idiom usually refers to young people who are brave and fearless due to their inexperience and ignorance. Although this can be valuable creative spirit, youngsters are often overwhelmed by their enthusiasm, which may bring unexpected troubles. Therefore, it is crucial to keep a calm and clear mind, and use reason to guide one's behavior, because the fearlessness caused by ignorance can be disastrous.

此地无银三百两

Cǐ dì wú yín sān bǎi liǎng

出自民间故事

[近义词：欲盖弥彰、不打自招；

反义词：相得益彰、讳莫如深]

古时候，有个叫张三的人，他攒下三百两银子，怕被别人偷走，便放在一个大箱子里，把箱子深埋在了自家后院的地下，还在东屋墙上写了个字牌："此地无银三百两"。邻居王二看到了字牌，明白过来，于是把箱子挖了出来，偷走了银子，也在东屋墙上写了个字牌："隔壁王二未曾偷"。

There Is No Three Hundred Taels of Silver Here

From Chinese Folktales

In ancient China, there was a man named Zhang San who saved up 300 taels of silver. He feared the money to be stolen, so he put it in a big box and buried it deep in his backyard. He also put a sign on the east wall that reads: "There is no 300 taels of silver here." His neighbor Wang Er saw the sign, understood what was going on, dug out the box, stole the silver, and put a sign on the east wall that says: "Neighbor Wang Er did not steal it." This idiom is a metaphor for trying to cover up a fact but ended up exposing it more.

打草惊蛇

Dǎ cǎo jīng shé

出自唐·段成式《酉阳杂俎》

[近义词：操之过急、因小失大；

反义词：欲擒故纵、引蛇出洞]

王鲁为当涂宰，颇以资产为务，会部民连状诉主簿贪贿于县尹。鲁乃判曰："汝虽打草，吾已惊蛇。"为好事者口实焉。

Stirring the Grass and Startling the Snake

From "Miscellaneous Sacrificial Utensils from Youyang"

by Duan Chengshi (800–863)

When Wang Lu was the magistrate in Dangtu county, he engaged in corruption. It happened that the people under his command filed a lawsuit against his chief clerk for bribery. Wang Lu wrote on the petition: "Although you are accusing my subordinate, I have already felt the situation is serious, it is like stirring the grass and startling the snake." Then Wang Lu suppressed the case. This idiom originally means to punish others and warn oneself. Later, it is used to describe doing things carelessly, causing the other party to be alert and take precautions.

大器晚成

Dà qì wǎn chéng

[近义词：后生可畏；反义词：不堪造就、冥顽不灵]

上德若谷；大白若辱；大方无隅；大器晚成；大音希声；大象无形；道隐无名。夫唯道，善贷且成。–春秋·老子《道德经·四十一章》

琰从弟林，少无名望，虽姻族犹多轻之，而琰常曰："此所谓大器晚成者也，终必远至。"–西晋·陈寿《三国志·魏志·崔琰传》

Great Talents Mature Late

From "Dao De Jing: Chapter 41"

by Laozi (Li Er, c.571–471 BCE)

The lofty virtue seems like a low valley; the purist innocence seems shameful; the perfect square has no corners; the most precious utensil is made last; the loudest voice sounds silent; the largest image is shapeless; the Dao is hidden and nameless. Yet only the Dao can make everything start and end well. This idiom "The most precious utensil is made last" originally refers to the fact that it takes a long time to make a big tool out of a large material. Later, it is used to describe people who can take on big tasks or accomplish great things but achieve success late.

呆若木鸡

Dāi ruò mù jī

出自《庄子·达生》

[近义词：瞠目结舌、目瞪口呆、呆头呆脑；
反义词：大智若愚、矫若游龙、神色自若]

鸡虽有鸣者，已无变矣，望之似木鸡矣；
其德全矣，异鸡无敢应者，反走矣。

As Dumb as a Wooden Chicken

From "Zhuangzi: Nurturing Life"

Even if other chickens crow, this one will not, it looks like a wooden chicken whose virtue is perfected; other fighting cocks dare not fight with it, they just turn around and run away. In this fable, the seemingly wooden chicken does not need to fight at all but makes other fighting cocks flee. It is used to illustrate the principle that "two opposite poles approach each other and transform at a certain height," which is the dialectical thinking in Daoist thought. This idiom originally means to collect all of one's spirit. Later, it describes a person who looks a little stupid or dumbfounded due to fear or shock.

东窗事发

Dōng chuāng shì fā

出自元·刘一清《钱塘遗事》

[近义词：露出马脚、破绽百出、原形毕露、

真相大白；反义词：秘而不宣]

秦桧欲杀岳飞，于东窗下谋。其妻王夫人曰："擒虎易，放虎难。"其意遂决。后桧游西湖，舟中得疾，见一人披发，厉声曰："当误国害民，我已诉于天，得请于帝矣。"桧死。未几，子熹亦死。夫人思亡，设醮，方士伏章，见蠢荷铁枷，因问秦太师所在，熹曰："吾父见在酆都。"方士如言而往，果见桧与万俟俱荷铁枷，备受诸苦。桧曰："可烦传与夫人，东窗事发矣！"

Plot Under the East Window Has Been Exposed

From "Qiantang Legacies"

by Liu Yiqing of the Yuan Dynasty (1271–1368)

Qin Hui (1091–1155) wanted to kill Yue Fei (1103–1142), so he discussed it with his wife Wang under the east window. Wang said: "It's easy to catch a tiger, but it's difficult to catch it again after letting it go." This was to hint Qin Hui to act quickly, and Qin Hui made up his mind to do so. Soon after, Qin Hui plotted to kill Yue Fei. After Yue Fei's death, Qin Hui once visited West Lake and suddenly fell ill on the boat. In a trance, he saw a man with disheveled hair shouting at him: "You have harmed the country and the people. I have appealed to heaven, and now I am here to arrest you!" Qin Hui returned home and soon died. Shortly after, Qin Hui's son Qin Xi also died. Hence, Wang invited a Daoist sage to set up an incense table to perform a ritual. In the smoke, Qin Xi was wearing an iron shackle. The Daoist sage asked: "Where is the Grand Master (Qin Hui)?" Qin Xi replied: "In Fengdu." The Daoist sage heard this, walked toward Fengdu, and saw Qin Hui and Moqi Xie (1083–1157, who falsely accused Yue Fei) both wearing iron shackles and undergoing various punishments. When Qin Hui saw the Daoist sage, he said: "Tell my wife what we had plotted under the east window has been exposed." This idiom means that a secret which cannot be told has been completely disclosed.

东山再起

Dōng shān zài qǐ

出自唐·房玄龄等《晋书·谢安传》

[近义词：重整旗鼓、卷土重来、死灰复燃；

反义词：一去不返、过眼烟云、一蹶不振]

隐居会稽东山，年逾四十复出为桓温司马，累迁中书、司徒等要职，晋室赖以转危为安。

Rising Again on the East Mountain

From "Book of Jin: Biography of Xie An"

by Fang Xuanling (579–648) *et al.*

Xie An (320–385) lived in seclusion in the East Mountain of Kuaiji Commandery (Hangzhou Bay area). At the age of 40, he re-entered the Imperial Court to serve as Sima (General) for Grand General Huan Wen (312–373) and was promoted to important posts such as Zhongshu (Official in Secretariat) and Situ (Minister of Revenue). Thereafter, the Eastern Jin dynasty (317–420) turned from danger to peace. This idiom means retaking an important position or regaining power after losing it; it also denotes making a comeback after withdrawal.

东施效颦

Dōng shī xiào pín

出自《庄子·天运》

[近义词：照猫画虎、生搬硬套、邯郸学步；

反义词：标新立异、择善而从、独辟蹊径]

西施病心而颦其里，其里之丑人见而美之，归亦捧心而颦其里。其里之富人见之，坚闭门而不出；贫人见之，挈妻子而去之走。彼知颦美，而不知颦之所以美。

Dong Shi Imitating Xi Shi's Frown

From "Zhuangzi: The Movement of Heaven"

Xi Shi (503–473 BCE), also known as Xizi from Yue State, was one of the renowned Four Beauties in ancient China. She had a pain in her chest and walked around the village with a frown on her face. An ugly woman in the village, named Dong Shi, saw Xi Shi and thought she was very beautiful in her frown. Dong Shi thus imitated Xi Shi by walking around the village with her hand covering her chest. When the rich saw Dong Shi's frown, they closed their doors without going out; when the poor saw Dong Shi's frown, they ran away with their wives and children. Dong Shi only knew that frowning made Xi Shi more beautiful, but she did not know why.

对牛弹琴

Duì niú tán qín

出自汉·牟融《弘明集·理惑论》

[近义词：对牛鼓簧、白费口舌；

反义词：对症下药、有的放矢]

公明仪为牛弹清角之操；伏食如故；非牛不闻；不合其耳矣。转为蚊虻之声，孤犊之鸣，即掉尾奋耳，蹀躞而听。

Playing the Guqin to a Cow

From "Master Mou's Treatise on Settling Doubts"

by Mou Rong (?–79)

Gong Mingyi was an excellent musician in the Warring States period (475–221 BCE). He played the guqin so well that all the local people enjoyed listening to it. One day, a cow was eating grass in a field. Gong played the Elegant Music for the cow, but the cow was indifferent and continued eating grass. Gong then used the guqin to imitate the buzzing sound of mosquitoes, and the mooing sound of a calf. The cow immediately stopped eating grass, raised its head, pricked up its ears, wagged its tail, and walked back and forth to listen. This idiom metaphorically satirizes the people who are being elegant to those who do not understand elegance; it further implies that education should be based on aptitude.

多行不义必自毙

Duō xíng bú yì bì zì bì

出自《左传·隐公元年》

[近义词：作茧自缚、作法自毙、
自食其果、玩火自焚]

多行不义必自毙，子姑待之。

Doing Evil Must Be Self-Destructive

From "The Zuo Tradition: The First Year of Yin Gong"

by Zuo Qiuming (556–452 BCE)

Duke Wu of Zheng (780–744 BCE) had two sons: Duke Zhuang of Zheng (757–701 BCE) and Gong Shuduan (754 BCE–?). His wife Wu Jiang had a difficult birth to the first son and thus disliked Duke Zhuang and wanted to make the second son Gong Shuduan the crown prince, but Duke Wu refused. When Duke Zhuang succeeded in the throne, Wu Jiang asked to let Gong Shuduan govern the city of Jing, and Duke Zhuang agreed. Gong Shuduan recruited soldiers, made weapons, and expanded the city boundaries. Soon, Gong Shuduan also asked for the border areas in the west and north to be under his control. Gong Shuduan took these two places as his own fiefdoms and expanded his territory all the way to Linyan (today north of Yanjin county, Henan province). Gong Shuduan strengthened the city walls, accumulated food, forged weapons, and strengthened the army, intending to attack the capital of Zheng, and Wu Jiang's army was willing to open the city gates for him as an internal response. When Duke Zhuang found out about the date of the rebellion, he ordered Prince Lü to lead 200 chariots to attack Jing city. The people in Jing revolted against Gong Shuduan who was forced to flee to Yan city (today's Yanling county, Henan province), and Duke Zhuang chased him to Yan. Later, Gong Shuduan fled to Gong State (today's Hui county, Henan province). Duke Zhuang also placed his mother under house arrest, removing the stumbling block to his governance. This idiom alerts people that doing too many evil things will eventually lead to self-destruction.

奉公守法

Fèng gōng shǒu fǎ

出自西汉•司马迁《史记•廉颇蔺相如列传》

[近义词：克己奉公；反义词：贪赃枉法、假公济私]

以君之贵，奉公如法则上下平，上下平则国强。

Serving the Public and Obeying the Law

From "Records of the Grand Historian:
Biographies of Lian Po and Lin Xiangru"
by Sima Qian (145–c.86 BCE)

In the Warring States period (475–221 BCE), there was a general in the state of Zhao named Zhao She (fl. 3rd century BCE). When he was young, Zhao She served as an official in charge of collecting land taxes. Although the position was minor, Zhao She was loyal to his duties, handled affairs impartially, and was not afraid of power. He once said to Zhao Sheng (Lord Pingyuan, 308–251 BCE), who was the son of King Wuling of Zhao (340–295 BCE) and the younger brother of King Huiwen of Zhao (310–266 BCE): "As a noble prince of the state, you should abide by the law and make the upper and lower classes equal, then the country will be strong." King Huiwen of Zhao shortly ordered him to manage the national taxes. After taking office, Zhao She still handled all affairs fairly. The taxes in Zhao State were just and reasonable, collected in time and according to the amount, the treasury was full, and the people's livelihoods improved. Later, Zhao She was appointed as a general and made many military achievements for Zhao State. This idiom is used to refer to serving the public and obeying the law.

改过自新

Gǎi guò zì xīn

出自西汉·司马迁《史记·孝文本纪》

[近义词：改过迁善、改邪归正；
反义词：顽固不化、死不改悔]

妾伤夫死者不可复生，刑者不可复属，
虽复欲改过自新，其道无由也。

Reforming Oneself

From "Records of the Grand Historian:
The Basic Annals of Emperor Xiaowen"
by Sima Qian (145–c.86 BCE)

In the early years of the Han dynasty (206 BCE–220 CE), there was a man named Chunyu Yi (205–150 BCE) in Linzi (district of the city of Zibo, Shandong province). He loved to study medicine at a young age and learned it from the prominent doctor Gongcheng Yangqing (c.251–c.176 BCE) who was over 70 years old at the time and was sonless. Thus, Gongcheng gave Chunyu all his secret formulas and books by the Yellow Emperor (2717–2600 BCE) and Bian Que (c.407–c.310 BCE). Chunyu Yi's medical skills improved day by day under the guidance of a great medical doctor. Three years later, he cured people's illnesses with ease, and many people came to seek his medical treatment. However, he socialized widely and was not always at home. Sometimes he refused to treat others, so many patients had complaints about him. Later, Chunyu Yi was accused by someone in a letter to the Imperial Court. According to the criminal law, he was to be escorted to Chang'an (today's Xi'an). Chunyu Yi had five daughters. The youngest daughter, Tiying, was determined to save her father. She followed him to Chang'an and wrote a letter to Emperor Wen of Han (203–157 BCE), in which it said: "When my father was an official, the locals praised him for his honesty and justice. Now he has broken the law and is being punished. I feel a deep sadness that a person who dies can never be reborn, and a person who is injured and disabled by punishment can never recover. Even if one wants to reform themselves, it will be impossible to do. To give my father a chance to reform himself, I am willing to be a servant in the court to atone for my father's flaws." Emperor Wen of Han read the letter, was moved by Tiying's filial piety, and ordered Chunyu Yi to be pardoned.

高山流水

Gāo shān liú shuǐ

出自《列子·汤问》

[近义词：阳春白雪]

伯牙鼓琴，志在高山，锺子期曰："善哉，峨峨兮若泰山！"志在流水，锺子期曰："善哉，洋洋兮若江河。"伯牙所念，锺子期必得之。子期死，伯牙谓世再无知音，乃破琴绝弦，终身不复鼓。

Lofty Mountains and Flowing Water

From "Liezi: Tang's Questions"

Yu Boya (?–354 BCE) was good at playing the guqin, and Zhong Ziqi was good at listening to it. When Boya played with his mind on the mountains, Ziqi praised: "Great, it looks like Mount Tai!" When Boya played with his mind on the flowing water, Ziqi cheered again: "Great! It sounds like the Yangzi River!" No matter what Boya was thinking while playing, Ziqi could always tell his thoughts accurately. After Ziqi died, Boya felt he would never find another soulmate who could understand his music better than Zhong Ziqi, so he smashed his guqin and never played music again for the rest of his life. This idiom refers to the difficulty of meeting a soulmate, or the excellence of a piece of music.

高瞻远瞩

Gāo zhān yuǎn zhǔ

出自汉·王充《论衡·别通篇》

[近义词：登高望远；反义词：鼠目寸光、目光如豆]

夫闭户塞意，不高瞻览者，死人之徒也哉。

Standing High and Having Foresight

From "Discussive Weighing: On Intelligence"

by Wang Chong (27–97)

Those who close their eyes and ears to stop thinking, and those who do not stand high to see far ahead, are the same as the dead. This idiom is used as a metaphor to suggest that one should train their foresight ability, perhaps by practicing imagining the future and what different scenarios might look like, then they can become better at making decisions.

刮目相看

Guā mù xiāng kàn

出自西晋·陈寿《三国志·吴志·吕蒙传》

[近义词：另眼相待、肃然起敬；

反义词：视同一律、等闲视之、一视同仁]

（鲁）肃拊蒙背曰："吾谓大弟但有武略耳。至于今者，学识英博，非复吴下阿蒙。"蒙曰："士别三日，即更刮目相待。"

Seeing in a New Light

From "Records of the Three Kingdoms: Records of Wu: Biography of Lü Meng"
by Chen Shou (233–297)

Lü Meng (178–220) was very courageous and had learned a great deal of martial arts since a young age. He had many military victories and became a general under Sun Quan (182–252). However, Lü Meng grew up in a poor family and had not studied much. Other officials and generals looked down on him despite his military achievements. Sun Quan suggested that he should read more books. Lü Meng listened and began to study very attentively. Lu Su (172–217) was a Confucian general of his contemporary who had heard about Lü Meng for a while, so he went to visit Lü Meng. The two talked about the past and present, and Lü Meng analyzed the situation of the state. Lu Su was very surprised to hear this. He quickly stood up and patted Lü Meng on the back and said: "I thought brother Lü only had military strategies. But now you are so well-educated and knowledgeable, no longer the warrior Lü Meng from Wu." Lü Meng said: "After 3 days of parting, you should look at a person in a new light." This idiom means to change one's old perspective and look at people with new eyes.

管鲍之交

Guǎn bào zhī jiao

[近义词：生死之交、莫逆之交、金兰契友；
反义词：点头之交]

生我者父母，知我者鲍叔也！
此世称管鲍善交者，小白善用能者。
–出自《列子·力命》

管仲夷吾者，颖上人也。少时常与鲍叔牙游，鲍叔知其贤。管仲贫困，常欺鲍叔，鲍叔终善遇之，不以为言。已而鲍叔事齐公子小白，管仲事公子纠。及小白立为桓公，公子纠死，管仲囚焉。鲍叔遂进管仲。管仲既用，任政于齐。齐桓公以霸，九合诸侯，一匡天下，管仲之谋也。管仲曰："吾始困时，尝与鲍叔贾，分财利多自与，鲍叔不以我为贪，知我贫也。吾尝为鲍叔谋事而更穷困，鲍叔不以我为愚，知时有利不利也。吾尝三仕三见逐于君，鲍叔不以我为不肖，知我不遭时也。吾尝三战三走，鲍叔不以我为怯，知我有老母也。公子纠败，召忽死之，吾幽囚受辱，鲍叔不以我为无耻，知我不羞小节而耻功名不显于天下也。生我者父母，知我者鲍子也。"鲍叔既进管仲，以身下之。子孙世禄于齐，有封邑者十余世，常为名大夫。天下不多管仲之贤而多鲍叔能知人也。–西汉·司马迁《史记·管晏列传》

Guan and Bao's Deep Friendship

From "Liezi: Endeavor and Destiny"; and
"Records of the Grand Historian:
Biographies of Guan and Yan"
by Sima Qian (145–c.86 BCE)

Guan Zhong (725–645 BCE) and Bao Shuya (c.723–644 BCE) were both from Qi State during the Spring and Autumn period. They were good friends from a young age. Bao Shuya admired Guan Zhong's talent and understood his aspirations. The two had done business together and never fought for the share of the profits. Later, Guan Zhong and Bao Shuya separated. Guan Zhong became the teacher of Duke Xiang of Qi's (c.729–686 BCE) younger brother, Prince Jiu (?–685 BCE); and Bao Shuya became the teacher of Duke Xiang of Qi's other younger brother, Prince Xiaobai (?–643 BCE). Duke Xiang of Qi was self-indulgent and drove all his brothers abroad. Soon, civil strife broke out and Duke Xiang of Qi was killed. After hearing the news, Prince Jiu and Prince Xiaobai rushed back to the state, each hoping to get the throne first. Guan Zhong sent people to escort Prince Jiu back to the state, while personally leading people to intercept Prince Xiaobai. They met Prince Xiaobai's caravan on the way. Guan Zhong persuaded Prince Xiaobai and Bao Shuya to go back, but they refused. Guan Zhong took out an arrow and shot at Xiaobai who screamed and fell backwards. Guan Zhong thought that Prince Xiaobai had been shot dead, so he returned and escorted Prince Jiu to Qi in a leisurely manner. Unexpectedly, Prince Xiaobai was not dead. Guan Zhong's arrow happened to hit his belt hook. He was afraid of being shot again, so he pretended to be shot and fell. Seeing Guan Zhong leaving, Prince Xiaobai ordered to take a shortcut; he finally rushed back to the capital and became the monarch. Prince Xiaobai was Duke Huan of Qi (r. 685–643 BCE). After ascending the throne, Duke Huan of Qi immediately sent troops and killed Prince Jiu and captured Guan

Zhong. Duke Huan hated Guan Zhong for almost killing him and wanted to execute him. Bao Shuya tried his best to recommend Guan Zhong to Duke Huan, saying that if Guan Zhong could be reused, the state would be strong. Duke Huan was finally persuaded. Not only did he not kill Guan Zhong but also made him the Grand Chancellor of Qi. Bao Shuya was willing to be Guan Zhong's assistant. With Guan Zhong's support, Qi quickly became strong. Guan Zhong said: "My parents gave me life, but Bao Shuya understood me best." The friendship between Guan Zhong and Bao Shuya became a legend at the time. The original meaning of this idiom refers to the deep friendship between Guan Zhong and Bao Shuya. Later, it is used to describe the deep friendship and mutual trust between friends.

国士无双

Guó shì wú shuāng

出自西汉·司马迁《史记·淮阴侯列传》

[近义词：海内无双、玉堂金马]

诸将易得耳，至如信者，国士无双。

Unparalleled in the Country

From "Records of the Grand Historian: Biography of the Marquis of Huaiyin" by Sima Qian (145–c.86 BCE)

At the end of the Qin dynasty (221–206 BCE), Han Xin (231–196 BCE) was not valued by Xiang Yu (232–202 BCE), so he defected to Liu Bang (c.256–195 BCE). However, he was not valued by Liu Bang at first and was recommended to Xiao He (257–193 BCE) by Duke Teng (Xiahou Ying, ?–172 BCE). Xiao He thought Han Xin was a rare talent and strongly suggested that Liu Bang should put him in an important position. But Liu Bang dealt with Han Xin perfunctorily, so Han Xin left without saying goodbye. Xiao He chased Han Xin under the moonlight and told Liu Bang that Han Xin was a peerless national talent. Hence, Liu Bang appointed Han Xin as a general. Later, Han Xin played a major role in helping Liu Bang to conquer territories and made great contributions.

过河拆桥

Guò hé chāi qiáo

[近义词：鸟尽弓藏、卸磨杀驴；反义词：饮水思源]

过桥便拆桥，得路便塞路。
–出自宋·大慧宗杲禅师《大慧普觉禅师语录》

参政可谓过河拆桥者矣。
–明·宋濂《元史·彻里帖木儿传》

Destroying the Bridge After Crossing the River

From "History of Yuan Dynasty:
Biography of Cheri Temur"
by Song Lian (1310–1381)

When the Yuan-dynasty minister Cheri Temur was serving in Zhejiang, he witnessed the corruption in the Imperial Examinations and secretly made up his mind that when he gained power, he would urge the court to abolish the system. Later, he was promoted to the position of manager of governmental affairs in the central secretariat, equivalent to the deputy chancellor. He then reported to Emperor Shundi (Toghon Temür, 1320–1370) and requested the abolition of the imperial examination system, which caused a huge response in the court. Boyan (Bayan of the Baarin, 1236–1295) expressed his support, but there were many opponents. Supervisory censor Lü Sicheng firmly opposed the abolition and asked Emperor Shundi to punish Cheri Temur. Unexpectedly, Emperor Shundi was very supportive of it; soon after, he ordered to draft an edict to abolish the imperial examination system. Before the verdict was issued, Xu Youren (1287–1364), a counselor with a slightly lower status than the manager of governmental affairs, came out to oppose the abolition. The next day, all the civil and military officials in the court were summoned to the Chongtian Gate to listen to the emperor's decree. Xu Youren was specially notified to kneel in front of the officials to listen to the imperial announcement. Xu Youren was very reluctant but was afraid of offending the emperor and being punished, so he had to follow the instructions. After listening to the edict, Xu Youren walked away. The imperial censor Puhua walked to his side and said sarcastically: "Counselor, you have become a person who has crossed the river and destroyed the bridge." What he meant was that Xu Youren became an official through the Imperial Examination. Now the emperor's edict on abolishing the imperial examination system was being read while Xu Youren was kneeling in the front, as if he was the leader of the abolition, just like a person who had crossed the bridge and then destroyed it. Xu Youren felt ashamed and quickly left. Afterwards, he used the excuse of being ill and never returned to court.

过门不入

Guò mén bú rù

出自战国·邹·孟轲《孟子·离娄下》；

西汉·司马迁《史记·夏本纪》

禹伤先人父鲧功之不成受诛，乃劳身焦思，

居外十三年，过家门不敢入。

Passing by One's Own House Without Entering

From "Mengzi: Li Lou Part 2"; and

"Records of the Grand Historian: Annals of Xia"

by Sima Qian (145–c.86 BCE)

Legend says that about 4,000 years ago, China was in the era of Yao and Shun, and there was a flood nearly every year. During Yao's reign, to stop the flood, everyone elected Gun to handle it. Gun used traditional earth-blocking method to control floods. However, the floods were so fierce that Gun spent 9 years without success. After Shun succeeded Yao as the leader of the tribal alliance, he found Gun ineffective and killed him. When Gun's son Yu grew up, he vowed to inherit his father's career to subdue floods. Later, Shun sent Yu to control floods. Yu learned from his father's failure, he and his followers traveled through mountains and rivers, surveyed the source, the upstream and downstream of the water flow. He also piled stones or cut down trees in important places as reference marks. Then he used the methods of opening canals to drain water and dredging rivers to divert floods to the sea. After 13 years of hard work, floods were finally stopped. It is said that when Yu received the mission from Emperor Shun, he and his wife Tushan were only married for 4 days. To control floods, Yu traveled everywhere and did not return home for 13 years. Legend has it that Yu led people build roads and passed by his house three times without entering. The story spread all over the country and people were very moved. Because of Yu's admirable service in controlling floods, when Shun was old, everyone elected Yu as the successor. After Shun died, Yu succeeded as the leader of the tribal alliance. Later, Yu's son Qi founded China's first slave state – Xia dynasty (c.2070–c.1600 BCE). Therefore, later generations also called him Xia Yu.

邯郸学步

Hán dān xué bù

[近义词：东施效颦、鹦鹉学舌、生搬硬套；

反义词：独辟蹊径、标新立异]

子往呼！且子独不闻夫寿陵余子之学行于邯郸与？未得国能，又失其故行矣，直匍匐而归耳。今子不去，将忘子之故，失子之业。–出自《庄子·秋水》

昔有学步于邯郸者，曾未得其仿佛，又复失其故步，遂匍匐而归耳。–东汉·班固《汉书·叙传上》

Learning to Walk by Imitating Others

From "Zhuangzi: Autumn Water"; and

"The Book of Han: Narrative Biography (Part 1)"

by Ban Gu (32–92)

In the Warring States period (475–221 BCE), there was a young man in Shouling of Yan State (today's Henan province) who heard that people in Handan, the capital of Zhao State, walked very gracefully. He wanted to go there to learn it. When he arrived in Handan, he saw that people on the streets indeed walked very elegantly. He thus imitated them but could not grasp it. Then he decided to learn to walk from scratch and carefully considered each step he would take next. After 3 months, he had not learned the walking posture of Handan people but forgot his own way of walking. In the end, he did not know how to walk at all and crawled back to Yan State. Later, this idiom describes blindly imitating others but losing one's own skill.

好大喜功

Hào dà xǐ gōng

出自宋·欧阳修、宋祁等《新唐书·太宗本纪》

[近义词：好高骛远、沽名钓誉；

反义词：稳扎稳打、脚踏实地]

赞曰："至其牵于多爱，复立浮图，好大喜功，勤兵于远，此中材庸主之所常为。"

Desiring to Be Great

From "New Book of Tang:
Chronicle of Emperor Taizong"
by Ouyang Xiu (1007–1072)
and Song Qi (998–1061) *et al*.

Emperor Taizong of Tang, Li Shimin (599–649), was the second emperor of the Tang dynasty (618–907). He followed his father, Emperor Gaozu of Tang, Li Yuan (566–635), raised an army at the end of the Sui dynasty (581–618), fought in the south and north, and won countless battles. He made great contributions to pacifying the Central Plains in China and establishing the Tang dynasty. Li Shimin hated the practice of killing meritorious officials by the successive emperors after the establishment of each new dynasty. To remind himself not to forget the contributions of the creditable officials, he ordered to have portraits of 24 commendable officials painted and hung on the walls in Lingyan Pavilion. Under the rule of Li Shimin, the country was prosperous and the government transparent, forming the famous "Zhenguan Reign" (627–649). But Li Shimin was fond of ostentation.

To expand his territory, he led his troops to Liaodong, which became a talk for future generations. Li Shimin was almost an invincible general, but because he was fond of ostentation and wanted to show off his power to neighboring states, he ended his military career with a defeat. This idiom originally refers to the emperor's love of expanding territory and showing off his power, later it refers to seeking great success boastfully.

好善嫉恶

Hào shàn jí è

出自后晋·刘昫等《旧唐书·李晟传》

[近义词：嫉恶如仇]

好善嫉恶，赏罚严明，治之材也。

Love Good and Hate Evil

From "Old Book of Tang: Biography of Li Sheng"

by Liu Xu (888–947) *et al*.

In the Mid-Tang dynasty (618–907), there was a general named Li Sheng (727–793) who made great contributions to quelling the rebellion and resisting the invasion of Tufan (Tibetan Empire). After the "An Lushan Rebellion" (755–763), a large area in the Central Plains of China was invaded, even the capital Chang'an (today's Xi'an) fell into the hands of the rebels. Li Sheng led his army and won a bloody battle to regain Chang'an. Emperor Dezong of Tang, Li Kuo (742–805), appointed Li Sheng as the governor of Fengxiang and Longyou, responsible for guarding the northwest border. At the time, the Tufan in the Western Regions wanted to invade the Central Plains. Shang Gyaltsen (?–796), the prime minister of Tufan, knew that if he wanted to attack the Central Plains, he first had to get rid of Li Sheng. He used a trick of personally leading the army to Longyou and Fengxiang, but instead of allowing their soldiers to plunder as they had done in the past, they just turned around as a demonstration, and spread the word everywhere: "Li Sheng summoned us, why didn't he reward us with wine and meat?" After Li Sheng knew about this, he sent troops to trap Tufan army. Tufan army was defeated, but unfortunately Shang Gyaltsen ran away.

Li Sheng led his troops to pursue the victory and conquered Tufan's Cuisha Fortress. Shang Gyaltsen hurriedly sent envoys to ask for peace with Emperor Dezong. Li Sheng rushed back to the capital and persuaded Emperor Dezong not to make peace. However, Emperor Dezong hated fighting after years of war, so he did not listen to Li Sheng's advice and even revoked Li Sheng's military post. Someone said to Li Sheng: "You have worked very hard and made great contributions, but you have been deprived of your military power. Since ancient times, those who have made great contributions have not had a good end. Why don't you prepare for your retreat?" Li Sheng knew this man was asking him to form a party and rebel, so he denounced him. People then all praised Li Sheng for "love good and hate evil."

后顾之忧

Hòu gù zhī yōu

出自北朝·北齐·魏收《魏书·李冲列传》

[近义词：后顾之虞；反义词：无忧无虑]

朕以仁明忠雅，委以台司之寄，使我出境无后顾之忧，一朝忽有此患，朕甚怀怆慨。

Worries from the Back

From "Book of Wei: Biography of Li Chong"

by Wei Shou (507–572)

Li Chong (450–498) was a well-known official of the Northern Wei dynasty (386–534) during the Southern and Northern dynasties. He was extremely intelligent, honest, loyal to the court, and highly valued by Emperor Xiaowen, Yuanhong (467–499), and respected by the ministers. A man named Li Biao (444–501) went to Li Chong when he first arrived in the capital city. After talking with him, Li Chong felt that Li Biao was very talented and appreciated him, so he recommended him to Emperor Xiaowen. Later, Li Biao became a lieutenant and minister, close to the emperor. Li Biao then felt great and looked down on all the ministers in the court. He was even arrogant and rude to Li Chong. The ministers hated Li Biao and went to Li Chong to express their discontent. Li Chong was also very angry, so he and the ministers jointly drafted a letter to Emperor Xiaowen to accuse Li Biao. When writing about Li Biao's ungratefulness, Li Chong was so furious that he became very sick and died 10 days later. Emperor Xiaowen was leading his troops to the south at the time. He hurried back to the capital after hearing the sad news. When he passed by Li Chong's tomb, Emperor Xiaowen cried and said: "Li Chong was a man of high moral character, loyal and reliable. He handled all the state affairs I entrusted to him very well, so that I had no worries every time I went out on the expedition. Unexpectedly, he died of a sudden illness. I'm so heartbroken!" This idiom refers to worrying about problems from the back in the process of advancement.

囫囵吞枣

Hú lún tūn zǎo

出自宋•圆悟克勤《碧岩录•卷三》

[近义词：生吞活剥、不求甚解；

反义词：细嚼慢咽、含英咀华、融会贯通]

若是知有底人，细嚼来咽；

若是不知有底人，一似浑仑吞个枣。

Swallowing Whole Jujubes

From "Blue Cliff Record: Volume 3"

by Chan/Zen Master Yuanwu Keqin (1063–1135)

Legend says in ancient China, there was a man who liked to be smart. Once, he asked an old doctor what fruit was most beneficial to the body. The doctor said: "Each type of fruit has its own characteristics and benefits the human body but eating too much of one type can also harm the body. For example, pears are good for teeth, but eating too much of them will damage the spleen and stomach. Jujubes nourish the spleen, but eating too much of them is not good for teeth. So, you must eat everything in moderation." The man shook his head and said: "I have a way to get the benefits of fruits without harming the body." The doctor asked: "What good method do you have? Can you tell me?" The man said: "My method is to eat different fruits in different ways. For example, when eating pears, just chew them in the mouth without swallowing them; when eating jujubes, don't bite them but swallow them whole. This way, it benefits without harm, and it will not hurt the teeth, the spleen, or the stomach." After hearing this, the doctor laughed and said: "Your method is no good. It is possible to chew pears without swallowing them, but it is difficult to swallow jujubes without chewing them. And you can't taste the jujubes if you swallow them whole like that!" This idiom is a metaphor for reading and accepting information without analyzing it.

狐假虎威

Hú jiǎ hǔ wēi

出自西汉·刘向《战国策·楚策一》

[近义词：仗势欺人、狗仗人势、攀龙附凤；

反义词：独擅胜场、独步天下]

荆宣王（楚宣王）问群臣曰："吾闻北方之畏昭奚恤也，果诚何如？"群臣莫对。江乙对曰："虎求百兽而食之，得狐。狐曰：'子无敢食我也。天帝使我长百兽，今子食我，是逆天帝命也。子以我为不信，吾为子先行，子随我后，观百兽之见我而敢不走乎？'虎以为然，故遂与之行。兽见之皆走。虎不知兽畏己而走也，以为畏狐也。今王之地方五千里，带甲百万，而专属之于昭奚恤；故北方之畏昭奚恤也，其实畏王之甲兵也，犹百兽之畏虎也。"

Fox Relying on Tiger's Might

From "Strategies of the Warring States: Strategies of Chu I" by Liu Xiang (77–6 BCE)

In the Warring States period (475–221 BCE), there was a high-ranking general in the state of Chu named Zhao Xixu who was very talented and had led his troops to victory many times. The northern states all feared him. Once the King Xuan of Chu (r. 369–340 BCE) summoned his ministers and asked: "I heard the northern states are very afraid of Zhao Xixu. Is that true?" The ministers were silent, not knowing how to answer. There was a minister named Jiang Yi who was very witty. He read the king's mind and said: "Your Majesty, those states are not afraid of Zhao Xixu, what they fear is Your Majesty's power!

I have heard such a story: Long ago, there was a tiger who was hungry and ran outside to look for food. When it came to a dense forest, it suddenly saw a fox walking in the front. So, the tiger jumped over and captured the fox. But when the tiger opened its mouth and was about to eat the fox, the cunning fox suddenly spoke: 'Humph! Don't think you are the king of beasts and dare to swallow me; you must know that heaven has ordered me to be the king of kings, whoever eats me will be severely punished.' The tiger was half-believing and half-doubting the fox's words. Even so, the tiger still thought to itself: 'Because I am the king of beasts, any beast in the world will fear me, how come this fox is ordered by heaven to rule us?' The fox saw the tiger hesitated, it then pointed at the tiger's nose and said: 'Why, don't you believe what I said? Then you walk behind me and see if all the beasts are scared when they see me.' The tiger thought this was a good idea. So, the fox led the way in front of the tiger, and the tiger followed behind the fox. Not long after they walked, they vaguely saw many small animals in the depths of the forest competing for food. When they saw the tiger walking behind the fox, they were frightened and ran away. The fox thus turned around, looking at the tiger proudly. Seeing this, the tiger felt a little scared, not knowing the beasts were afraid of itself, but thought they were afraid of the fox! The cunning fox's plot was successful, but it was entirely due to the might of the tiger, so the fox used the misleading situation to threaten the other animals. The tiger was fooled and didn't even know it!"

华而不实

Huá ér bù shí

出自春秋·左丘明《左传·文公五年》

[近义词：金玉其外、虚有其表；

反义词：表里如一、朴实无华]

天为刚德，犹不干时，况在人乎？

且华而不实，怨之所聚也。

Flashy but Insincere

From "The Zuo Tradition: Duke Wen's Fifth Year"

by Zuo Qiuming (556–452 BCE)

In the Spring and Autumn period (770–476 BCE), there was a nobleman in Jin State named Yang Chufu (?–621 BCE) who was handsome, well-mannered, and always gave others a good first impression. Once he was on a mission trip to Wei State, on his way back to Jin State, he passed by Ningyi (today's Huojia county, Henan province) and stayed in an inn. The innkeeper was surnamed Ying, who saw Yang Chufu was handsome with extraordinary manners, he immediately liked him and took extra care of him. In the evening, the innkeeper said to his wife: "I have long wanted to seek refuge with a person of noble character and do a great cause. For many years, I have been looking for such a person, I think Yang Chufu who came today looks like a person who can accomplish great things. Maybe he is sent by heaven to guide me. I decide to go with him." The next day, after getting Yang Chufu's permission, the innkeeper said goodbye to his wife and left with

Yang. A few days later, the innkeeper returned home. His wife was very puzzled and asked him: "You have finally met such a person, why have you returned only after a few days?" The innkeeper said: "I saw this person was handsome and I had a good impression of him, but through these few days of contact, I found he had extreme thoughts, and he was flashy but insincere. Such a person is easy to make enemies. I am worried that following him is not only unbeneficial to me, but will also bring me disasters, so I'd better leave him as soon as possible." Later, Yang Chufu was indeed killed. This idiom originally refers to the flowers that look beautiful but do not bear fruit; later it is used to refer to something that looks good but is useless.

画饼充饥

Huà bǐng chōng jī

出自西晋·陈寿《三国志·魏志·卢毓传》

[近义词：望梅止渴、纸上谈兵；

反义词：名副其实、货真价实]

选举莫取有名，名如画地作饼，不可啖也。

Drawing Cakes to Relieve Hunger

From "Records of the Three Kingdoms:
Records of Wei: Biography of Lu Yu"
by Chen Shou (233–297)

Lu Yu (183–257) was a well-known minister of Wei State during the Three Kingdoms period (220–280). He was from a poor family and his parents died when he was very young. Then he lived with his elder brother who also died soon after. Nevertheless, he was very talented and studied very hard. Finally, he became an official in the capital city and was highly valued by Emperor Wen of Wei, Cao Pi (187–226). Lu Yu was upright and honest in his administration, which won praise from many people. So, he was soon promoted to the position of Palace Attendant and served the emperor by the side. Later, he became the Minister of Personnel while still maintaining his upright and outspoken personality. Before Lu Yu was promoted to the Minister of Personnel, he served as the Secretary of the Central Secretariat. After he was transferred, the position became vacant and needed to be filled. At this time, Emperor Wen of Wei asked Lu Yu to recommend a suitable person and give his own advice: "The most important quality in selecting talents is their ability to do things. Many people are famous, but they can't perform real deeds. Don't select those who only have big names but can't fulfil their duties. People's fame is like a pie drawn on the ground, which can be viewed but can't be tasted." Lu Yu replied: "Your Majesty, the problem you mentioned exists. When we select outstanding candidates, we really can't just look at their fame but also must see if they can fulfil the duty. Oftentimes, a person's moral character may be more important than their other qualities. Therefore, we should consider people with good moral character as our reserve candidates. If their abilities are also qualified, they can hold important positions. I suggest strengthening the assessment method. People with both moral cultivation and real talents are the ones we need." Emperor Wen of Wei thought that Lu Yu's words made sense, so he ordered the formulation of an assessment method. This idiom originally refers to drawing cakes to relieve hunger. Later, it is extended to mean imagining something that is urgently needed to comfort oneself.

画龙点睛

Huà lóng diǎn jīng

出自唐·张彦远《历代名画记·张僧繇》

[近义词：锦上添花、点石成金、妙笔生花；

反义词：画蛇添足、弄巧成拙]

张僧繇于金陵安乐寺画四龙于壁，不点睛。每云："点之即飞去。"人以为妄诞，固请点之。须臾，雷电破壁，二龙乘云腾去上天，二龙未点眼者皆在。

Drawing Dragon's Eyes as the Finishing Points

From "Records of Famous Paintings of All Ages: Zhang Sengyao" by Zhang Yanyuan (815–907)

During the Southern and Northern dynasties (420–589), there was a great painter named Zhang Sengyao (479–?) in the Liang-dynasty capital Jinling (today's Nanjing). His paintings always looked vibrant and magnificent. The imperial families, nobles, and wealthy merchants all competed to collect his paintings. Legend says that one year, Zhang Sengyao was commissioned by Emperor Wu of Liang (464–549) to paint four golden dragons on the wall of Anle Temple. In just 3 days, he painted four lifelike dragons which amazed all the viewers. However, when looked closely, these dragons had no eyes, which made everyone puzzled. The viewers asked Zhang Sengyao to add eyes to the dragons. Zhang Sengyao smiled and said: "It's not difficult to paint eyes for the dragons, but once the eyes are painted, these four dragons will fly away." When the viewers heard this, they all laughed and thought he was joking. No one believed it. So, Zhang Sengyao first painted eyes for two of the dragons. In front of everyone, he picked up the brush and lightly dotted the eyes on the painting. As soon as he finished this, the sky suddenly became overcast, followed by a burst of lightning and thunder. In the storm, the two dragons broke through the wall, flew to the sky, and finally disappeared in the clouds. Everyone was stunned. When the clouds dispersed and the sky cleared, everyone saw that there were only two dragons left on the wall. Zhang Sengyao just stood aside, smiling and saying nothing. This idiom is often used as a metaphor to refer to using a few key sentences to make an article or a speech clearer or make the content more vivid and powerful.

画蛇添足

Huà shé tiān zú

出自西汉·刘向《战国策·齐策二》

[近义词：多此一举、节外生枝、弄巧成拙；

反义词：画龙点睛、恰到好处、恰如其分]

陈轸曰："令尹贵矣，王非置两令尹也。臣窃为公譬可也？楚有祠者，赐其舍人卮酒。舍人相谓曰：'数人饮之不足，一人饮之有余。请画地为蛇，先成者饮酒。'一人蛇先成，引酒且饮之，乃左手持卮，右手画蛇，曰：'吾能为之足。'未成，人之蛇成，夺其卮曰：'蛇固无足，子安能为之足？'遂饮其酒。为蛇足者，终亡其酒。今君相楚而攻魏，破军杀将得八城，不弱兵，欲攻齐。齐畏公甚，公以是为名居足矣。官之上非可重也。战无不胜，而不知止者，身且死，爵且后归，犹为蛇足也。"昭合以为然，解军而去。

Drawing a Snake with Feet

From "Strategies of the Warring States: Strategies of Qi II" by Liu Xiang (77–6 BCE)

There was a nobleman in the state of Chu who, after offering sacrifices to his ancestors, gave a pot of libation wine to his guests. The guests held the pot of wine and did not know what to do with it. They thought that one pot of wine would not be enough for so many people, it would be better to give it to one person to drink it entirely. But who should they give it to? The guests discussed an idea that each person should draw a snake on the ground, and whoever finished the drawing first would get the pot of wine. Everyone agreed with the idea. The guests each took a small stick and began to draw snakes on the ground. One person drew very quickly, and soon he finished drawing the snake, he took over the wine pot. Just as he was about to drink it, he saw that others had not finished drawing the snake. He held the wine pot in his left hand and continued to draw the snake with his right hand and said: "I still have time to add a few feet to the snake." Before he finished drawing the feet for the snake, unexpectedly, another person had already finished drawing the snake. That person grabbed the wine pot and said: "Snakes don't have feet; how can you add feet to it? This wine belongs to me!" Then he drank the wine. The man who added feet to the snake did not get to drink the wine in the end. This idiom refers to doing something unnecessary that is not only useless but also inappropriate; it also refers to fabricating facts and making something out of nothing.

黄粱一梦

Huáng liáng yí mèng

出自唐·沈既济《枕中记》

[近义词：黄粱美梦、一枕黄粱、一枕槐安、南柯一梦、邯郸一梦、庄周梦蝶；

反义词：如梦初醒、梦想成空、梦想破灭]

开元七年，道士有吕翁者，得神仙术，行邯郸道中，息邸舍，摄帽弛带隐囊而坐，俄见旅中少年，乃卢生也。……卢生欠伸而悟，见其身方偃于邸舍，吕翁坐其傍，主人蒸黍未熟，触类如故。生蹶然而兴，曰："岂其梦寐耶？"翁谓生曰："人生之适，亦如是矣。"生怃然良久，谢曰："夫宠辱之道，穷达之运，得丧之理，死生之情，尽知之矣。此先生所以窒吾欲也。敢不受教！"稽首再拜而去。

A Dream Under the Yellow Beam

From "The Pillow Book" by Shen Jiji (? –800)

During the Kaiyuan period (713–741) of the Tang dynasty (618–907), a young man named Lu went to take the Imperial Examination in the capital city. In the evening, he stayed in an inn. The inn owner was cooking yellow rice, and a Daoist old man named Lü was also staying there. Lu chatted with Lü, and the two had a very good conversation. Lu said passionately: "A real man should be a general or a chancellor, but I have achieved nothing!" Lü smiled and said: "This is not difficult." Lü then took out a pillow and said: "If you sleep on this pillow, you will fulfil your desire." Although being skeptical, Lu took the pillow, with his clothes on, he soon fell asleep. He dreamed that he passed the Imperial

Examination and married the beautiful Miss Cui. Later, he became the governor of Hexi, defeated Tufan, returned victoriously, and became the chancellor. Unexpectedly, a treacherous official accused him of rebellion, the emperor ordered to arrest him and exiled him to a distant place. A few years later, the emperor rehabilitated him, reinstated him, and gave him many treasures. He lived past 80 years old, with many children and grandchildren, enjoying all the splendor and wealth. When Lu woke up, he found himself still sleeping in the inn, with Lü sitting next to him. He looked at the stove, the yellow rice cooked by the innkeeper was still not ready! This idiom suggests that a fulfilling life cannot be achieved by an illusory dream; only through hard work can one turn their wishes into reality.

家徒四壁

Jiā tú sì bì

出自西汉·司马迁《史记·司马相如列传》

[近义词：环堵萧然、家徒壁立、一贫如洗；
反义词：家给人足、富甲一方、富可敌国]

文君夜亡奔相如，相如乃与驰归成都，
家居徒四壁立。

Only Four Walls Around the House

From "Records of the Grand Historian:
Biography of Sima Xiangru"
by Sima Qian (145–c.86 BCE)

During the Western Han dynasty (206 BCE–23 CE), Sima Xiangru (179–118 BCE) was a well-known poet and writer who had literary talent and was good at playing the guqin. Being elegant and unrestrained, many people wanted to associate with him. When Emperor Jing of Han, Liu Qi (188–141 BCE) and King Xiao of Liang, Liu Wu (?–144 BCE) were alive, Sima Xiangru worked as a minor official. Later, he returned to his hometown of Chengdu and lived a leisurely life. When his friends in the town saw that Sima Xiangru had come back, they all visited him. Sima Xiangru also went to visit his friends. He had a friend named Wang Ji, who was the Linqiong county magistrate. Once Sima Xiangru went to visit Wang Ji and stayed in a small inn there. Wang Ji met Sima Xiangru in the inn, the two friends talked so much, making their friendship known to wealthy people in the city.

There was a rich man named Zhuo Wangsun who saw that Wang Ji respected Sima Xiangru so much, he also wanted to get to know Sima Xiangru. So, he prepared a banquet and invited Wang Ji and Sima Xiangru to come. But Sima Xiangru did not want to meet Zhuo Wangsun, so he pretended to be sick and refused to come, which made Zhuo Wangsun anxious. Zhuo Wangsun had a daughter named Zhuo Wenjun (175–121 BCE), who returned to her parental home after her husband's death. Zhuo Wenjun loved poetry and music since childhood and had heard of Sima Xiangru's name. Zhuo Wangsun invited hundreds of guests and begged Wang Ji to personally invite Sima Xiangru, thus Sima Xiangru accepted the invitation. The banquet was very lively. Sima Xiangru played several pieces of music, which won the praise of all the guests. Zhuo Wenjun heard Sima Xiangru's pleasant guqin performance through the window, and saw that he was handsome and gracious, she fell in love with him immediately. After knowing this, Sima Xiangru also liked Zhuo Wenjun's talent and appearance. The two contacted each other privately and secretly agreed to spend their lives together. After finding out about this, Zhuo Wangsun despised Sima Xiangru's poverty and disapproved the marriage. Zhuo Wenjun and Sima Xiangru then secretly left Linqiong at night and returned to Sima Xiangru's home in Chengdu. Zhuo Wenjun saw that Sima Xiangru's house had only four walls with nothing inside, he was penniless, but she still loved him. After learning about this, Zhuo Wangsun was very angry and refused to give them any money. Zhuo Wenjun had no complaints and was willing to live a humble life with Sima Xiangru. They returned to Linqiong and opened a small restaurant. Zhuo Wenjun personally sold wine while Sima Xiangru worked as a waiter. Zhuo Wangsun was afraid of losing face, so he gave Zhuo Wenjun some money to allow the couple to return to Chengdu. Later, Emperor Wu of Han, Liu Che (156–87 BCE) read Sima Xiangru's writings and was very impressed, he called Sima Xiangru to the capital and appointed him as a secretary.

价值连城

Jià zhí lián chéng

出自西汉·司马迁《史记·廉颇蔺相如列传》

[近义词：无价之宝、连城之价；

反义词：一钱不值、无足轻重]

赵惠文王时，得楚和氏璧。秦昭王闻之，

使人遗赵王书，愿以十五城请易璧。

Its Price Worthy of Many Connected Cities

From "Records of the Grand Historian:
Biographies of Lian Po and Lin Xiangru"
by Sima Qian (145–c.86 BCE)

During the Spring and Autumn period (770–476 BCE), there was a man named Bian He from Chu State. One day, he found a piece of jade in Jing Mountain. The jade was covered with a layer of stone. If the stone was removed, it could be carved into a rare jade disk. Bian He was a loyal man; he took the piece to the palace and presented it to King Li of Chu (?–741 BCE), who asked his ministers to pass it around. The ministers looked at it and said it was a piece of stone, which made King Li very angry. At this time, Bian asked for a jade carver to examine it. When the jade carver saw this big piece, he said with certainty that it was stone. King Li was furious, he charged Bian He with deceiving the monarch, and ordered others to cut off his left foot, which made Bian He very sad. Not long after, King Li died and King Wu of Chu (?–690 BCE) ascended the throne. Bian thought that King

Wu would recognize the treasure, so he brought the piece to King Wu again. After King Wu passed it around to his ministers, and personally observed the piece, he felt it did not look like jade. So, he called the jade carver to identify it. The carver insisted that it was a stone, which made King Wu enraged and ordered Bian He's right foot to be cut off.

Bian cried out that he was unjustly treated. After King Wu died, King Wen of Chu (?–675 BCE) ascended the throne. Bian He no longer went to the palace, but at the foot of Jing Mountain while holding the jade, he cried bitterly for 3 days and 3 nights. The news reached the palace, and King Wen sent officers to investigate the matter. The officers asked him why, Bian He said confidently: "I'm sad because the jade is unparalleled in the state, but it is considered a stone and not being valued as it should be. I am an honest man, but I am considered guilty of deceiving the king. This is too unfair!" After hearing about this, King Wen immediately called Bian He to the palace and ordered the jade carver to remove the layer of stone outside the jade. After the carver did this, King Wen finally obtained a crystal jade disk, which was indeed rare and priceless. King Wen regarded this jade disk as a national treasure and called it "Heshi Bi." During the Warring States period (475–221 BCE), Zhao State acquired Heshi Bi. When King Zhaoxiang of Qin (325–251 BCE) knew about this, he pretended that he wanted to exchange 15 cities with Zhao State for this jade disk. King Huiwen of Zhao (310–266 BCE) was afraid of offending King Zhaoxiang, so he sent Lin Xiangru to Qin State with the jade disk to negotiate. It turned out that King Zhaoxiang had no real intention of exchanging 15 cities for Heshi Bi. Lin Xiangru, with his wit and courage, fulfilled his mission and brought Heshi Bi back to Zhao. The original meaning of this idiom is that the value of an item is equal to many cities connected, it is priceless.

兼听则明，偏听则暗

Jiān tīng zé míng, piān tīng zé àn

出自汉·王符《潜夫论·明暗》

[近义词：广开言路、集思广益；

反义词：独断专行、闭目塞听]

君之所以明者，兼听也；其所以暗者，偏信也。

Listening to Both Sides Leads to Enlightenment, Listening to Only One Side Leads to Ignorance

From "Qianfu's Theory: Enlightenment and Ignorance"

by Wang Fu (c.85–c.163)

The reason why some monarchs are bright and can discern right from wrong is because they listen to opinions from both sides; and the reason why some monarchs are foolish and make wrong judgments is because they only listen to one-sided opinion and believe it as true. Therefore, only by listening to opinions from both sides can a monarch understand the truth and become intelligent and wise; if he only listens to one-sided opinion, he will eventually become foolish.

将欲取之，必先与之

Jiāng yù qǔ zhī, bì xiān yǔ zhī

出自春秋·老子《道德经·第三十六章》

[近义词：将取姑也、欲取姑与]

将欲废之，必固兴之；将欲取之，必固与之。

If You Want to Take, You Must First Give

From "Dao De Jing: Chapter 36"

by Laozi (c.571–471 BCE)

The phrase "If you want to take, you must first give" has different meanings in different contexts. In military, it means to retreat to advance. In social life, it means to give before receiving. In agriculture, it means to sow and plow before harvest. Using the "Theory of Contradiction" to explain it, "taking" and "giving" are two aspects of the contradiction that cannot occur at the same time, but they are inseparable. There is no reward without giving. Giving is the necessary premise for asking for something and asking for something or getting something is also the inevitable logical result of giving. In methodological significance, it requires that the relationship between the two cannot be separated. If one only wants to take without knowing how to give, one will bring about their own discontent.

狡兔三窟

Jiǎo tù sān kū

出自西汉·刘向《战国策·齐策四》

[近义词：移花接木、掩人耳目；

反义词：瓮中之鳖、坐以待毙]

狡兔有三窟，仅得其免死身，今君在一窟，

未得高枕而卧也，请为君复凿二窟。

A Cunning Rabbit Has Three Burrows

From "Strategies of the Warring States: Strategies of Qi IV" by Liu Xiang (77–6 BCE)

During the Spring and Autumn and the Warring States periods (770–221 BCE), there was an aristocrat and statesman in Qi State, known as Lord Mengchang (Tian Wen, ?–279 BCE), who kept many retainers at home as his counselors. Among the retainers was a man named Feng Xuan, who was from a poor family and often stayed in Mengchang's house for a long period of time. Nevertheless, Mengchang still entertained him. Once, Feng Xuan went to Xuedi to collect debts for Mengchang, not only did he not ask the local people for the debts but also burned all the bonds. The people of Xuedi thought it was Mengchang's kindness and were grateful to him. Later, Mengchang was dismissed from his position as Grand Chancellor by the King of Qi and went to Xuedi to settle down. He was warmly welcomed by Xuedi people, only then Mengchang knew Feng Xuan's talent. At this time, Feng Xuan, who usually did not talk much, said to Mengchang: "A cunning rabbit has three burrows to avoid the misfortune of being beaten to death. I want to dig another burrow for you." Later, Feng Xuan used a trick to let the King of Qi send gold, horses, and swords as gifts to respectfully invite Mengchang to resume his official position. Mengchang had therefore served as an official for several decades, and Feng Xuan offered him many strategies. In modern Chinese, this idiom refers to someone who is scheming.

脚踏实地

Jiǎo tà shí dì

出自宋·邵伯温《邵氏闻见录：卷十八》

[近义词：足履实地；反义词：好高骛远]

公尝问康节曰："某何如人？"

曰："君实脚踏实地人也。"

Keeping Your Feet Firmly on Solid Ground

From "Shao's Records of What Heard and Saw: Volume 18" by Shao Bowen (1057–1134)

Sima Guang (1019–1086) was a renowned historian in the Northern Song dynasty (960–1127). He was diligent and studious since childhood and had a special preference for history. When he was very young, he was determined to become a historian and later fulfilled his wish. During the reign of Emperor Yingzong of Song, Zhao Shu (1032–1067), Sima Guang was commissioned to edit "Zizhi Tongjian" (*Comprehensive Mirror in Aid of Governance*). During the compilation process, he worked day and night and often forgot to eat and sleep. To prevent from sleeping too soundly or too long to delay his work, he made a round wooden "alarm pillow" so that he could get up early to write. With the assistance of many other historians, Sima Guang spent 19 years studying countless historical records, extensively collecting materials, carefully arranging them in chronological order, and finally completed the 294-volume *Zizhi Tongjian*. This rich and valuable history book starts from the early Warring States period (475–221 BCE) and ends at the Five Dynasties (907–979), covering nearly 1,500 years, with more than 3 million words – the largest chronological records in Chinese history. Sima Guang's work ethics has been widely praised. Once, Sima Guang asked his good friend Shao Yong: "What kind of person am I?" Shao Yong replied admiringly: "You are a person who keep your feet firmly on solid ground!" This idiom is a metaphor for doing things in a down-to-earth and surefooted manner.

揭竿而起

Jiē gān ér qǐ

出自西汉·贾谊《过秦论》

[近义词：逼上梁山；反义词：忍辱偷生]

将数百之众，转而攻秦，斩木为兵，揭竿为旗。

Raising the Pole to Uprise

From "The Faults of the Qin Dynasty"

by Jia Yi (200–168 BCE)

At the end of the Qin dynasty (221–206 BCE), regardless of the people's livelihoods, the Imperial Court levied heavy taxes and recruited soldiers from farmers all over the country to defend the border. Among the group of recruited poor farmers from Yangcheng, were Chen Sheng (?–208 BCE) and Wu Guang (?–208 BCE), who marched to Yuyang. Chen Sheng was a farmhand with great ambition and believed that one day he would get ahead. The two official guards saw that Chen Sheng and Wu Guang were physically strong, they asked Chen and Wu to be the leaders of the troop to lead 900 people to the designated place within the prescribed time limit. When the troop arrived in Daze township, it happened to encounter heavy rains for several days in a row. The road was flooded, and they could not move forward. According to the Qin-dynasty law, those who failed to arrive on time would be executed. All the soldiers sighed. Chen and Wu secretly discussed: "It is still thousands of *li* to Yuyang from here, it is impossible to arrive on time. If we miss the deadline, we will die. If we rebel, we will also die. Why not rebel?"

Chen Sheng and Wu Guang then set a plan. To create public opinion, they decided to act on two strategies. Wu Guang first wrote the three characters "King Chen Sheng" on a piece of white cloth in advance and stuffed it into the belly of the fish he bought. The next day, the chef cut the fish, found the white cloth and spread the news. The soldiers all talked about it and looked at Chen Sheng differently. On that night, Wu Guang lit a bonfire in the distant jungle and imitated the voice of a fox and shouted: "Great Chu Rise, King Chen Sheng!" The soldiers heard the shouting in the middle of the night and said that it was heaven's will that Chen Sheng would become the emperor soon. They all supported him and were determined to follow him. Chen Sheng and Wu Guang saw that the time was ripe, they deliberately angered the two official guards and killed them. Afterwards, Chen Sheng and Wu Guang summoned 900 soldiers and announced an uprising. The soldiers were well prepared and cheered in unison, unanimously agreeing to the uprising and nominating Chen Sheng and Wu Guang as leaders. So, Chen Sheng appointed himself as general and Wu Guang as captain, under the banner of the crown prince of the Qin dynasty, Fusu (241–210 BCE), and the former general of Chu State, Xiang Liang (?–208 BCE), they named it Zhang Chu and officially started the uprising. The rebels first occupied Daze township, the villagers offered them food and water, and the young men rushed to join the rebel army. The army suddenly increased in number. Without weapons and flags, they picked up wooden sticks as swords and guns and cut down bamboos as flagpoles. Chen Sheng and Wu Guang rose up and led the rebel army to the battlefield.

捷足先登

Jié zú xiān dēng

出自西汉·司马迁《史记·淮阴侯列传》

[近义词：捷足先得；反义词：姗姗来迟]

蒯通至，上曰："若教淮阴侯反乎？"对曰："然，臣固教之。竖子不用臣之策，故令自夷于此。如彼竖子用臣之计，陛下安得而夷之乎！"上怒曰："亨之。"通曰："嗟乎，冤哉亨也！"上曰："若教韩信反，何冤？"对曰："秦之纲绝而维弛，山东大扰，异姓并起，英俊乌集。秦失其鹿，天下共逐之，于是高材疾足者先得焉。跖之狗吠尧，尧非不仁，狗因吠非其主。当是时，臣唯独知韩信，非知陛下也。且天下锐精持锋欲为陛下所为者甚众，顾力不能耳。又可尽亨之邪？"

Walking Faster Can Get There First

From "Records of the Grand Historian:
Biography of the Marquis of Huaiyin"
by Sima Qian (145–c.86 BCE)

During the Chu-Han Contention (206–202 BCE), Emperor Gaozu of Han, Liu Bang (c.256–195 BCE) had a general named Han Xin (231–196 BCE) who was very good at using troops. Once, Liu Bang sent Han Xin to lead troops to attack the King of Qi, Tian Guang (?–204 BCE). Han Xin quickly defeated Tian Guang and broke through Qi's capital city. Liu Bang was besieged by Xiang Yu (232–202 BCE) in Xingyang at the time, and was worried that Han Xin would rebel, so Liu Bang made Han Xin the King of Qi. Han Xin had an advisor named Kuai Tong who saw that Han Xin was powerful, thus advised him to take the opportunity to divide the country into three states alongside Liu Bang and Xiang Yu. However, Han Xin thought of the favors that Liu Bang had given him and felt that it would be unloyal to do so; he did not accept Kuai Tong's advice. After Liu Bang became emperor, he no longer trusted Han Xin. So, he first removed Han Xin's military power and changed his title from King of Qi to King of Chu and then took him to Luoyang and demoted him to Marquis of Huaiyin. Han Xin lived in Chang'an (today's Xi'an) with much discontent. It happened that his good friend Chen Xi (?–196 BCE) was sent to garrison in Julu, Han Xin then secretly contacted Chen Xi and conspired to start a rebellion. After Liu Bang learned the news, he crusaded against Chen Xi. Han Xin pretended to be sick and secretly prepared for the details of the day of action, but the plan was exposed. Liu Bang's wife, Empress Lü (c.241–180 BCE) discussed with Grand Chancellor Xiao He (257–193 BCE), tricked Han Xin into the palace, and executed him on the spot. When Han Xin was dying, he said: "I really regret not listening to Kuai Tong's advice, so now I die in vain at the hands of a woman!" After Liu Bang defeated Chen Xi and returned to Chang'an, he heard about this and immediately arrested Kuai Tong and interrogated him: "Did you persuade Han Xin to rebel?" Kuai Tong admitted it and said: "Han Xin didn't listen to my advice at the beginning, so he ended up like this!" Liu Bang was furious and ordered him to be boiled to death. Kuai Tong cried out that he was wronged and said confidently: "At that time, the Qin regime was like a fleeing deer. Only those with outstanding talents and quick actions could get it first. I was Han Xin's advisor, of course I gave him advice. There were many people fighting to get the power of the country, and many people said such things. Do you want to catch them all and boil them all to death?" Liu Bang was speechless after hearing this. He felt that Kuai Tong's words made sense, so he released him. This idiom originally means that the one who walks faster will reach the top first; it also means that those who act more quickly can get what they want before others.

解铃还须系铃人

Jiě líng hái xū xì líng rén

[近义词：心病还须心药医；反义词：越俎代庖]

法灯泰钦禅师少解悟，然未为人知，独法眼禅师深奇之。一日法眼问大众曰："虎项下金铃，何人解得？"众无以对。泰钦适至，法眼举前语问之。泰钦曰："大众何不道：'系者解得。'"由是人人刮目相看。–出自宋·惠洪《林间集》

金陵清凉寺泰钦法灯禅师在众日，性豪逸，不事事，众易之，法眼独契重。眼一日问众："虎项金铃，是谁解得？"众无对。时师适至，眼举前语问。师曰："系者解得。"眼曰："汝辈轻渠不得。"–明·翟汝稷《指月录》

The One Who Tied the Bell Must Be the One Who Can Untie It

From "Forest Collection"

by Hui Hong (1071–1128); and

"Record of Pointing to the Moon"

by Qu Ruji (1548–1610)

During the Southern Tang dynasty (937–975), there was an eminent monk named Master Fayan, who lived in Qingliang Temple in Jinling (today's Nanjing), and who founded the Fayan School, one of the five schools of Chan Buddhism in the history of Chinese Buddhism. Many monks in the temple learned Buddhism from him. Everyone was diligent, attended classes on time, practiced meditation, abided by the rules and regulations, and chanted scriptures and worshiped Buddha. There was another master named Taiqin, known as Monk Fadeng, who also lived in Qingliang Temple. He was proficient in Buddhism, had great wisdom and intelligence, but his words were often incomprehensible. Fadeng had a bold and unrestrained character. He did not ask about the affairs of the temple and often ignored the rules and regulations. Therefore, many monks disliked him, kept a distance from him, and some even looked down on him. But Fadeng did not care at all and continued to do his own things. Master Fayan saw this, but never said anything about Fadeng and still respected him very much, knowing that Fadeng was not an ordinary monk. One day, Master Fayan was giving a talk to all the monks who were sitting upright and listening attentively. As usual, Master Fadeng did not come to the class. No one knew where he had gone. Master Fayan asked a question: "There is a ferocious tiger with a golden bell tied around its neck. Who can take the bell off?" The monks looked at each other, none of them could answer the question. At this time, Fadeng walked by the door. Master Fayan called him in and asked him to answer the question. Master Fadeng answered without hesitation: "The one who tied the bell must be the one who can untie it." All the monks suddenly realized what was going on and admired Fadeng's wisdom. Master Fayan was very satisfied and took the opportunity to say to all the monks: "From now on, you can no longer look down on him!"

金石为开

Jīn shí wéi kāi

[反义词：无动于衷]

昔者楚熊渠子夜行，见寝石以为伏虎，关弓射之，灭矢饮羽，下视，知石也。却复射之，矢摧无迹。熊渠子见其诚心，而金石为之开，况人心乎？–出自西汉·刘向《新序·杂事四》

李广……复猎于冥山之阳，又见卧虎，射之，没矢饮羽，进而视之，乃石也，其形类虎。退而更射，更镞折而石不伤。余尝以问扬子云，子云曰："至诚则金石为开。" – 西汉·刘歆《西京杂记·第五》

Opening the Stone

From "New Order: Miscellaneous Matters 4"

by Liu Xiang (77–6 BCE); and

"Miscellaneous Records of the Western Capital:

Volume 5" by Liu Xin (46 BCE–23 CE)

During the Zhou dynasty (1046–221 BCE), there was a man named Xiong Quzi from Chu State, who loved archery since childhood. When he first started practicing archery, he had very little strength and could not pull a slightly stronger bow. Some people laughed at him and said that he would not be a good archer in the future. Xiong Quzi was very unconvinced and insisted on practicing arm strength every day. Gradually, he developed strength. When he pulled the bow and shot arrows again, the arrows flew out no longer lightly. However, the arrows he shot could not accurately hit the target, so he continued to practice his eyesight.

After hard training, he had achieved very good archery skills. For every ten arrows he shot, seven or eight hit the target. People then said he was an expert in archery. However, he felt that his skills were not good enough and he could not improve, which made him very worried. Someone said to him: "You can shoot very well now, but you shoot with skills. You should shoot every arrow with your heart, that is the real skill." Xiong Quzi heard this, pondered over it, and practiced even harder.

One night, Xiong Quzi was walking alone on a mountain road. Suddenly, he saw a tiger lying not far in front of him. If he got closer, it would pounce on him. Xiong Quzi was shocked, but then he calmed down. He thought that this was a good opportunity to test his archery skills. With his skills, he must be able to shoot the tiger to death. So, he was not afraid and quickly took the bow and arrow, aimed at the tiger, pulled the bow to the full and shot an arrow. With a "whoosh" sound, there was no movement at all. Xiong Quzi was surprised. He thought that this arrow must not only hit the tiger but also kill it. Who would expect that the tiger did not move at all? What had happened? He took up his courage and strode over to look at it. He could not help laughing. It turned out to be a big stone lying on the ground. Looking more closely, the arrow shot into the hard stone, and even the arrow feathers were deeply embedded in the stone, almost invisible. This incident spread quickly, and everyone praised his excellent archery skills. The man who had encouraged him before said that it was not only because Xiong Quzi was strong and good at archery, but also because he concentrated his energy and faced the opponent with the confidence of winning, so even the stone was opened by him. This idiom means that the hardest things are opened, which suggests that enough sincerity can move people's hearts; it also implies that a strong will can overcome all difficulties. In modern times, the idiom is often used to describe that sufficient preparations have been made and only a suitable opportunity is needed to succeed.

锦囊妙计

Jǐn náng miào jì

出自明·罗贯中《三国演义·第五十四回》

[近义词：神机妙算；反义词：无计可施、一筹莫展]

汝保主公入吴，当领此三个锦囊。

囊中有三条妙计，依次而行。

Smart Strategies in Brocade Bags

From "Romance of the Three Kingdoms: Chapter 54"

by Luo Guanzhong (c.1330–c.1400)

During the Three Kingdoms period (220–280), Liu Bei (161–223) competed with Sun Quan (182–252) and Cao Cao (155–220) for the country. He invited Zhuge Liang (181–234) to Longzhong to serve as a military advisor, which made him more powerful. Later, Liu Bei occupied Jingzhou as his own territory, recruited soldiers, bought horses, and became very mighty. Liu Bei's existence made Sun Quan deeply worried. In addition, Jingzhou originally belonged to the jurisdiction of Eastern Wu, and Sun Quan always wanted to take Jingzhou back. Liu Bei's wife Gan died in the Battle of Changbanpo, and Liu Bei had not remarried at the time. Zhou Yu (175–210) thought of an opportunity.

Zhou Yu and Sun Quan planned to let Sun Quan's sister marry Liu Bei, trick Liu Bei to Wu capital, Nanxu (today's Zhenjiang city), then get rid of him and take the opportunity to regain Jingzhou. When Liu Bei heard about this, he thought it was a scam and refused to take the risk of going to Wu capital to get married. Zhuge Liang had already seen through

Zhou Yu's plan and decided to use it against him to put Liu Bei and Sun Quan in a marriage relationship and let Sun Quan reap what he sow. Zhuge Liang advised Liu Bei to go there and get married. He said: "Why don't you accept someone who has sent you a good wife? I'll ask Zhao Yun to accompany you there. Rest assured that you will get your wife and not lose Jingzhou." Zhuge Liang then called Zhao Yun, gave him three brocade bags with three ingenious strategies, and asked him to follow them one by one in the correct order. Zhao Yun took the bags, protected Liu Bei, and led 500 people on speedboats to Nanxu. When Liu Bei arrived in Wu capital, everything was as Zhuge Liang expected. Zhao Yun followed Zhuge Liang's instructions, opened one bag at every critical moment, and acted according to the scheme. After the three ingenious strategies were used, Liu Bei successfully married Sun Quan's sister and safely returned to Jingzhou. Sun Quan adopted Zhou Yu's plan but ended up "losing his sister and the soldiers."

惊弓之鸟

Jīng gōng zhī niǎo

出自西汉·刘向《战国策·楚策四》

[近义词：心有余悸、谈虎色变、一朝被蛇咬，

十年怕井绳；反义词：初生之犊]

更羸与魏王处京台之下，仰见飞鸟。更羸谓魏王曰："臣为王引弓虚发而下鸟。"魏王曰："然则射可至此乎？"更羸曰："可。"有间，雁从东方来，更羸以虚发而下之。魏王曰："然则射可至此乎？"更羸曰："此孽也。"王曰："先生何以知之？"对曰："其飞徐而鸣悲。飞徐者，故疮痛也，鸣悲者，久失群也，六故疮未息而惊心未至也，闻弦音，引而高飞，故疮陨也。"

A Frightened Bird

From "Strategies of the Warring States: Strategies of Chu IV" by Liu Xiang (77–6 BCE)

In the state of Wei, there was a man named Geng Lei who was very good at archery. One day, he was talking with the King of Wei and heard the cry of a wild goose. He looked up and saw a wild goose flying in the sky. Geng Lei watched for a while and said to the king: "Your Majesty, I can shoot this wild goose down by just pulling the bow without putting an arrow on it." The king laughed and said: "You are joking! I don't believe your archery skills can be so high." Geng Lei took out the bow, waited for the wild goose to fly close, and immediately pulled the bow open, aimed at the wild goose, and flicked it with a "bang." The arrow did not shoot, but the wild goose fell headfirst to the ground with the sound of the bowstring. The king was so surprised that he could not help but praise him: "You are indeed worthy of being a sharpshooter." Geng Lei put down his bow, pointed at the goose, and said modestly: "It's not that I am skilled, but this goose was wounded by an arrow." The king approached the goose and took a closer look. It was indeed true. He was even more surprised and asked: "How do you know it was wounded by an arrow?" Geng Lei said calmly: "I found that it flew very slowly, and its cry was sad. Flying slowly means that the wound is painful; crying sadly means that it is lonely and separated from the flock. The old wound had not healed, and it was frightened. When it heard the bowstring, it thought someone shot it with an arrow, so it flew high and the wound broke, so it fell by itself." This idiom is used to describe a person who has been wounded and is scared at the slightest advancement.

开天辟地

Kāi tiān pì dì

出自三国·吴·徐整《三五历纪》

天地混沌如鸡子，盘古生在其中，万八千岁，
天地开辟，阳清为天，阴浊为地，盘古在其中。

Opening Heaven and Earth
(Chinese Cosmogonic Myth)

From "Three Five Historic Records"
by Xu Zheng (220–265)
[Note: "Three Five" refers to
"Three Sovereigns and Five Emperors"]

Legend says that in the most ancient times, the world was like a huge egg, with no distinction between heaven and earth. In this chaotic "egg," a giant named Pangu began to grow. At first, Pangu was like a fetus, breathing the vitality of heaven and earth and growing slowly. After 18,000 years, Pangu grew up and became extremely powerful. He stood up, stretched his body, and moved his hands and feet. Unexpectedly, the big "egg" broke and opened, part of the light and transparent gas gradually rose and became the sky; the other part of the heavy and turbid things gradually settled down and condensed to become the earth. At this time, the heaven and the earth were very close. Pangu was tall, with his head in the sky and his feet on the ground. He could not move and sometimes could not even straighten his waist. It was very strenuous and uncomfortable. He supported himself between heaven and earth like this. His body grew 10 feet taller every day, so the sky also grew 10 feet higher every day, and the earth also became 10 feet thicker every day.

　　Days passed, the distance between heaven and earth became further, and Pangu became taller, always supporting the heaven and earth, preventing them from closing again. Eighteen thousand years passed, the sky rose very high, the earth became very thick, and Pangu's body was already 90,000 miles tall. Pangu stood between heaven and earth like a mountain towering into the clouds, a truly majestic giant. Then the sky stopped rising, the earth stopped getting thicker, the dark and chaotic scene was gone forever, and Pangu's energy was exhausted. He relaxed his body, the sky did not collapse, and the earth was very solid, so he fell like a mountain, cried out a few times, and died. When Pangu was dying, his whole body underwent tremendous changes. The breath he exhaled turned into spring wind and clouds, his voice turned into thunder, his left eye turned into the shining sun, his right eye turned into the bright moon, his hair and beard turned into stars in the sky, his limbs turned into the four cardinal points of east, south, west, and north, his body turned into the five famous mountains, his blood turned into rushing rivers, his tendons and veins turned into roads that extend in all directions, his muscles turned into fertile fields, his hair turned into lush vegetation, his teeth, bones, and marrow turned into jade and metal deposits, his sweat and tears turned into rain and dew... Pangu fell down, but his good name and achievements in creating the world will be remembered forever. This idiom has two meanings. The first meaning refers to opening and starting a business with hard work and is often used to describe the creation of an unprecedented and magnificent career. The second meaning is something that has never happened before and is the first time in history.

坎井之蛙

Kǎn jǐng zhī wā

出自《庄子·秋水》

[近义词：井底之蛙、坐井观天；

反义词：见多识广、智周万物]

公子牟隐机大息，仰天而笑曰："子独不闻夫埳井之蛙乎？谓东海之鳖曰：'吾乐与！出跳梁乎井干之上，入休乎缺甃之崖。赴水则接腋持颐，蹶泥则没足灭跗。还虷蟹与科斗，莫吾能若也。且夫擅一壑之水，而跨跱埳井之乐，此亦至矣。夫子奚不时来入观乎？'东海之鳖左足未入，而右膝已絷矣。于是逡巡而却，告之海曰：'夫千里之远，不足以举其大；千仞之高，不足以极其深。禹之时，十年九潦，而水弗为加益；汤之时，八年七旱，而崖不为加损。夫不为顷久推移，不以多少进退者，此亦东海之大乐也。'于是埳井之蛙闻之，适适然惊，规规然自失也。"

A Frog in the Well

From "Zhuangzi: Autumn Water"

A frog in a well boasted to a turtle from the East China Sea: "Look, I'm so happy living here! When I'm cheery, I would jump around the well curb; and when I'm tired, I would rest in the brick hole on the well wall. I may soak my body in the water with my head and mouth stretching out; I may also walk in the mud of less than a foot deep. Then I look around and see those mosquito larvae, crabs, and tadpoles, none of them can compare with me! Besides, I occupy this pit of water alone, and I enjoy this happiness in the well alone.

I can be said having reached the pinnacle. Why don't you visit me more often?"

After hearing what the frog said, the turtle really wanted to go in, but its right leg was stuck by the well curb before its left foot stepped in. So, it quickly retracted its legs and said to the frog: "Have you seen the sea? It's so vast that one cannot describe it as a thousand miles wide, and it's so deep that one cannot describe it as a thousand feet high. During Yu the Great [?–2025 BCE], there were floods 9 out of 10 years, but the sea level did not increase; and during Tang the Great [c. 17th century BCE –16th century BCE], there were droughts 7 out of 8 years, but the coastline did not decrease. Thus, the sea water does not change with the passing of time, nor does it increase or decrease with the rainfall or the lack of it. Living in such a sea is real happiness indeed!" After hearing what the turtle said, the frog was astonished and felt insignificant.

刻舟求剑

Kè zhōu qiú jiàn

出自吕不韦《吕氏春秋·察今》

[近义词：一成不变、依样葫芦、守株待兔；

反义词：借坡下驴、因地制宜、因时制宜]

楚人有涉江者，其剑自舟中坠于水。遽契其舟，曰："是吾剑之所从坠。"舟止，从其所契者入水求之。舟已行矣，而剑不行，求剑若此，不亦惑乎！

Marking the Boat to Look for the Sword

From "Master Lü's Spring and Autumn Annals: Observing the Present"

by Lü Buwei (291–235 BCE)

There was a man from Chu State who was crossing the river by boat. His sword fell into the water. So, he hurriedly used a knife to mark the side of the boat and said: "This is where my sword fell." The boat stopped at the destination, and he followed the mark carved on the side of the boat to look for the sword. The boat had travelled a long way, but the sword was still in the same place. Isn't it a foolish way to find the sword like this?

孔融让梨

Kǒng róng ràng lí

续汉书曰:"孔融,字文举,鲁国人,孔子二十世孙也。高祖父尚,钜鹿太守。父宙,泰山都尉。"融别传曰:融四岁,与兄食梨,辄引小者。人问其故。答曰:"小儿,法当取小者。" –出自《世说新语笺疏》

《融家传》曰:"年四岁时,与诸兄共食梨,融辄引小者。"大人问其故,答曰:"我小儿,法当取小者。"由是宗族奇之。–《后汉书·孔融传》李贤注

Kong Rong Giving up the Bigger Pears

From "A New Account of the Tales of the World Annotations"; and

"Book of the Later Han: Biography of Kong Rong"

Li Xian's (655–684) Annotations

Kong Rong (151–208) was born in Qufu, the state of Lu (today's Shandong province). He was the 20th-generation grandson of Confucius. His great-grandfather Kong Shang was the governor of Julu, and his father Kong Zhou was the commander of Mount Tai. According to Kong Rong's supplementary biography, when he was 4 years old, he always took the smallest pear while eating with his two elder brothers. His father asked him why, he replied: "I am the youngest child, so I should take the smallest pear."

口蜜腹剑

Kǒu mì fù jiàn

出自北宋·司马光《资治通鉴·唐玄宗天宝元年》

[近义词：甜言蜜语、佛口蛇心、笑里藏刀；

反义词：心直口快、心口如一]

尤忌文学之士，或阳与之善，啖以甘言，而阴陷之。世谓李林甫"口有蜜，腹有剑。"

Sweet in the Mouth but Bitter in the Stomach

From "Comprehensive Mirror in Aid of Governance: The First Year of Emperor Xuanzong of Tang's Tianbao Period" by Sima Guang (1019–1086)

During the reign of Emperor Xuanzong of Tang (685–762, r. 712–756), there was an official in the court named Li Linfu (683–753) who belonged to the same clan as the emperor, and who concurrently held the positions of the Minister of War and the Director of the Central Secretariat. His positions were prime and powerful. Li Linfu was very talented, he had good handwriting, was good at painting, and was appreciated and valued by Emperor Xuanzong. However, Li Linfu's morality was very bad. To keep his official positions, Li Linfu used flattery to win the favor of the eunuchs and the concubines who were close to the emperor and did his best to deceive the emperor's praise. He relied on this special skill to mislead the emperor and the people around him and served in the court for 19 years.

When dealing with his colleagues, Li Linfu always pretended to be humble and approachable, like a fair and considerate loyal minister. In fact, he was insidious, cunning, and vicious in his method. He specifically made friends with powerful people and formed gangs to expand his power. He was very jealous of anyone who was talented and knowledgeable. If an official who had more merit than him, was favored by the emperor, and whose status threatened him, he would find ways to get rid of the person. To learn about Emperor Xuanzong's preferences, Li Linfu bribed the eunuchs and the concubines with money and jade. Therefore, he could always know any news of the emperor immediately. Once, he heard that the emperor was going to put Lu Xuan, the assistant of the Ministry of War, in an important position, he soon transferred Lu to another place, demoted him, but told the emperor that Lu Xuan was ill and unable to take the position. Another time, he knew that the emperor wanted to give Yan Tingzhi (673–742) an important role, he thus invited Yan to the capital for medical treatment, and then told the emperor that Yan was old, weak, and being treated. Li Linfu was two-faced, jealous of talents, and framed many people who were more talented than him. People who knew Li Linfu all said that he was a double-faced person with a treacherous heart. They hated him and kept their distance from him. This idiom describes the cunning and insidiousness of a double-dealer who speaks sweet words but has a sinister heart and wants to frame others all the time.

滥竽充数

Làn yú chōng shù

出自《韩非子·内储说上》

[近义词：名不副实、鱼目混珠；

反义词：名副其实、货真价实]

齐宣王使人吹竽，必三百人。南郭处士请为王吹竽，宣王说之，廪食以数百人。宣王死，湣王立，好一一听之，处士逃。

Unskilled Yu Performer Making up the Number

From "Han Feizi: On Internal Storage (Part 1)"

King Xuan of Qi (c.350–301 BCE) wanted to have a group of 300 people play the *yu* (an ancient Chinese musical instrument) for him. A south-city retired scholar asked to play the *yu* for the king. King Xuan was pleased and provided him plentiful food, enough for serving several hundred people. After King Xuan died, King Min of Qi (323–284 BCE) succeeded to the throne, but King Min liked to listen to individual performances, thus the retired scholar ran away.

狼狈不堪

Láng bèi bù kān

出自西晋•陈寿《三国志•蜀志•马超传》

[近义词：惊慌失措、手足无措；

反义词：镇定自若、从容不迫]

进退狼狈，乃奔汉中依张鲁。

In Distressing and Embarrassing Situation

From "Records of the Three Kingdoms:
Records of Shu: Biography of Ma Chao"
by Chen Shou (233–297)

During the Three Kingdoms period (220–280), there was a distinguished general named Ma Chao (176–222), who was brave and resourceful, and who later became one of the "Five Tiger Generals" in Liu Bei's (161–223) Shu Han army. Before defecting to Liu Bei, Ma Chao and Han Sui (145–215) merged their troops to fight Cao Cao (155–220), the leader of Wei army. During the Battle of Tong Pass, Ma Chao met Cao Cao in front of the combat and tried to capture him but was blocked by Cao Cao's bodyguard Xu Chu (?–230). Cao Cao's army was large; thus, Ma Chao did not act rashly. Cao Cao hated Ma Chao to the core but could not do anything about him. After this battle, Cao gathered many more soldiers and horses, ready to make a desperate move, cross the Wei River to attack Ma Chao and Han Sui, and annihilate them all at once. After hearing this, Ma Chao said to Han Sui: "Cao's army has come from afar. We should set up a blockade on the north side of

Wei River to trap Cao's army. When they run out of food, we can defeat them."

However, Han Sui refused to adopt Ma Chao's strategy. Cao Cao found out about this and thought Ma Chao was vicious, he said bitterly: "If Ma Chao doesn't die, I will have no place to bury my body!" So, Cao Cao used his adviser's strategy to sow discord between Ma Chao and Han Sui, making them suspicious of each other. Cao's army took the opportunity to attack and defeated Ma Chao and Han Sui. Ma Chao led his troops to break out of the siege. With nowhere to stay, he captured Jicheng, killed the state official, and self-proclaimed General of the Western Expedition, taking over the military and political power of Bingzhou and Liangzhou. The subordinates of the former state official were dissatisfied and attacked Ma Chao, forcing Ma Chao and his troops to leave Jicheng and to attack Lucheng, but was fiercely resisted and could not capture it. When he led his troops back to Jicheng, the city had already been reoccupied by the subordinates of the former state official, and the city gates were closed, making it impossible for Ma Chao to enter. Once again, Ma Chao had nowhere to stay; he was in a distressing and embarrassing situation. He had no choice but to go to Hanzhong to seek refuge with Zhang Lu, who was a mediocre person, and whom Ma Chao could not work with on important matters. At this time, Ma Chao heard that Liu Bei was leading his army to fight in Chengdu, so, he wrote a secret letter to Liu Bei, asking for surrender. Liu Bei was very pleased and solemnly welcomed Ma Chao and his troops to surrender. Liu Bei liked Ma Chao very much and appointed him as General Pingxi and later promoted him to General of Agile Cavalry. Together with Guan Yu (160–220), Zhang Fei (?–221), Huang Zhong (148–220), and Zhao Yun (?–229), they became the "Five Tiger Generals."

老当益壮

Lǎo dāng yì zhuàng

出自南朝·宋·范晔《后汉书·马援传》

[近义词：宝刀不老、老而弥坚；

反义词：未老先衰、年老力衰]

丈夫为志，穷当益坚，老当益壮。

Older but Should Be Stronger

From "Book of the Later Han: Biography of Ma Yuan" by Fan Ye (398–445)

During the Eastern Han dynasty (25–220), Emperor Guangwu of Han, Liu Xiu (5 BCE–57 CE) had a renowned general named Ma Yuan (14 BCE–49 CE), who was a descendant of Zhao She (an eminent general of Zhao State during the Warring States period). Ma Yuan made many military achievements in pacifying the frontiers and played an important role in the social stability of early Eastern Han dynasty. During the reign of Wang Mang (45 BCE–23 CE), Ma Yuan served as postal inspector of Fufeng county. Once, the county magistrate sent him to take prisoners to Chang'an (today's Xi'an). On the way, he saw that the prisoners were crying sorrowfully, he let them go and thus lost his official post. He fled to Beidi county to hide. To make a living, Ma Yuan farmed and raised livestock, in only a few years, he had bred several thousand cattle and sheep and stored much grain. But he did not want to live a pastoral life of "working at sunrise and resting at sunset." He had the world in his heart and often said: "A real man should have great ambitions. The poorer he is, the stronger he should be. The older he is, the stronger he should be."

Later, when Wang Mang's regime collapsed, Ma Yuan defected to Liu Xiu – Emperor Guangwu of Han and served as the Generals of Longxi and Fubo. He fought in many battles in the south and north and made many military achievements. In the autumn of 44 CE, Ma Yuan came back from fighting. Someone said to him: "You have worked hard enough; you should rest at home now." Ma Yuan replied: "No, the Xiongnu and Wuhuan are still making the border chaotic. I am about to ask the emperor to defend the north. A real man should die on the frontier and let others wrap his body in horsehide and bury it. How can I stay at home and live with my wife and children all the time?" Then he went to the battlefield. Not long after the north was pacified, in the south, a tribe invaded in Wuxi (today's junction of Hunan and Guizhou). Emperor Guangwu sent troops to fight twice but was defeated by the Wuxi tribe. The emperor was very troubled by this situation. At the time, Ma Yuan was 62 years old, but he still asked to lead troops to fight. The emperor looked at Ma Yuan and saw that his beard was all white, he said: "General, you are old, you'd better not go!" But Ma Yuan refused to admit his old age, he put on his armor in front of the palace, mounted his warhorse, and galloped back and forth in a vigorous manner. The emperor could not help but admired him and said: "What a strong old man!" So, he sent him to lead two generals, Ma Wu (?–61) and Geng Shu, and 40,000 soldiers to attack Wuxi. When Ma Yuan's army arrived in Wuxi, many soldiers died of heatstroke because they could not adapt to the southern climate. Ma Yuan himself also fell ill and finally died in the army, fulfilling his ambition to die on the battlefield. This idiom is a metaphor for being old but having stronger physical and mental strength.

老马识途

Lǎo mǎ shí tú

出自《韩非子·说林上》

[近义词：老当益壮、驾轻就熟、轻车熟路；

反义词：老气横秋、老态龙钟、乳臭未干]

管仲、隰朋从于桓公伐孤竹，春往冬返，迷惑失道。管仲曰："老马之智可用也。"乃放老马而随之。遂得道。

The Old Horses Know the Way

From "Han Feizi: A Forest of Speeches (Part 1)"

In 663 BCE, at the request of Yan State, Duke Huan of Qi (718–643 BCE) sent troops to fight Shanrong who invaded Yan State. The Grand Chancellor Guan Zhong (725–645 BCE) and the sovereign's advisor Xi Peng (?–645 BCE) accompanied the troops. The Qi army set out in the spring, but their triumphant return was in the winter when the grass and trees had withered. The army wandered around, but got lost in the valley, and could not find the way back. Although they sent out many spies to explore the path but still could not figure out where to get out of the valley. As time went on, the army had difficulty in getting supplies. The situation was very critical. If they could not find a way out, the army would be trapped there. Guan Zhong thought for a long time and came up with an idea: since dogs can find their way home even if they are far away from home, then the horses in the army, especially the old horses, can also recognize the road. So, he said to Duke Huan of Qi: "Your Majesty, I think the old horses can recognize the road. Let them lead the way in the front to let the army out of the valley." Duke Huan of Qi agreed to give it a try. Guan Zhong immediately chose a few old horses, untied the reins, and let them walk freely in front of the army. It was surprising that these old horses all walked in one direction without hesitation. The army followed the horses east and west and finally got out of the valley and found the way back to Qi State. This idiom suggests that the old horses know the road they have traveled, which is a metaphor for experienced people being familiar with things.

乐不思蜀

Lè bù sī shǔ

出自西晋·陈寿《三国志·蜀志·后主禅传》

东晋·裴松之注引《汉晋春秋》

[近义词：随遇而安、流连忘返、乐而忘返；

反义词：归心似箭、饮水思源]

司马文王与禅宴，为之作故蜀技，旁人皆为之感怆，而禅喜笑自若……。他日，王问禅曰："颇思蜀否？"禅曰："此间乐，不思蜀。"

Being Happy in the Hostland and Forgetful of the Homeland

From "Records of the Three Kingdoms: Records of Shu: Biography of the Later Lord Chan" Pei Songzhi's (372–451) notes cited from "Annals of the Han and Jin"

During the Three Kingdoms period (220–280), the ruler of Shu State, Liu Bei (161–223) died, his son Liu Chan (207–271) succeeded to the throne, and was known as the "Later Lord of Shu." However, Liu Chan was an incompetent monarch. Although he was assisted by Zhuge Liang (181–234) and others, he could not revive Shu. After Zhuge Liang's death, Liu Chan trusted the eunuch Huang Hao (fl. 220s–263), causing the government increasingly corrupt, and was eventually destroyed by Wei State.

Cao Huan (246–302), the ruler of Wei State at the time, was only a nominal emperor; all the power was in the hands of Sima Zhao (211–265), who accepted Liu Chan's surrender and forced his family to leave Shu capital Chengdu to move to Wei capital Luoyang. Sima Zhao reprimanded Liu Chan first, and then named him "Duke of Comfort," granted him a house, allocated funds, and hosted him. When Liu Chan was reprimanded by Sima Zhao, he was scared to death, fearing that he would be executed. Unexpectedly, he was conferred a title instead, so he was relieved. The next day, Liu Chan personally went to Sima Zhao's house to thank him, and Sima Zhao held a banquet for him. At the banquet, Wei songs and dances were performed first. The former Shu officials felt embarrassed, but Liu Chan was pleased. Sima Zhao then asked for Shu songs and dances to be performed. The former Shu officials were tearful, but Liu Chan was laughing and joking without showing any sign of hatred for the loss of his homeland. A few days later, Sima Zhao met Liu Chan and asked him: "Do you miss Shu?" Liu Chan replied with a smile: "I'm very happy here. I don't miss Shu!" This idiom refers to being very happy in a hostland that one forgets to return to their homeland. In China, it has negative connotations.

乐此不疲

Lè cǐ bù pí

出自南朝·宋·范晔《后汉书·光武帝纪下》

[近义词：其乐无穷、乐而忘返；

反义词：心猿意马、心不在焉]

皇太子见帝勤劳不怠，承间谏曰："陛下有禹、汤之明，而失黄、老养性之福。愿颐养精神，优游自宁。"帝曰："我自乐此，不为疲也。"

Enjoying It Without Feeling Tired

From "Book of the Later Han:

Chronicle of Emperor Guangwu (Part 2)"

by Fan Ye (398–445)

Emperor Guangwu of Han, Liu Xiu (5 BCE–57 CE), was a diligent and hardworking monarch. Whether in the war years or in peaceful times, he worked tirelessly and set a good example for his ministers. After Liu Xiu became the emperor of Eastern Han dynasty (25–220), his work became even more intense. Since the war times had just subsided, the state affairs were under repair and the people hoped for stability. Liu Xiu shifted his focus to developing production and making the people live and work in peace. He and his ministers were busy with work every day and never mentioned the war.

The crown prince once asked his father about war, Liu Xiu replied: "Duke Ling of Wei once asked Confucius how to attack and fight. Confucius said, 'I often hear people talk about sacrifices and rituals, but I don't know anything about leading the army to fight.'

You see, Confucius was so concerned about the governance of the country. You should do the same and don't study things related to war." Since the establishment of the Eastern Han dynasty, Liu Xiu personally handled government affairs every day and worked very diligently: he went to court from dawn and returned to his bedchamber at night. He often discussed the government policies and formulated the decrees with the civil and military officials and could not go to bed until midnight. The crown prince saw that Liu Xiu worked so hard; he was very concerned about his father's health. Once, when Liu Xiu was resting, the crown prince persuaded him boldly: "Your Majesty, you're so diligent in serving the people. You can be said to have the wise characters of Yu the Great, Tang the Perfect [Tang of Shang, c.17th–16th BCE], and King Wu of Zhou [1076–1043 BCE], but you don't have the self-cultivation of longevity like the Yellow Emperor or Laozi. I hope you take care of yourself. Your good health is also a blessing for the people of the country." After hearing this, Liu Xiu laughed and said: "I'm happy to do this work, I'm used to it, and I don't feel tired at all!" The crown prince was deeply moved. This idiom means to be interested in something, immersed in it, and not feeling tired or exhausted.

两袖清风

Liǎng xiù qīng fēng

[近义词：洁身自好、廉洁奉公；

反义词：贪得无厌、贪赃枉法]

两袖清风身欲飘，杖藜随月步长桥。

–元·陈基《次韵吴江道中》

清风两袖朝天去，免得闾阎话短长。

–明·于谦《入京诗》

Two Sleeves of Cool Breeze

From "Secondary Rhyme on the Way to Wujiang"

by Chen Ji (1314-1370); and

"Poem on Entering Beijing"

by Yu Qian (1398–1457)

Yu Qian (1398–1457) was a native of Qiantang, Zhejiang province in the Ming dynasty (1368–1644). He passed the Imperial Examination at the age of 24 and became an investigating censor. He sympathized with the sufferings of the people and did many good things during his tenure. Emperor Xuanzong of Ming (1398–1435) appreciated and valued him very much. After Yu Qian was promoted to Governor of Henan and Shanxi, he still had lived a very frugal life. Emperor Yingzong of Ming (1427–1464) ascended the throne at the age of 9 and gave power to the eunuch Wang Zhen (?–1449), who was an insatiable corrupt official. When representatives from other provinces came to Beijing, they always presented Wang Zhen with jewelry and silver to please him. But whenever Governor Yu Qian came to Beijing, he never brought any gifts.

Yu Qian's colleagues advised him: "Although you don't offer gold and treasures, or seek the rich and powerful, you should at least bring some famous local specialties such as incense sticks, mushrooms, handkerchiefs, and so on, to show your favor!" Yu Qian smiled, raised his sleeves, and said humorously: "I've brought the breeze!" His attitude was to mock those flattering corrupt officials, as expressed in his poem:

> Silk handkerchiefs, mushrooms, and incense sticks,
>
> Meant for people to enjoy but have turned disasters.
>
> I go to court with two sleeves of cool breeze,
>
> To avoid gossips from the people.

This idiom refers to having clean hands and being an honest official, it may also refer to being poor and having nothing.

毛遂自荐

Máo suì zì jiàn

出自西汉·司马迁《史记·平原君虞卿列传》

[近义词：自告奋勇、挺身而出、当仁不让；

反义词：自惭形秽、让位于贤]

门下有毛遂者，前，自赞于平原君曰："遂闻君将合从于楚……合少一人，愿君即以遂备员而行矣。"

Self-Recommendation

From "Records of the Grand Historian: Biographies of Lord Pingyuan and Yu Qing" by Sima Qian (145–c.86 BCE)

During the Warring States period (475–221 BCE), Lord Pingyuan, Zhao Sheng (308–251 BCE) recruited a group of talented retainers to make suggestions for the political and military affairs of Zhao State. Among them, there was a man named Mao Sui, who had lived in Lord Pingyuan's house for 3 years without doing anything, but Lord Pingyuan did not care. In 259 BCE, the Qin army besieged Handan, the capital of Zhao State. The situation was very critical. King Wuling of Zhao (340–295 BCE) ordered Lord Pingyuan to go to Chu State to ask for help. Lord Pingyuan selected 19 civil and military retainers to set off. At this time, Mao Sui, who had always been quiet, suddenly came to Lord Pingyuan and volunteered to accompany them to Chu. Lord Pingyuan was surprised at Mao Sui's self-recommendation and said to him: "If a person has virtue and talent, it will soon show up, just like putting an awl into a pocket, the tip of the awl will immediately expose. You have been in my house for 3 years, but you have not shown any talent."

Mao Sui smiled and said: "If you had allowed me to make suggestions before, my talent would have been revealed long ago. It's not too late now. If you take me with you, you will be able to use my talent!" Lord Pingyuan felt that Mao Sui's words made sense, he allowed him to join the group. Lord Pingyuan and his group arrived in Chu, while the King of Chu received them with a great ceremony. After the negotiation began, Lord Pingyuan discussed the importance of sending troops to fight against the Qin army, but the King of Chu could not get to the point. From morning to noon, there was no result. Lord Pingyuan was very anxious because the Qin army was at the gates of the city and Zhao State was in great danger. At this time, Mao Sui walked angrily to the king, holding a sharp sword in one hand and pulling the King of Chu's clothes with the other hand, making it impossible for the king to avoid. Then, Mao Sui argued convincingly, explained the importance of Chu sending troops. His words were passionate and clear. The king was shocked by his courage and admired him very much. Instead of blaming him for being rude, he sympathized with his feelings. The King of Chu immediately agreed to sign an alliance with Lord Pingyuan to send troops to rescue Zhao State. Lord Pingyuan was very pleased with Mao Sui's courageous act and admired his talent very much. Afterwards, Lord Pingyuan held Mao Sui's hand and praised him, he said: "Mr. Mao Sui's eloquence is better than a million troops!" From then on, Lord Pingyuan looked at Mao Sui with new eyes and treated him as a distinguished guest. This idiom refers to volunteering or recommending oneself to take on an important task.

盲人摸象

Máng rén mō xiàng

[近义词：管中窥豹、坐井观天；

反义词：洞若观火、一目了然]

尔时大王，即唤众盲各各问言："汝见象也？"众盲各言："我已得见。"王言："象为何类？"其触牙者，即言象形如芦菔根；其触耳者，言象如箕；其触头者，言象如石；其触鼻者，言象如杵；其触脚者，言象如木臼；其触背者，言象如床；其触腹者，言象如瓮；其触尾者，言象如绳。–出自《大般涅槃经》

有僧问："众盲摸象，各说异端，忽遇明眼人又作么生？"–北宋·释道原《景德传灯录·洪进禅师》

Blind Men Touching the Elephant

From "Nirvana Sutra"; and

"Transmission of the Lamp: Chan Master Hong Jin"

by Daoyuan of the Northern Song Dynasty (960–1127)

Once a king summoned all the blind men in the country and asked them one by one: "Have you seen an elephant?" The blind men all answered: "Yes, I have." The king asked again: "What kind of thing is an elephant?" The blind man who touched the elephant's tusk immediately answered its shape was like a carrot root. The blind man who touched the elephant's ear said it was like a dustpan. The blind man who touched the elephant's head said it was like a stone. The blind man who touched the elephant's trunk said it was like a pestle. The blind man who touched the elephant's feet said it was like a wooden mortar. The blind man who touched the elephant's spine said it was like a bed. The blind man who touched the elephant's belly said it was like a pottery pot. The blind man who touched the elephant's tail said it was like a rope. This fable describes that people tend to make random guesses due to an incomplete understanding of things. It suggests that we need to examine things from multiple angles and in all directions to draw the correct conclusion.

名列前茅

Míng liè qián máo

出自春秋·左丘明《左传·宣公十二年》

[近义词：榜上有名、首屈一指；

反义词：榜上无名、名落孙山]

蒍敖为宰，择楚国之令典，军行，右辕，左追蓐，前茅虑无，中权，后劲，百官象物而动，军政不戒而备，能用典矣。

Front Thatch

From "The Zuo Tradition: The 12th Year of Duke Xuan"

by Zuo Qiuming (556–452 BCE)

During the Spring and Autumn period (770–476 BCE), the struggle for supremacy between Jin and Chu states was fierce. Zheng State in the middle between the two great powers was in a dangerous situation. One year, the Chu army invaded Zheng. Zheng asked Jin for help while resisting resolutely. As a result, the Zheng army failed before the reinforcements arrived. Jin sent General Xun Linfu (?–593 BCE) as the commander of the central army to lead the soldiers to rescue Zheng. However, before they crossed the Yellow River, they heard that Zheng had already surrendered to Chu, and the Chu army had crossed the Yellow River and retreated. Xun Linfu called the generals to discuss countermeasures and said: "The battle is over, and the Chu army has withdrawn. It is meaningless for us to rush here now. It is better to retreat." However, the deputy general Xian Gu disagreed with this idea; he thought that they should cross the Yellow River immediately to pursue the Chu army.

The commander-in-chief of the upper army, Shi Hui, analyzed the situation of the Jin and Chu armies, and believed that it was right to withdraw the troops and return home. Shi Hui said: "One of the primary principles of commanding military operations is to be good at observing opportunities. Only by seizing the enemy's loopholes to launch an attack can we achieve victory. Now the virtues, political orders, laws, and etiquette of Chu are all in line with the norm. They sent troops to attack Zheng because Zheng was ambivalent about them. The King of Chu had appointed talented people and reorganized their army. The army is well-trained. When they go out, the teams are in good order. The right army closely guards the commander's chariot. The left army is responsible for cutting grass to arrange overnight stays. The vanguard uses thatch as a signal and raises the thatch to warn the rear when they find the enemy. The central army is responsible for formulating battle plans and issuing orders. The rear army is an elite force. When fighting, all the soldiers have clear division of labor, and the military discipline is very strict. Besides, Chu is now well managed, and everyone is eager to contribute to the state. How can we rashly attack them? I think we should withdraw our troops and return home to reorganize our army, strengthen training, and improve the combat effectiveness of the troops." Xun Linfu agreed with Shi Hui's suggestion. However, Xian Gu insisted on his own way and led his army across the Yellow River to attack the Chu army, which resulted in a disastrous defeat. Thatch was a specialty of Chu State. The Chu soldiers used thatch as signal flags. They walked in front and sent signals with thatch when they found any movement of the enemy. Therefore, the vanguard was called "front thatch." This is how the idiom came. Later, the idiom refers to a top of the list, or an excellent performance.

南柯一梦

Nán kē yí mèng

出自唐·李公佐《南柯太守传》

[近义词：黄粱一梦、白日做梦、一枕黄粱；

反义词：心想事成、天从人愿]

东平淳于棼，吴楚游侠之士。……生解巾就枕，昏然忽忽，仿佛若梦。……累日，（王）谓生曰："吾南柯政事不理，太守黜废，欲借卿才，可曲屈之，便与小女同行。"……二使因大呼生之姓名数声，生遂发悟如初。见家之僮仆拥篲于庭，二客濯足于榻，斜日未隐于西垣，余樽尚湛于东牖。梦中倏忽，若度一世矣。……生感南柯之浮虚，悟人世之倏忽，遂栖心道门。

A Dream Under the Southern Branch

From "An Account of the Governor of the Southern Branch" by Li Gongzuo (778–848)

Once upon a time, there was a scholar named Chun Yufen, who loved to drink wine. Outside the south wall of his courtyard, there was an old Chinese scholar tree with luxuriant branches and leaves. One day, he got drunk under the tree and was helped into the house by his two friends. He lay down to rest while his two friends sat beside him and washed their feet. In the dim light, Chun Yufen saw two envoys coming in and inviting him to visit the Dahuai'an Kingdom. So, he followed the envoys out and got on the carriage and soon entered a cave. Suddenly, the sunny sky, mountains, wilderness, cities, and villages were all in front of him, as if he had come to a new world.

Chun Yufen entered the palace and met the king of the Dahuai'an Kingdom. The king talked to him cordially and showed admiration for his talents. Sure enough, he was appointed as the "Governor of the Southern Branch" and was allowed to marry the princess. Chun Yufen suddenly became rich and powerful. He served as a senior official in the Dahuai'an Kingdom for 30 years with outstanding political achievements. He was very popular with the people, and the king also valued him very much. Thereafter, he had five sons and two daughters, and lived a happy, rich, and comfortable life. Unexpectedly, the Tanluo Kingdom suddenly invaded, and the king ordered him to lead the army to fight. Because he did not understand military affairs, he rushed to fight and was defeated by the Tanluo army and fled. After returning, he found that his wife had died, and the king no longer trusted him. Later, he was dismissed from his official position, was placed under house arrest for a period, and then sent back to his hometown…

At this point, Chun Yufen woke up and found that it was a dream. He saw that the sun had not yet set outside the window, the leftover wine was still on the table, and the two friends' feet had not finished washing. Chun Yufen was very curious, he went back to the big scholar tree outside the courtyard, dug a hole in the tree, and saw a big ant hole inside. A group of ants lived in the hole; two of them were particularly large, protected by dozens of smaller ants. There were also pavilions and small cities made of mud in the hole. Chun Yufen thought: "This is probably the palace of the Dahuai'an Kingdom. There is a tunnel outside the palace, which goes up to a branch in the south. This is probably the 'Southern Branch County' where I was the governor." Chun Yufen could not help but sighed and said: "Thirty years of wealth and glory, turned out to be just a dream!" This idiom is a metaphor for life being like a dream, while wealth, gains, and losses are all temporary.

南山可移

Nán shān kě yí

出自后晋·刘昫等《旧唐书·李元纮传》

[近义词：执法如山；反义词：言而无信]

元纮早修谨，仕为雍州司户参军。时太平公主势震天下，百司顺望风指，尝与民竞碾硙，元纮还之民。长史窦怀贞大惊，趣改之，元纮大署判后曰："南山可移，判不可摇也。"

South Mountain Can Be Moved

From "Old Book of Tang: Biography of Li Yuanhong" by Liu Xu (888–947) *et al*.

During the Tang dynasty (618–907), there was a well-known Princess Taiping (665–713), who was the youngest daughter of Emperor Gaozong of Tang, Li Zhi (628–683), and Empress Wu Zetian (624–705). Relying on the power of the court, this princess often occupied common people's fields and robbed other people's properties. The civil and military officials in the palace were very afraid of her. Once, Princess Taiping went to a temple near Chang'an (today's Xi'an) city to play, and she took a fancy to a stone mill in the temple and wanted to take it for herself. The monk refused, so Princess Taiping ordered her followers to rob it and then left.

The monk was so angry that he reported it to the state government. Li Yuanhong (?–733), the officer in charge of household registration and hearing civil disputes in Yongzhou county, accepted the case. Li Yuanhong was an upright official who was not afraid of power and handled cases fairly. After he learned about the incident, he immediately ruled that Princess Taiping must return the stone mill to its original owner, and the monk left with satisfaction. However, when Li Yuanhong's superior, the chief officer of Yongzhou, Dou Huaizhen (?–713) found out about this, he was very anxious. He called Li Yuanhong and scolded him: "Don't you know how powerful Princess Taiping is? She is not easy to mess with! If you offend her, you and I will be in trouble. Hurry up and change the verdict!" Li Yuanhong thought about it, picked up the brush and wrote another line of big characters on the original verdict: "South Mountain can be moved, this verdict will never be changed." South Mountain refers to Zhongnan Mountain in the south of Chang'an city. Li Yuanhong used this sentence to express that his verdict was firmer than Zhongnan Mountain. This idiom means that the case has been judged and cannot be overturned. It also means that the order has been issued and cannot be modified.

南辕北辙

Nán yuán běi zhé

出自西汉·刘向《战国策·魏策四》

[近义词：背道而驰、相背而行、适得其反；

反义词：瞻予马首、马首是瞻、殊途同归]

今者臣来，见人于大行，方北面而持其驾，告臣曰："我欲之楚。"臣曰："君之楚，将奚为北面？"曰："吾马良。"臣曰："马虽良，此非楚之路也。"曰："吾用多。"臣曰："用虽多，此非楚之路也。"曰："吾御者善。"此数者愈善，而离楚愈远耳。

Wanting to Go to South but the Wheels Going North

From "Strategies of the Warring States: Strategies of Wei IV" by Liu Xiang (77–6 BCE)

When the King Anxi of Wei (?–243 BCE) was about to send troops to attack Zhao State, Minister Ji Liang told the king the following story to persuade him to give up the plan:

"During the Warring States period (475–221 BCE), there was a man who was going to Chu State. He met a fellow traveler on the way while driving a horse-drawn carriage, and they started chatting. When the fellow traveler learned that he was going to Chu, he was shocked and asked him: 'Chu is in the south, why are you going north and how long will it take you to reach Chu?' The man said calmly: 'It doesn't matter, my horse runs fast, I won't worry about not reaching Chu.' The fellow traveler reminded him: 'You will get farther and farther away from Chu if you keep going this way.' The man pointed to his luggage and said: 'I have a lot of travel expenses and dry food that can last for many days. It doesn't matter if the journey is long.' The fellow traveler said anxiously: 'You are going the wrong direction; you won't reach Chu if you keep going this way.' The man said confidently: 'My coachman is a very good driver, don't worry.' Seeing this man so confused, the fellow traveler shook his head helplessly and sighed."

After hearing the story, the King of Wei remained silent. Finally, he gave up his plan to attack Zhao State. In Ji Liang's view, the way to achieve supremacy is to establish prestige through honesty and gain the support of the people. If using force to obtain power, it is just like the person who was going north to Chu. This idiom refers to the opposite direction between action and purpose.

弄巧成拙

Nòng qiǎo chéng zhuó

[近义词：画蛇添足、画虎类狗、多此一举；

反义词：弄假成真、化险为夷、画龙点睛]

适来弄巧成拙。–出自唐·马祖道一《五灯会元》

弄巧成拙，为蛇添足。–宋·黄庭坚《拙轩颂》

Overdoing Something

From "Combined Sources for the Five Lamps"

by Mazu Daoyi (709–788); and

"Ode to My Humble Home"

by Huang Tingjian (1045–1105)

During the Northern Song dynasty (960–1127), there was a notable painter named Sun Zhiwei who was good at figure painting and had a group of students learning painting from him. Once, he was asked by the Shouning Temple in Chengdu to paint a picture of the Nine Star Gods, which would show Mercury Bodhisattva and a servant boy holding an empty crystal vase. He carefully painted the picture with a brush, and the characters were lifelike, with fluttering clothes and ribbons, just like immortals. Only the last step of coloring was left. It happened that a friend invited him to drink. He put down his brush, looked at the painting carefully for a while, and felt satisfied. So, he asked his students to color the painting and then left.

The students were very happy to gain the trust of their teacher. When they were about to color the painting, they suddenly found that the vase in the boy's hand was empty. They were all very surprised and said: "Our teacher usually paints a bunch of beautiful flowers in it when drawing a vase. Why did he forget it today? It must be that he left in a hurry and neglected it." So, they painted a bright and blooming lotus in the vase. The next day, Sun Zhiwei came back and found a lotus flower growing out of the vase in the boy's hand. His face immediately changed. He asked angrily: "Who told you to add the lotus flower?" The students answered: "We did it ourselves! Look, doesn't it look better with the lotus flower?" Sun Zhiwei said: "You have done a fool's errand! You don't know that the Daoist scriptures say that the vase of Mercury Bodhisattva is a treasure he uses to suppress demons and water. It cannot and should not have flowers. If you add a lotus flower, it will not be a treasure but an ordinary vase. Although you have done a good job in coloring, the painting has been ruined." The students then realized what they have done wrong and lowered their heads in regret. This idiom means that one wants to show off their intelligence but ends up doing something foolish or messing things up.

呕心沥血

Ǒu xīn lì xuè

[近义词：煞费苦心、殚精竭虑、苦心孤诣；

反义词：漫不经心、敷衍塞责]

（李贺）恒从小奚奴，骑距驴，背一古破锦囊，遇有所得，即书投囊中。及暮归，太夫人使婢受囊出之，见所书多。辄曰："是儿要当呕出心乃已尔。"–出自唐·李商隐《李贺小传》

刳肝以为纸，沥血以书辞。–韩愈《昌黎先生集·归彭城》

Making Painstaking Efforts, Shedding Heart's Blood

From "A Brief Biography of Li He"

by Li Shangyin (813–858); and

"Mr. Chang Li's Collection: Return to Pengcheng"

by Han Yu (768–824)

In mid Tang dynasty (618–907), there was a renowned young poet named Li He (790–816) who was intelligent and studious since childhood, and whose poems written at the age of 7 were praised by many. The writers of the time, such as Han Yu (768–824) and Huangfu Shi (777–835), specially interviewed him and said that this child was indeed a genius. Hence, Li He was recognised at a young age. However, he was unable to move forward in politics and was never valued by the court. So, he put all his energy into poetry writing.

When Li He wrote poems, he usually did not decide on the subject first but focused on field investigation and accumulated materials. He often rode a horse, walking slowly in the suburbs while chanting on the spot. When he encountered a good topic, he would write lines and put them in his brocade book bag. After returning home, he would organize the lines into a poem. He was very diligent and serious in his writing and slept very late every night. He once said: "Writing long poems wear my clothes out, and writing short poems break my white hair." Li He was physically weak, and his mother felt sorry for him. So, every day when Li He came home, his mother would ask the maid to check his bag. If she found too many poems written in it, she would say angrily: "You child, are you going to shed your heart's blood before you stop?" He died at the age of 26 due to excessive fatigue from writing poems; it was also because he felt that his talent was not appreciated and he had depression. He left behind more than 240 poems, many of which are masterpieces. Han Yu once wrote these two lines: "Cut the liver to make paper and let the blood drip out to write words." Later, people combined the stories of these two poets into an idiom to describe the painstaking efforts of writing and literary creation.

排难解纷

Pái nàn jiě fēn

出自西汉·刘向《战国策·赵策三》

[近义词：排忧解难、息事宁人；

反义词：搬弄是非、火上浇油、推波助澜]

所贵于天下之士者，为人排患释难解纷乱而无取也；即有所取者，是商贾之人也。仲连不忍为也。

Eliminating Dangers and Resolving Disputes

From "Strategies of the Warring States: Strategies of Zhao III" by Liu Xiang (77–6 BCE)

During the Warring States period (475–221 BCE), King Zhaoxiang of Qin (325–251 BCE) sent troops to attack Zhao State and approached its capital city Handan. King Xiaocheng of Zhao (?–245 BCE) asked Wei State for help, thus King Anxi of Wei (r. 277–243 BCE) sent General Jin Bi (?–257 BCE) to lead troops to rescue Zhao. But then the King of Qin sent people to intimidate the King of Wei and said: "I will soon conquer Zhao State. Whoever dares to save Zhao, I will attack them immediately afterwards." The King of Wei was frightened and ordered Jin Bi not to fight with the Qin army, but to stay at the border between Wei and Zhao states. The King of Wei also sent General Xin Yuanyan as an envoy to enter Handan from a small road.

Xin Yuanyan said to the King of Zhao: "The King of Qin is the hegemon of the country, and everyone is afraid of him. Now his army has surrounded Handan, but his intention is to make other states honor him as the emperor. If Zhao sends people to Qin to express your willingness to honor him as the emperor, Handan will be relieved."

At this time, a man from Qi State named Lu Zhonglian (c.305–245 BCE) was in Handan. He was very talented and often helped people resolve disputes. After hearing that Xin Yuanyan persuaded the King of Zhao to "honor the King of Qin as the emperor," he visited the Grand Chancellor of Zhao, Lord Pingyuan (308–251 BCE), and asked him to introduce Xin Yuanyan. The two met, and Lu Zhonglian said to Xin Yuanyan: "Qin State is already very strong. If you honor the King of Qin as the emperor, he will be even more tyrannical. At that time, Wei may also become its vassal state. He will do whatever he wants, and I am afraid your position will also be difficult to maintain." Xin Yuanyan was deeply impressed by Lu Zhonglian's words and bowed to express his gratitude. He then wanted to give up the compromising policy of "honoring the King of Qin as the emperor." Lord Pingyuan was very grateful to Lu Zhonglian and intended to give him a fiefdom, but he refused. Lord Pingyuan then offered him a thousand gold coins, he also refused. Lu Zhonglian said: "True wise men believe that it is their duty to help others resolve disputes without asking for compensation. Otherwise, wouldn't they be the same as merchants?"

盘根错节

Pán gēn cuò jié

出自南朝宋·范晔《后汉书·虞诩传》

[近义词：错综复杂、千丝万缕；

反义词：井然有序、简明扼要、一目了然]

志不求易，事不避难，臣之职也；

不遇盘根错节，何以别利器乎？

Tangled Tree Roots and Intertwined Joints (Deep-Rooted Issues Are Difficult to Solve)

From "Book of the Later Han: Biography of Yu Xu" by Fan Ye (398–445)

During the Eastern Han dynasty (25–220), there was an official named Yu Xu (?–137) in Wuping, Chen State (now Luyi, Henan province), who served successively as Chief of Chaoge, Prefect of Wudu, Colonel Director of Retainers, and Minister of the Eastern Han. He dared to speak out and was not afraid of power. However, he was condemned nine times and punished three times for offending the powerful. In 110, the Qiang and the Xiongnu invaded the Eastern Han from the west and the north, respectively. Emperor An of Han (94–125) summoned the ministers to discuss a strategy. General Deng Zhi (?–121) advocated abandoning the west and concentrating troops to deal with the Xiongnu in the north, which was agreed by most ministers.

At that time, Yu Xu held a relatively low position, but he rejected Deng Zhi's strategy, believing that such action would lead to disastrous consequences. Deng Zhi was furious when he heard someone dared to openly oppose his ideas and was ready to find an opportunity to retaliate. Soon, turmoil broke out in Chaoge. The common people attacked and killed local officials and rose up in rebellion. The situation became worse. Deng Zhi thought that the opportunity to punish Yu Xu had come, so he suggested sending Yu Xu to Chaoge as a county magistrate. Anyone with a discerning eye could tell Deng Zhi's intentions, and Yu Xu's friends were also concerned about him, fearing that he would encounter difficulties after getting there. But Yu Xu did not care and said frankly: "A man with ambition does not seek easy things to do, nor does he avoid difficulties. This is what a minister should do. How can you identify the sharpness of a knife or an axe without encountering tangled tree roots and intertwined joints?" He resolutely went to Chaoge to take office, quickly quelled the unrest, and won the trust and praise of the emperor. Later, he led the troops to repel the invasion of the Qiang people and made great contributions to the Eastern Han dynasty. This idiom describes that complex issues are difficult to solve.

旁若无人

Páng ruò wú rén

出自西汉·司马迁《史记·刺客列传》

[近义词：不可一世、目中无人；反义词：众目睽睽]

荆轲嗜酒，日与狗屠及高渐离饮于燕市，酒酣以往，高渐离击筑，荆轲和而歌市中，相乐也，已而相泣，旁若无人者。

As If There Is No One Around

From "Records of the Grand Historian:
Biographies of Assassins"
by Sima Qian (145–c.86 BCE)

Jing Ke (?–227 BCE) was an assassin during the late Warring States period (475–221 BCE). A native of Wei State, he was generous and loyal and always stood up when seeing something unfair. When Jing Ke was a child, he often practiced martial arts and swordsmanship, hoping to build a strong physique to serve his homeland. Wei State was weak, and Qin State was strong. The powerful Qin, located in the west, kept expanding to the east of Mount Xiao little by little, aiming to unify the country. Jing Ke's homeland Wei State had always been under Qin's threat. Jing Ke saw this and was anxious about it. However, the general trend had been determined, and the weak Wei State was no match for Qin State at all.

Soon, Wei State perished. Thereafter, Jing Ke left his homeland and wandered around. He met a musician named Gao Jianli in Yan State and befriended a butcher who made a living by selling dog meat. The three of them had a great talk and felt like old friends at first sight. They kept giving speeches in the teahouse, exposing the ambitions and conspiracies of Qin to the public. However, the general trend of the country was not something that people like them could reverse. Therefore, they could only express their grief by drinking and singing. Gao Jianli was good at playing the zither, and Jing Ke always sang loudly to the sound of Gao Jianli's zither, but the song was tragic and fervent. They sometimes cried and sometimes laughed, as if there was no one around. The people on the street treated them as crazy. In the 20th year of the reign of Qin Shi Huang (259–210 BCE), Jing Ke went to assassinate Qin Shi Huang under the persuasion of Yan State Crown Prince Dan (?–226 BCE), but Jing Ke failed and was killed, leaving behind the tragic lyric:

>The wind is whistling,
>
>The Yi River is cold.
>
>The warrior has left,
>
>He never returned.

This idiom describes one's own doing without being influenced by others, as if there is no one around. It can also describe an arrogant attitude and looking down on others.

披肝沥胆

Pī gān lì dǎn

出自西汉·司马迁《史记·淮阴侯列传》

臣愿披腹心，输肝胆，效愚计，恐足下不能用也。

Cutting Liver and Dripping Bile
(Being Frank and Loyal)

From "Records of the Grand Historian:
Biography of the Marquis of Huaiyin"
by Sima Qian (145–c.86 BCE)

In 199 CE, Cao Cao (155–220) led 20,000 troops to march into Xuzhou to attack Liu Bei (161–223), who was weak at the time and was defeated without Zhuge Liang's (181–234) advice. Zhang Fei (?–221) broke through and went to Mangdang Mountain. Liu Bei had nowhere to go and surrendered to Yuan Shao (?–202). Guan Yu (160–220) was trapped and unable to escape. To save Liu Bei's family, Guan Yu had to temporarily surrender to Cao Cao. Liu Bei was with Yuan Shao, and he did not know where Zhang Fei and Guan Yu were. He only knew that his wife and children were in Cao's camp, he missed them and worried about them day and night. Yuan Shao learned of Liu Bei's pain and decided to send troops to attack Cao Cao and capture Xudu. After the two armies fought, Cao Cao adopted counselor Xun You's (157–214) strategy, luring the enemy to split up, making a feint to the east and attacking in the west. Guan Yu was sent to attack Baima first. The general of the Yuan army in Baima was Yan Liang (?–200) who relied on the large number of soldiers and the support of Yuan army, but he underestimated the enemy and was killed by Guan Yu in front of the battle, Baima was also occupied.

Yuan Shao was unwilling to give up, he sent his general Wen Chou (?–200) to confront the enemy. Cao Cao parked all the vehicles and equipment on the road where Wen Chou was going to pass and asked the soldiers to ambush nearby. When Yuan army arrived, they saw that there were many valuables on the vehicles, they dismounted to rob them. Cao Cao then gave an order; the ambushes attacked from all sides. Yuan army was defeated, and Wen Chou was killed by Guan Yu, who was in the lead. Yuan Shao learned that Guan Yu, Liu Bei's second brother, killed his two favorite generals, he was furious and wanted to kill Liu Bei. Liu Bei knew that Guan Yu was in Cao's camp, he expressed his willingness to write a letter to persuade Guan Yu to come back and assist Yuan Shao. Yuan Shao was overjoyed and immediately sent someone to deliver the letter. After reading the letter, Guan Yu knew that Liu Bei was with Yuan Shao. Guan Yu immediately wrote a letter in reply, saying: "I will go to see Cao Cao immediately, say goodbye to him, and take your wives back. I am frank and loyal to my brother, and I have no second thoughts." After that, Guan Yu went to bid farewell to Cao Cao. Cao Cao knew his intention, was reluctant to let him go, and deliberately avoided him. Guan Yu was determined to leave, he took his old followers, escorted the carriage carrying Liu Bei's wife, and rushed out. Cao Cao sent people to stop him along the way, but Guan Yu did not turn back. He passed five passes, killed six generals, and went through many hardships. Finally, he reunited with Liu Bei and Zhang Fei in the ancient city. This idiom literally means cutting the liver and dripping bile as a metaphor for being frank and loyal.

匹夫有责

Pǐ fū yǒu zé

出自清·顾炎武《日知录·正始》

[近义词：责无旁贷、义不容辞；反义词：敷衍塞责]

有亡国，有亡天下。亡国与亡天下奚辨？曰："易姓改号，谓之亡国；仁义充塞，而至于率兽食人，人将相食，谓之亡天下。是故知保天下，然后知保其国。保国者，其君其臣肉食者谋之；保天下者，匹夫之贱与有责焉耳矣。"

Everyone Has a Responsibility

From "Records of Daily Gains in Knowledge: Beginning of the Year"

by Gu Yanwu (1613–1682)

In the late Ming (1368–1644) and early Qing (1644–1911) dynasties, there was a prominent thinker and patriot named Gu Yanwu (1613–1682), who was born in a rural official family with a large collection of books at home. When Gu Yanwu was 6 years old, his stepmother Wang taught him to read and often told him stories of loyal and righteous men. His grandfather repeatedly asked him to read books related to economy and people's livelihoods. At the age of 14, Gu Yanwu participated in the activities of Fushe, a political and academic society seeking reform, whose members were mostly patriotic intellectuals. All of these had a great influence on Gu Yanwu's future growth.

In 1645, the Qing army went south to conquer Nanjing. Gu Yanwu participated in the anti-Qing struggle and defended Kunshan with the magistrate Yang Yongyan. However,

Kunshan was eventually taken, Gu Yanwu's two younger brothers were killed by the Qing army, and his stepmother Wang also starved herself to death. Before her death, she told Gu Yanwu: "Don't be a Qing minister!" Gu Yanwu agreed. From then on, he disguised himself as a merchant, running around to contact the anti-Qing forces along the coastal areas. To swallow up Gu Yanwu's property, Ye Fangheng (1615–1682), a Jinshi (one who passed the final Imperial Examination) in the Qing dynasty, colluded with Gu's servant Lu En to denounce that Gu Yanwu had connections with the coastal anti-Qing organization. Gu Yanwu was hunted by the government and had to flee Jiangnan to Shandong. During his more than 20 years in the north, Gu Yanwu traveled to Hebei, Shanxi, Shaanxi, Henan, among other provinces, and stayed in hotels every half year. With his more than 20 friends, they established a secret activity base in the north of Yanmen and insisted on anti-Qing. Later, he settled in Huayin, Shaanxi province. To expound his thoughts and ideas, after the age of 50, Gu Yanwu concentrated on writing the "Records of Daily Gains in Knowledge," in which he wrote: "Even an ordinary person is responsible for the rise and fall of the country." He always adhered to national integrity until his death at the age of 69.

匹夫之勇

Pǐ fū zhī yǒng

[近义词：一夫之勇、有勇无谋；

反义词：深谋远虑、大智大勇]

吾不欲匹夫之勇也，欲其旅进旅退也。–出自春秋·左丘明《国语·越语上》

（孟子）对曰："王请无好小勇。夫抚剑疾视曰，'彼恶敢当我哉！'此匹夫之勇，敌一人者也。王请大之！"–《孟子·梁惠王下》

A Commoner's Courage

From "States and Languages:
Yue/Shaoxing Dialect (Part 1)"
by Zuo Qiuming (556–452 BCE); and
"Mengzi: King Hui of Liang (Part 2)"

A native of Huaiyin, Jiangsu province, Han Xin (231–196 BCE) was proficient in military tactics. He first joined Xiang Liang (?–208 BCE) and then followed Xiang Yu (232–202 BCE), but neither of them gave him an important position. Later, Han Xin joined Liu Bang (c.256–195 BCE). Nevertheless, he was still not given an important post, only appointed as the commander in charge of the production of military rations. Han Xin was unwilling to accept it and ran away. Xiao He (257–193 BCE) knew Han Xin's talents. When he heard this news, he immediately rode a fast horse to chase Han Xin back. Liu Bang then decided to appoint Han Xin as a general, and held a grand ceremony for his taking office, which shocked the entire army. After the ceremony, Liu Bang asked Han Xin for advice on how to compete with Xiang Yu for the country.

Han Xin asked Liu Bang directly: "How do you think you compare with Xiang Yu in terms of courage, benevolence, and strength?" Liu Bang was silent for a while, then he answered: "I'm not as good as him." Han Xin said: "Yes, I think so, too. But I have been with Xiang Yu for years and know him very well. Xiang Yu is brave enough to overwhelm thousands of people with a shout. But he is not good at employing talented people. His is but a commoner's courage. When it comes to benevolence, Xiang Yu does care about people, but he does not reward those who have made big contributions and only offers small favors, which is hypocrisy. Moreover, he has not divided the land fairly, and the feudatories were dissatisfied. His army disturbed the locals, and the people were resentful. Therefore, although he is strong now, he will soon become weak. If you do the opposite, it will not be difficult to regain Guanzhong, and it will not be difficult to conquer the entire country." Liu Bang thought that Han Xin's words were sensible, he did what Han Xin suggested and led the army to quietly set out from Nanzheng to Guanzhong. In less than 3 months, he occupied Guanzhong, defeated Xiang Yu, unified the country, and established the Western Han dynasty (206 BCE–23 CE).

破釜沉舟

Pò fǔ chén zhōu

出自西汉·司马迁《史记·项羽本纪》

[近义词：孤注一掷、背水一战、义无反顾；

反义词：急流勇退、优柔寡断]

项羽乃悉引兵渡河，皆沉船，破釜甑，烧庐舍，持三日粮，以示士卒必死，无一还心。

Breaking the Cauldrons and Sinking the Boats

From "Records of the Grand Historian:

Biography of Xiang Yu"

by Sima Qian (145–c.86 BCE)

Toward the end of the Qin dynasty (221–206 BCE), the Qin army besieged Zhao State at Julu. King Huai of Chu (328–296 BCE) sent troops to rescue Zhao State. He appointed Song Yi (?–207 BCE) as the general, and Xiang Yu (232–202 BCE) as the second general, along with 200,000 soldiers. After Song Yi led the troops to Anyang (now east of Cao County, Shandong province), he feared the Qin army and did not move for 46 days. Xiang Yu could not bear it any longer and falsely conveyed the order of the King of Chu, killed Song Yi, and seized the military power. Then, Xiang Yu led the army cross the river to rescue the Zhao army. After landing, he ordered to sink all the boats, smash all the cooking cauldrons, and burn all the houses nearby. The soldiers set out with only 3 days of dry food, which meant to fight with the Qin army to the death. When they arrived at Julu, the Chu army fought one for ten and finally defeated the Qin army after nine fierce battles. This idiom is a metaphor for being decisive and leaving no way out.

破镜重圆

Pò jìng chóng yuán

出自唐·韦述《两京新记》与孟棨《本事诗·情感》

[近义词：和好如初、言归于好；

反义词：覆水难收、一去不返、鸾飘凤泊]

陈太子舍人徐德言之妻，后主叔宝之妹，封乐昌公主，才色冠绝。时陈政方乱，德言知不相保，谓其妻曰："以君之才容，国亡必入权豪之家，斯永绝矣。傥情缘未断，犹冀相见，宜有以信之。"乃破一镜，人执其半，约曰："他日必以正月望日卖于都市，我当在，即以是日访之。"及陈亡，其妻果入越公杨素之家，宠嬖殊厚。德言流离辛苦，仅能至京，遂以正月望日访于都市。有苍头卖半镜者，大高其价，人皆笑之。德言直引至其居，设食，具言其故，出半镜以合之，仍题诗曰："镜与人俱去，镜归人不归。无复嫦娥影，空留明月辉。"陈氏得诗，涕泣不食。素知之，怆然改容，即召德言，还其妻，仍厚遗之。闻者无不感叹。仍与德言、陈氏偕饮，令陈氏为诗，曰："今日何迁次?新官对旧官。笑啼俱不敢，方验作人难。"遂与德言归江南，竟以终老。

Broken Mirror Reunited

From "New Records of the Two Capitals"
by Wei Shu (?–757); and
"Poetry of Original Stories: Emotions"
by Meng Qi in the Tang Dynasty (618–907)

At the end of the Northern and Southern dynasties (420–589), Emperor Wen of Sui, Yang Jian (541–604), marched southward and had prepared to destroy Chen State to unify the country. Chen Shubao (553–604), the last emperor of Chen State, only knew how to drink wine, write poetry, and have fun, but ignored government affairs. When the Sui army approached, the Chen Court was in chaos. There was a man named Xu Deyan, who was the husband of Princess Lechang (who was the sister of Emperor Chen Shubao). Xu Deyan had a premonition that Chen State was about to perish, and the couple would not be together for long, so he said to the princess in tears: "The country is about to fall, and the family is about to be ruined. You and I can no longer stay together. With your beauty and talent, you will enter the Imperial Family or a wealthy household. If we both survive, I hope we can be reunited one day." He took out a round bronze mirror, broke it into two halves, gave one half to Princess Lechang, and kept the other half for himself. They agreed to each other: on the 5th Lantern Festival after separation, while people were busy on the streets of Chang'an (today's Xi'an), they would pretend to sell the broken mirror to look for each other.

Soon after, Chen State was taken by the Sui army. Princess Lechang was captured and sent to Chang'an to become the concubine of Yang Su (544–606), a military general and minister of the Sui dynasty. Xu Deyan missed his wife and traveled to Chang'an to look for her. As promised, on the 5th Lantern Festival, he took the half-bronze mirror to sell on the street. While walking around in the lantern market, he suddenly found an old servant also selling a half-bronze mirror. He went forward to examine it and saw that it exactly matched his half-bronze mirror. Xu Deyan recalled the princess by the sight of the mirror and burst into tears. He got to know from the old servant that Princess Lechang had entered the Yang Mansion, and thought that he would never see her again, he became even more sad. He could not help but wrote a "Broken Mirror Poem" on the half-mirror and asked the old servant to take it back. The poem reads: "The mirror and the woman left, while the mirror returned but the woman did not. There is no shadow of Chang'e, only the bright moonlight." After seeing Xu Deyan's poem, Princess Lechang refused to eat and sleep and cried for several days. When Yang Su learned about the whole story, he was very sympathetic to the couple and summoned Xu Deyan and returned Princess Lechang to him. He also held a banquet to celebrate the couple's "reunion." This idiom refers to a couple getting back together after separation or a breakup.

扑朔迷离

Pū shuò mí lí

出自《木兰诗》（又名《木兰辞》）

[近义词：眼花缭乱、千头万绪、错综复杂；
反义词：一清二楚、一目了然、显而易见]

雄兔脚扑朔，雌兔眼迷离，

双兔傍地走，安能辨我是雄雌。

Bewildering and Confusing

From "The Ballad of Mulan"

Legend has it that during the Northern Wei dynasty (386–534) of the Northern and Southern dynasties in Chinese history, the nomadic Rouran Khaganate in the north kept invading the south, and the Northern Wei dynasty was forced to recruit soldiers for defense. There was a hardworking and brave girl named Hua Mulan, whose father was on the list of conscription. But her father was old and in poor health, and her brother was still young and could not join the army, Mulan wanted to dress up as a man and join the army in place of her father. When Mulan first told her parents about the idea, her father firmly disagreed, but later he was moved by her filial piety. As there was nothing they could do, her parents finally agreed.

Mulan said goodbye to her parents in the morning, followed the army, and lived on the Yellow Riverbank at night. In the vast twilight, with the roar of the river and the neighing of war horses, Mulan was prepared to fight for her country. In the following 10 years, Mulan fought in hundreds of bloody battles and achieved notable military services.

After the war, the emperor wanted to reward Mulan with an official post, but she refused. Mulan returned to her hometown, accompanied by her comrades. When Mulan walked out of her boudoir, they were all stunned. They did not expect that Mulan, the handsome general who had been with them for 12 years, was a woman! Mulan said to them mischievously: "When the rabbits are caught and their ears are suspended in the air, the male rabbit kicks its four legs, and the female rabbit half closes its eyes. But when the two rabbits run together on the ground, who can tell which one is male and which one is female?" The comrades all laughed and even more admired this heroine who loved her country and was filial to her parents. This idiom describes things that are so complicated that it is difficult to see the truth.

齐眉举案

Qí méi jǔ àn

出自南朝·宋·范晔《后汉书·梁鸿传》

[近义词：举案齐眉、相敬如宾、夫唱妇随；

反义词：琴瑟不调]

梁鸿字伯鸾，扶风平陵人也。…势家慕其高节，多欲女之，鸿并绝不娶。同县孟氏有女，状肥丑而黑，力举石臼，择对不嫁，至年三十。父母问其故。女曰："欲得贤如梁伯鸾者。"鸿闻而娉之。女求作布衣、麻屦，织作筐、缉绩之具。及嫁，始以装饰入门；七日而鸿不答。妻乃跪床下请曰："窃闻夫子高义，简斥数妇，妾亦偃蹇数夫矣。今而见择，敢不请罪："鸿曰："吾欲裘褐之人，可与俱隐深山者尔？今乃衣绮缟，傅粉墨，岂鸿所愿哉？"妻曰："以观夫子之志耳。妾自有隐居之服。"乃更为椎髻，着布衣，操作而前。鸿大喜曰："此真梁鸿妻也。能奉我矣！"字之曰德曜，名孟光。…遂至吴，依大家皋伯通，居庑下，为人赁舂；每归，妻为具食，不敢于鸿前仰视，举案齐眉。

Holding the Tray up to the Eyebrows

From "Book of the Later Han:

Biography of Liang Hong" by Fan Ye (398–445)

During the Eastern Han dynasty (25–220), there was a young man named Liang Hong (26–?) whose parents were poor and died early. Nevertheless, Liang Hong had high aspirations and studied diligently. After graduating from the Imperial Academy, Liang Hong did not seek officialdom but returned to his hometown, immersed himself in studying classics and history, and became very knowledgeable. Some wealthy and powerful families admired Liang Hong's virtue and asked matchmakers to propose marriage, but Liang Hong rejected all of them.

In his hometown, there was a girl surnamed Meng who was dark and ugly, but kind-hearted. She was over 30 years old yet had not married. Her parents wanted to propose marriage for her, but she said: "I'm willing to marry only someone as knowledgeable and virtuous as Liang Hong!" After knowing this, Liang Hong agreed to marry her. On the wedding day, the girl came to Liang Hong's house in a sedan chair, wearing silk and satin, and her face was covered with makeup powder. When Liang Hong saw that the woman was dressed in jewels, he was disappointed and said: "How can this be the wife I want to marry?!" Then he walked into his study and did not speak to her for several days. On the 7th day after the marriage, the wife took off her gorgeous clothes, wiped off the makeup on her face, and changed into coarse clothes. Next, she cooked a bowl of millet porridge, put it on a tray, and walked into Liang Hong's study.

Liang Hong lowered his head to read, ignoring his newlywed wife. His wife knelt in front of him, raised the tray to the level of her eyebrows, and said softly: "Please have a meal, husband." Liang Hong was surprised to see his wife dressed like this, and he stood there not knowing what to do. His wife continued: "I heard that you have high ambitions, and that you have different criteria for choosing a wife. I'm honored to be chosen by you. But you didn't talk to me for 7 days. Please tell me what mistakes I've made." Liang Hong explained sincerely: "I want to marry a simple and honest woman who can live in seclusion with me in the mountains. But on the wedding day, you were wearing gold and silver and putting on makeup. This was not what I wanted." As soon as Liang Hong finished speaking, his wife smiled and said: "My dear, the reason I dressed like that on that day was just to see if your ambition was true or not." After hearing this, Liang Hong realized that she was testing him on purpose! He hurriedly helped her up and said excitedly: "This is the good wife in my mind!" He was so happy that he gave his wife a name, Meng Guang (lit.

"Light"). Soon, the couple went to Baling Mountain where they lived a secluded life. This idiom refers to holding the tray as high as the eyebrows when serving food to show respect; later it is used to describe the love and respect between husband and wife.

歧路亡羊

Qí lù wáng yáng

出自《列子·说符》

[近义词：误入歧途；反义词：改邪归正]

杨子之邻人亡羊，既率其党，又请杨子之竖追之。杨子曰："嘻！亡一羊，何追者之众？"邻人曰："多歧路。"既反，问："获羊乎？"曰："亡之矣。"曰："奚亡之？"曰："歧路之中又有歧焉，吾不知所之，所以反也。"杨子戚然变容，不言者移时，不笑者竟日。门人怪之，请曰："羊，贱畜，又非夫子之有，而损言笑者，何哉？"杨子不答。门人不获所命。

弟子孟孙阳出，以告心都子。心都子他日与孟孙阳偕入，而问曰："昔有昆弟三人，游齐鲁之间，同师而学，进仁义之道而归。其父曰：'仁义之道若何？'伯曰：'仁义使我爱身而后名。'仲曰：'仁义使我杀身以成名。'叔曰：'仁义使我身名并全。'彼三术相反，而同出于儒。孰是孰非邪？"杨子曰："人有滨河而居者，习于水，勇于泅，操舟鬻渡，利供百口。裹粮就学者成徒，而溺死者几半。本学泅，不学溺，而利害如此。若以为孰是孰非？"

心都子嘿然而出。孟孙阳让之曰："何吾子问之迂，夫子答之僻？吾惑愈甚。"心都子曰："大道以多歧亡羊，学者以多方丧生。学非本不同，非本不一，而末异若是。唯归同反一，为亡得丧。子长先生之门，习先生之道，而不达先生之况也，哀哉！"

Lost Sheep at a Crossroads

From "Liezi: On Symbols"

During the Warring States period (475–221 BCE), there was a well-known thinker named Yang Zhu (c.395–c.335 BCE). One day, Yang Zhu's neighbor lost a sheep and asked their relatives and friends to look for it. They also asked Yang Zhu's servant to help find it. Yang Zhu was puzzled and asked: "Hey, you only lost a sheep, why do you ask so many folks to chase it?" The neighbor replied: "There are too many forks in the road." After the people seeking the sheep came back, Yang Zhu asked the neighbor: "Have you found the sheep?" The neighbor replied: "We didn't catch it, it ran away." Yang Zhu asked: "Why did it run away?" The neighbor replied: "There was another fork in the road, and we didn't know which road it ran from, so we had to come back." After hearing this, Yang Zhu felt sad, he did not speak and did not smile all day. His students thought it strange and asked him: "Sheep are worthless animals, and they are not yours, why don't you say anything?" Yang Zhu did not answer, and the students did not know what Yang Zhu was thinking. A student named Meng Sunyang told another student named Xin Duzi about this matter.

One day, Xin Duzi and Meng Sunyang went together to see Yang Zhu. Xin Duzi said to Yang Zhu: "Once upon a time, there were three brothers who studied with the same teacher in the Qi and Lu area. They returned home after having mastered the principles of benevolence and righteousness. Their father asked them: 'What are the principles of benevolence and righteousness?' The eldest son replied: 'Benevolence and righteousness make me cherish my life and put reputation after life.' The second son replied: 'Benevolence and righteousness make me willing to sacrifice my life for reputation.' The third son replied: 'Benevolence and righteousness make me able to preserve both my life and reputation.' The three brothers gave different and even opposite answers, but they all came from learning Confucianism. Who do you think is right and who is wrong among the three brothers?" Yang Zhu said: "There was a man who lived by the river. He was familiar with water and dared to swim across the river. He made a living by rowing a boat and ferrying people across the river. The profit from ferrying could support a hundred people. There were groups of people who brought their own food to learn how to swim from him. Among them, almost half drowned. They were originally learning how to swim, not to learn how to drown. The benefits and losses were so opposite. Who do you think was right and who was wrong?"

After hearing this, Xin Duzi walked out with Meng Sunyang silently. Meng Sunyang blamed Xin Duzi and said: "Why did you ask the teacher such roundabout questions, and the teacher's answers were so strange? The more I listened, the more confused I got." Xin Duzi said: "The neighbor has lost the sheep because there are too many forks in the road, and those who seek to learn how to swim have lost their lives because there are too many methods. What we learn are not fundamentally different, but the results are so different. Only by returning to the same root and essence can we have no sense of gain or loss, and we will not lose our direction. You have been learning from our teacher for a long time, and you are his senior disciple. How sad that you don't understand his metaphors!" This idiom refers to the fact that things can be complex and changeable, without the right direction, one may go astray which might have serious consequences.

旗鼓相当

Qí gǔ xiāng dāng

出自南朝·宋·范晔《后汉书·隗嚣传》

[近义词：势均力敌、棋逢对手；

反义词：相形失色、天差地别]

如令子阳到汉中、三辅，愿因将军兵马，鼓旗相当。

Equally Matched by Flags and Drums

From "Book of the Later Han: Biography of Wei Ao"

by Fan Ye (398–445)

In 25 CE, Liu Xiu (5 BCE–57 CE) established the Eastern Han dynasty (25–220 CE) in Luoyang and became Emperor Guangwu of Han. However, the remote areas had not been completely unified. Wei Ao (c.1st century BCE – 33 CE) claimed to be the General in Gansu, and Gongsun Shu (?–36) claimed to be the Emperor in Sichuan. Both sides held heavy troops and often launched wars for territory. These two forces posed a serious threat to the Eastern Han dynasty, which had just been established without enough troops to quell the rebellions. Liu Xiu tried every means to win over Wei Ao to isolate Gongsun Shu's forces and unify the country. To seek a political way out, Wei Ao took the opportunity to write to Liu Xiu, expressing his willingness to surrender to the Eastern Han.

Thus, Liu Xiu sent the Grand Administrator of Land, Deng Yu (2–58), to Sichuan and appointed Wei Ao as the General in Sichuan. Soon, Lü Wei launched a rebellion in Chencang with tens of thousands of troops. Then, Lü Wei colluded with Gongsun Shu and sent soldiers to attack the central part of Shaanxi and approached Chang'an (today's Xi'an) city. The situation was extremely critical. At this time, Wei Ao led a large army to arrive in time and cooperated with Liu Xiu's troops to fight the enemy tenaciously and finally defeated the rebels and made them flee. Liu Xiu was very pleased to hear that the front line had won a victory, and personally wrote a tactful letter to Wei Ao, hoping that he could unite his troops with the Eastern Han army to deal with Gongsun Shu. Liu Xiu said in the letter: "I am now busy fighting in the east, and the main forces are deployed there. My forces in the west are extremely weak. If Gongsun Shu invades Chang'an, I hope to unite with the general's troops so that we can fight Gongsun Shu on equal terms." Wei Ao accepted Liu Xiu's advice. Soon after, Wei Ao and Liu Xiu jointly led an army to attack Gongsun Shu, and Gongsun Shu was defeated. This idiom refers to the fact that during ancient warfare, there were similar numbers of military flags and drums used to direct advances, retreats, and movements; it is a metaphor that the strength or ability of both sides is equal.

杞人忧天

Qǐ rén yōu tiān

出自《列子·天瑞》

[近义词：庸人自扰、杞人之忧；

反义词：无忧无虑、乐天安命]

杞国有人忧天地崩坠，身亡所寄，废寝食者。

A Man from Qi Feared the Sky Falling (Unfounded and Unnecessary Worries)

From "Liezi: Heaven's Gifts"

Legend has it that in ancient times, there was a man in Qi State who was always worried that the sky would fall, and the earth would collapse, leaving him with nowhere to reside. As a result, he was so anxious and frightened that he could not eat or sleep.

A friend of his saw how worried he was and felt sorry for him. The friend came to enlighten him and said: "The sky is nothing, but gas piled up together. There is no place between heaven and earth without this gas. Your every move and breath relate to the gas. You live in the middle of the sky all day, why are you still worried that the sky will collapse?" After hearing this, the Qi man became even more anxious and asked: "If the sky is really made of gas, then the sun, the moon, and the stars are hanging on the gas, won't they fall down?" The friend replied: "The sun, the moon, and the stars are also made of gas, they just shine. Even if they fall, they will never hurt anyone." The Qi man pondered for a while, still worried, and asked again: "What if the earth collapses?" The friend patiently explained: "The earth is nothing but piled up dirt. These dirt and rocks are everywhere, filling every corner. Dogs can run and jump on it as they please, so why worry about the earth collapsing?" After such enlightenment, the Qi man suddenly realized the fact, and finally he was relieved and lived happily. This idiom refers to unfounded and unnecessary worries and is often used to ridicule those who worry excessively about things that are unlikely to happen.

起死回生

Qǐ sǐ huí shēng

出自西汉•司马迁《史记•扁鹊仓公列传》

[近义词：妙手回春、死而复生、绝处逢生；

反义词：不可救药、病入膏肓、回天乏术]

行三十六术甚效，起死回生，救人无数。

Bringing the Dead Back to Life

From "Records of the Grand Historian:
Biographies of Bian Que and Cang Gong [Chunyu Yi]"
by Sima Qian (145–c.86 BCE)

Bian Que (401–310 BCE) was an eminent medical doctor in the Warring States period (475–221 BCE) who was very skilled in traditional Chinese medicine. Once, Bian Que was practicing medicine in Guo State and heard that the prince had just "died" of a sudden illness. Bian Que hurried to the palace to check and found that the prince still had a slight pulse and weak breathing. Bian Que said to the king of Guo: "The prince is not dead, he just fainted." Bian Que used acupuncture to treat the prince, and soon the prince came back to life. The king and ministers of Guo were overjoyed and praised Bian Que for his ability to bring the dead back to life. Bian Que said: "It's not that I have the ability to bring the dead back to life, but because the prince is not really dead!" The original meaning of this idiom is to bring back to life a dead or dying person. It is used to describe excellent medical skills; it also describes an ingenious method.

千变万化

Qiān biàn wàn huà

出自《列子·周穆王》

[近义词：变化多端、变化莫测、瞬息万变；
反义词：一成不变、依然如故]

周穆王西巡狩，越昆仑，不至弇山。反还，未及中国，道有献工人名偃师。穆王荐之，问曰："若有何能？"偃师曰："臣唯命所试。然臣已有所造，愿王先观之。"穆王曰："日以俱来，吾与若俱观之。"翌日偃师谒见王。王荐之，曰："若与偕来者何人邪？"对曰："臣之所造能倡者。"穆王惊视之，趋步俯仰，信人也。巧夫！领其颅，则歌合律；捧其手，则舞应节。千变万化，惟意所适。王以为实人也，与盛姬内御并观之。技将终，倡者瞬其目而招王之左右侍妾。王大怒，立欲诛偃师。偃师大慑，立剖散倡者以示王，皆傅会革、木、胶、漆、白、黑、丹、青之所为。王谛料之，内则肝胆、心肺、脾肾、肠胃，外则筋骨、支节、皮毛、齿发，皆假物也，而无不毕具者。合会复如初见。王试废其心，则口不能言；废其肝，则目不能视；废其肾，则足不能步。穆王始悦而叹曰："人之巧乃可与造化者同功乎？"诏贰车载之以归。夫班输之云梯，墨翟之飞鸢，自谓能之极也。弟子东门贾、禽滑釐闻偃师之巧以告二子，二子终身不敢语艺，而时执规矩。

Being Ever-Changing

From "Liezi: King Mu of Zhou"

Legend says that during the Western Zhou dynasty (1046–771 BCE), King Mu of Zhou (992–922 BCE) crossed the Kunlun Mountains and went hunting in the west. On his way back, he met a skilled man named Yanshi. King Mu had long heard of Yanshi's name, so he asked him: "I heard that you have extraordinary skills and can do whatever you want. Is this true?" Yanshi answered without hesitation: "Whatever the king asks me to make; I can make it. I have recently made a group of puppets who can sing and dance. I wonder if the king is interested in seeing them." King Mu was skeptical and said: "Sure, bring the puppets who can sing and dance to my palace tomorrow so that I can see what they are like." The next day, Yanshi really brought the puppets he made into the palace. These dummies walked slowly into the palace with small steps, lined up in a horizontal line, and stood in front the king. King Mu was stunned when he saw them. These dummies looked like real people, and it was hard to tell the real from the fake.

At this time, Yanshi turned on the switch on the dummies, and they began to sing and dance under his control. Yanshi played the harp, and the dummies sang loudly to the rhythm of his music, sometimes high-pitched and sometimes weeping. Yanshi beat the rhythm with his hands and feet, and the dummies danced gracefully to the beat, sometimes twisting their waists and sometimes waving their long sleeves, which was ever-changing! After the dummies finished singing and dancing, they all stood motionlessly in front of the king. King Mu was still discontented and wanted to continue watching. Seeing this, Yanshi was very proud, he took the dummies apart one by one and let the king take a closer look. It turned out that these dummies were made of animal skins, wood, glue, paint, and some pigments. The liver, gallbladder, heart, lungs, kidneys, spleen, intestines, and stomach were all complete, and the teeth, hair, tendons, flesh, skin, and bones were also made lifelike.

King Mu stared at them, and it took him a long time to come back to his senses. He exclaimed: "The reputation of Yanshi's skills is truly well-deserved, and they are really ingenious!" This idiom refers to something that is ever-changing.

千里送鹅毛，礼轻情意重

Qiān lǐ sòng é máo, lǐ qīng qíng yì zhòng

出自宋·罗泌《路史》

将鹅贡唐朝，山高路远遥。

沔阳湖失去，倒地哭号号。

上复唐天子，可饶缅伯高？

礼轻情意重，千里送鹅毛！

Delivering a Goose Feather a Thousand Miles, Friendship Is Deep Though the Gift Is Light

From "Grand History" by Luo Mi (1131–c.1189)

During the Zhenguan period (627–649) of Tang dynasty (618–907), local officials often sent people to pay tribute to Emperor Taizong of Tang (598–649). A local official from a remote area sent Mian Bogao to please the emperor with a live swan. When Mian Bogao came to the Mianyang River, he saw the white swan stretching its neck, opening its mouth, and panting. Mian Bogao opened the cage to let the swan drink the water. Unexpectedly, after drinking enough water, the swan spread its wings and flew away. Mian Bogao pounced forward and only pulled off a feather. He held the goose feather in his hand and cried. After much thought, he decided to continue his journey eastward. He took out a piece of white silk, carefully wrapped the goose feather, and wrote a poem on the silk:

I planned to present a swan to the Emperor of Tang,

The mountains are high, and the journey is very long.

I accidentally lost the treasure gift at Mianyang Lake,

I fell to the ground and cried out loud.

I report this incident to the emperor,

And Mian Bogao asks for his mercy.

I traveled a thousand miles to deliver a goose feather,

Although the gift is light, our friendship is deep.

After reading the poem and listening to Mian Bogao's story, Emperor Taizong did not punish him but rewarded him instead, because he felt that Mian Bogao was loyal and honest, and he fulfilled his mission.

前功尽弃

Qián gōng jìn qì

[近义词：前功尽废、功亏一篑；

反义词：功德圆满、大功告成]

今又将兵出塞，过两周，倍韩，攻梁，一举不得，前功尽弃。–出自西汉·司马迁《史记·周本纪》

一攻而不得，前功尽灭，不若称病不出也。

–西汉·刘向《战国策·西周策》

All the Previous Efforts Would Have Been Wasted

From "Records of the Grand Historian: Annals of Zhou"

by Sima Qian (145–c.86 BCE);

"Strategies of the Warring States:

Strategies of Western Zhou"

by Liu Xiang (77–6 BCE)

During the Spring and Autumn (770–476 BCE) and the Warring States (475–221 BCE) periods, Qin State rapidly enhanced its strength through Shang Yang's (c.390–338 BCE) reforms. By the time of King Zhao of Qin (325–251 BCE), Qin State had developed into an economic and military power. To achieve supremacy, King Zhao of Qin sent Bai Qi (332–257 BCE), the left General, to lead troops to attack Han State. While resisting, Han State asked Wei State for help. Seeing Han was attacked, Wei wanted to rescue it, but was afraid of Qin, and even more afraid of Bai Qi, so it could only watch Bai Qi defeat the Han army and occupy the cities. Later, Qin State took advantage of the incompetent King Qingxiang of Chu (329–263 BCE) to order General Bai Qi to conquer the capital of Chu State. Then the Qin army defeated the Zhao army in Changping, the Shangdang area of Shanxi. The Qin army was greatly boosted, and Bai Qi took advantage of the situation to lead the victorious army to move to Wei State and besiege the Wei capital Daliang. The court and the people of Wei were in a panic.

The King Hui of Wei (400–319 BCE) said to his ministers angrily: "When the Qin army attacked Han State, we should have sent troops to resist Qin, but you thought the Qin army was a fierce military and dared not fight against it. Now, our neighboring states of Han and Zhao were defeated by Qin, and the Qin army is at the gates of our city, but we have no place to ask for help. What should we do?" A minister immediately said: "Su Li, the younger brother of Su Qin [382–284 BCE], the former Grand Chancellor of the Six Kingdoms, is now in Daliang. Your Majesty may wish to ask him for advice. Perhaps he has a good plan to repel the Qin army." The King of Wei immediately summoned Su Li and said: "Sir, the capital of Wei State is in danger. Do you think there is any way to resolve this disaster?" Su Li said: "Qin's military action this time is ill-intentioned. They have long planned to destroy the six states. It is indeed difficult to deal with. However, I am willing to meet the King Nan of Zhou [336–256 BCE], perhaps he can stop Qin from continuing to use military force." After hearing Su Li's words, the King of Wei fully supported his actions. Su Li rushed to Luoyi, where the Zhou emperor lived, and said to King Nan of Zhou: "Qin State has been too aggressive and domineering in recent years. King Zhao of Qin sent General Bai Qi to take over Chu State, and defeated Zhao and Han States in succession. Now it is besieging the capital of Wei State, Daliang. If you don' stop it, I'm afraid the Zhou dynasty will be in danger of overthrowing." The King Nan of Zhou just nodded helplessly but did not take any action. So, Su Li went to see Bai Qi and said to him: "You have made many military contributions. Now you must lead troops out of the border, travel a long way, pass through Zhou and Han, and attack Daliang of Wei. If you cannot win this battle, all your previous efforts will be wasted. You should immediately withdraw your troops and use illness as an excuse." Bai Qi ignored Su Li's words and continued the annexation war. Bai Qi had served as the commander of the Qin army for more than 30 years and conquered over 70 cities. If Bai Qi had listened to Su Li's advice, all his previous efforts would have been wasted. This idiom suggests that to succeed, one must persevere and never give up halfway.

黔驴技穷

Qián lǘ jì qióng

出自唐·柳宗元《三戒·黔之驴》

[近义词：无计可施、束手无策；

反义词：神通广大、力大无穷]

黔无驴，有好事者船载以入。至则无可用，放之山下。虎见之，庞然大物也，以为神，蔽林间窥之。稍出近之，慭慭然，莫相知。他日，驴一鸣，虎大骇，远遁；以为且噬己也，甚恐。然往来视之，觉无异能者；益习其声，又近出前后，终不敢搏。稍近，益狎，荡倚冲冒。驴不胜怒，蹄之。虎因喜，计之曰："技止此耳！"因跳踉大㘎，断其喉，尽其肉，乃去。

Guizhou Donkey Run out of Skills

From "Three Admonitions: The Donkey of Guizhou"

by Liu Zongyuan (773–819)

There were no donkeys in Guizhou. A nosy man brought a donkey there by boat but found it useless and placed it at the foot of a hill. A tiger saw the huge creature and regarded it as a deity, hid in the woods and secretly watched it. The tiger gradually came out to approach the donkey carefully, not knowing what it was. One day, the donkey brayed, the tiger was very scared and ran away, as it thought the donkey was going to bite it. Then the tiger observed back and forth, felt the donkey had no special skills, gradually got used to the donkey's bray, and approached it from front to back, but never fought with it. The tiger slowly neared the donkey, colliding, leaning, bumping into, and offending it. The donkey was very angry and kicked the tiger with its hoof. The tiger was thus pleased and said cunningly: "Your skill is but like this!" Then the tiger jumped up and roared, bit off the donkey's throat, ate all its meat, and walked away.

请君入瓮

Qǐng jūn rù wèng

[近义词：以毒攻毒、以牙还牙]

唐秋官侍郎与来俊臣对推事。俊臣别奉进止鞫兴，兴不之知也。及同食，谓兴曰："囚多不肯承，若为作法？"兴曰："甚易也。取大瓮，以炭四面炙之，令囚人处之其中，何事不吐？"即索大瓮，以火围之，起谓兴曰："有内状勘老兄，请兄入此瓮。"兴惶恐叩头，咸即款伏。–出自唐·张鷟《朝野佥载·周兴》

或告文昌右丞周兴与丘神勣谋反，太后命来俊臣审之。俊臣与兴方推事对食，谓兴曰："囚多不承，当为何法？"兴曰："此甚易耳！取大瓮，以炭四周炙之，令囚入中，何事不承？"俊臣乃索大瓮，火围如兴法，因起谓兴曰："有内状推兄，请兄入此瓮！"兴惶恐，叩头伏罪。–宋·司马光《资治通鉴·唐纪·则天皇后天授二年》

Please Enter the Urn

From "Collected Records of Court and Country:
Zhou Xing" by Zhang Zhuo (658–730/660–740);
"Comprehensive Mirror in Aid of Governance:
Records of Tang:
The Second Year of Tianshou Under Empress Zetian"
by Sima Guang (1019–1086)

Empress Wu Zetian (624–705) of the Tang dynasty appointed cruel officials to suppress those who opposed her. Two of them were most vicious: one was named Zhou Xing (c.651–691), and the other was named Lai Junchen (651–697). They used false accusations and cruel punishments to kill many upright civil and military officials and civilians.

Once, a whistleblower letter was delivered to Wu Zetian to accuse Zhou Xing of contacting others to rebel. Wu Zetian was furious and ordered Lai Junchen to investigate the matter. Lai Junchen was worried and thought: "Zhou Xing is a cunning and treacherous person, a whistle-blowing letter alone cannot make him tell the truth. But if there were no result, the empress would blame me. What should I do?" After much thought, he came up with a clever idea. He invited Zhou Xing to his house for a banquet. The two persuaded each other to drink. After three rounds of drinking, Lai Junchen sighed and spoke: "Brother, I often encounter prisoners who refuse to confess. What can you do?" Zhou Xing said proudly: "This is not difficult to handle!" Lai Junchen pretended to be very sincere and said: "Oh, please tell me quickly!" Zhou Xing smiled sinisterly and said: "Find a big urn, heat it up with charcoal fire all around, and then let the prisoner enter it. Think about it, what else can he not confess?" Lai Junchen nodded repeatedly in agreement, then ordered someone to bring a large urn, and lit charcoal fire around it as Zhou Xing had said. Then he turned to Zhou Xing and said: "Someone in the palace has reported you for treason, and the empress has ordered me to investigate it. I'm sorry, but please enter the urn now." At this moment, Zhou Xing realized that he had fallen into a trap. He was so frightened that he quickly knelt on the floor and kowtowed to plead guilty.

罄竹难书

Qìng zhú nán shū

[近义词：擢发难数、作恶多端、不胜枚举；

反义词：宅心仁厚]

此皆乱国之所生也，不能胜数，

尽荆越之竹犹不能书。–出自《吕氏春秋·明理》

罄南山之竹，书罪未穷；决东海之波，流恶难尽。

–刘昫等《旧唐书·李密传》

Cannot Write Everything Down Even If Using All the Bamboo Slips

From "Master Lü's Spring and Autumn Annals:
Understanding the Reasons"; and
"Old Tang Book: Biography of Li Mi"
by Liu Xu (888–947) *et al.*

At the end of the Sui dynasty (581–618), Emperor Yang of Sui, Yang Guang (569–618), was extremely cruel. He not only lived an extravagant and dissolute life and ignored the suffering of the people, but also continued to build large-scale projects annually, and constantly recruited a great number of soldiers and laborers in the country. Young and strong men either went to war or worked for the court. As a result, enormous areas of land were barren, and the people were living in poverty. The toiling masses could not bear it any longer, and sweeping peasant uprisings broke out. Among the numerous uprising armies, there was one called the "Wagang Army" led by Zhai Rang (?–617) based in

Wagangzhai (now south of Hua County, Henan province). Many of the rebels were fishermen and hunters who were brave and good at fighting. Zhai Rang was extraordinarily courageous, and his army quickly grew to more than 10,000 people.

As early as the 9th year of Emperor Yang's Daye reign (613), Yang Xuangan (571–613), Duke of Yue, took advantage of the peasant uprisings to raise an army against the Sui dynasty, but was defeated and killed soon after. His subordinate, Li Mi (582–619), was arrested after the failure but escaped during the escort. In the 12th year of Daye (616), Li Mi joined the Wagang army and persuaded Zhai Rang to unite the nearby forces to win the battle against the Sui army, thus gained Zhai Rang's trust. In the following year (617), Li Mi took the leadership of the entire army and was promoted to the Duke of Wei. Li Yuan (566–635) was the cousin of Emperor Yang of Sui and the governor of Taiyuan at the time, he was sent by the emperor to suppress the peasant uprising, which was developing rapidly and had spread all over the country. Li Yuan knew that it was impossible to suppress it, but he also knew that the emperor was suspicious and bloodthirsty. In this turbulent era, it was difficult to ensure his own safety, let alone protect the incompetent emperor. Later, Li Yuan and his second son Li Shimin (599–649) launched a mutiny in the 13th year of Daye (617), named themselves generals, and led troops to attack the Sui army. At this time, Li Mi, who was in the eastern part of Henan province, was expanding his power. To further unite the various rebel forces and attract civil and military officials of the Sui dynasty to join him, Li Mi, after gaining power and while attacking Luoyang (capital of the Sui dynasty), issued a manifesto against Emperor Yang of Sui, calling on people from all sides to overthrow the rule of the Sui dynasty.

After listing 10 major crimes of Emperor Yang's brutal rule and his harm to the people, Li Mi's manifesto continues: "Even if all the bamboos in the South Mountain were used to make bamboo slips, we cannot write down all the faults of Yang Guang. Even if all the water in the East China Sea was drained, we cannot wash away his sins." As soon as this manifesto was spread, it caused a great sensation. Everyone rushed to circulate it, and Li Mi's momentum grew. As Li Mi's power continued to expand, Li Yuan wanted to win him over and sent him a letter to express his intention. Li Mi was self-righteous and did not take Li Yuan seriously, so he asked Li Yuan to bring his army over to form an alliance, but the leader of the alliance was Li Mi. Li Yuan feared offending Li Mi at this time, but he did not want to go to Li Mi's territory, as he thought: "Li Mi is arrogant and conceited. I'm about to march into Guanzhong. If I refuse him now, I will have another enemy. It's better to flatter him and let him be proud for a few more days. Then I can reap the benefits." So, Li Yuan asked his subordinate to write back to Li Mi, saying that: "Among the people in the country, there must be a leader. Who else can be the next emperor except you? I am over 50 years old now and no longer have this ambition. I am willing to follow you, my big younger brother, to climb the ladder of success." After reading the letter, Li Mi was even more pleased with himself, thinking that he was great, and never doubted Li Yuan again. However, in the end, Li Yuan won the country. This idiom describes that there are so many crimes that a person has committed, it is difficult to record them all.

取而代之

Qǔ ér dài zhī

出自西汉·司马迁《史记·项羽本纪》

[近义词：改朝换代；反义词：一如既往]

秦始皇游会稽，渡浙江，梁与籍俱观，籍曰："彼可取而代也。"

Replacing Someone

From "Records of the Grand Historian:
Biography of Xiang Yu"
by Sima Qian (145–c.86 BCE)

Xiang Yu (232–202 BCE) was a native of Chu State during the late Warring States period (475–221 BCE). He was strong and brave, cheerful and open-minded, decisive and capable, and was therefore highly appreciated by his fourth Uncle Xiang Liang (?–208 BCE). Xiang Yu once studied literature with Xiang Liang, but after a short while, he found reading boring, so he gave up literature and studied swordsmanship with Xiang Liang, but he failed it again. Xiang Liang was angry about this and scolded him for being useless. Xiang Yu said: "Reading is just remembering names, which is not very useful; no matter how proficient I am in swordsmanship, I can only fight with one person, which is not worth learning. What I am interested in is learning the skills to defeat 10,000 enemies."

After hearing Xiang Yu's words, Xiang Liang felt that this young man had great ambitions, so he began to teach Xiang Yu the *Art of War*. Although Xiang Yu was very interested in these books, he was not bound by books and had his own opinions on the strategies described in the books. One year, Qin Shi Huang (259–210 BCE) went to Kuaiji and was about to cross the Qiantang River. Xiang Liang and Xiang Yu went there to watch. Seeing the mighty and majestic procession of the first emperor of China, Xiang Yu could not help but pointed at him and said: "I will replace him in the future!" Xiang Liang was frightened and quickly covered Xiang Yu's mouth and whispered: "You can't talk nonsense! You're committing the crime of exterminating the entire clan!" But in his heart, Xiang Liang secretly admired his nephew's courage and thought that he would achieve great things in the future. As Qin Shi Huang implemented torture and tyranny, the people were miserable and rose up in rebellion. Chen Sheng (?–208 BCE) and Wu Guang (?–208 BCE) took the lead in revolting against Qin in Daze township. Xiang Yu also followed Xiang Liang to raise troops in Kuaiji to respond. Xiang Yu personally killed the governor of Kuaiji county and led 8,000 soldiers from Wu to fight against Qin. Later, Xiang Yu killed the King of Qin Ziying (?–206 BCE), self-proclaimed the Ruler of Western Chu, and became a powerful figure. This idiom means to take over someone else's position, or to replace one thing with another.

人死留名

Rén sǐ liú míng

出自北宋·欧阳修《新五代史·王彦章传》

[近义词：流芳百世；反义词：默默无闻]

彦章武人不知书，常为俚语谓人曰：

"豹死留皮，人死留名。"

其于忠义，盖天性也。

Leaving a Good Name Behind After Passing Away

From "New History of the Five Dynasties:
Biography of Wang Yanzhang"
by Ouyang Xiu (1007–1072)

During the Five Dynasties (907–979), a prominent general of the Liang dynasty (907–923), Wang Yanzhang (863–923), loved to use an iron spear when fighting, known as the "Iron Spear Wang." When he was young, Wang Yanzhang followed Liang Taizu Zhu Wen (852–912) to fight in battles in the north and south, and repeatedly made extraordinary military achievements, which won Zhu Wen's appreciation and respect. After the last emperor of Later Liang, Zhu Youzhen (888–923) succeeded to the throne, the power of the court was controlled by a group of treacherous officials, and Wang Yanzhang was not valued. As a result, Liang State frequently lost its land. One year, the Jin army broke through the Yunzhou city and penetrated deep into Liang's heartland, making Liang people terrified.

At this time, the last emperor of Liang took the advice of Grand Chancellor Jing Xiang (?–923) and appointed Wang Yanzhang as the recruitment envoy to lead the army to confront the enemy. Wang Yanzhang with the elite force conquered Huazhou and Nanzhou in just 3 days. However, the Liang army was not well supported, and the troops were outnumbered and lost. The last emperor believed a calumny and ordered Wang Yanzhang to be removed from his military position. Soon, the Tang army attacked Liang again, heading straight for Yanzhou, an important place in Liang State. Seeing this critical situation, the last emperor resumed Wang Yanzhang's post and provided him 500 imperial guards. However, due to these guards' lack of training, Wang Yanzhang lost again in the Yanzhou battle, he was also seriously injured and captured by the Tang army. Emperor Zhuangzong of Later Tang (885–926) persuaded Wang Yanzhang to surrender. Wang Yanzhang said righteously: "I am a minister of the Liang dynasty and have received our emperor's grace. I cannot repay him even if I die, how can I serve the Tang dynasty? Liang people often say this phrase: 'A leopard dies but leaves its skin; a man dies but leaves his name.' If I surrender to you, I will be cursed by future generations. I, Wang Yanzhang, am a man of integrity and will never live in humiliation!" Soon after, Wang Yanzhang was killed. This idiom refers to someone who has made great achievements during their lifetime, and their reputation will be respected by future generations after their death.

如火如荼

Rú huǒ rú tú

出自春秋·左丘明《国语·吴语》

[近义词：方兴未艾、轰轰烈烈；

反义词：冷冷清清、无声无息]

万人以为方阵，皆白裳，白旗，素甲，白羽之矰，望之如荼。……左军亦如之，皆赤裳，赤旃，丹甲，朱羽之矰，望之如火。

Look Like Red Fire and White Flowers

From "States and Languages: Wu Dialect"

by Zuo Qiuming (556–452 BCE)

In the late Spring and Autumn period (770–476 BCE), Wu State grew increasingly powerful, it defeated Chu, Yue, and Qi states successively, which had shocked all the states. The last king of Wu, Fuchai (?–473 BCE), thus planned to call the monarchs to form an alliance, attempting to suppress Duke Ding of Jin (?–475 BCE) by showing off his military power to win the position of overlord of all the states. In 482 BCE, Fuchai led his army to Wei State's Huangchi (now southwest of Fengqiu county, Henan province) to meet the various states' monarchs. Duke Ding of Jin had always been the leader of the states and was unwilling to be surpassed, so the two sides argued endlessly regarding the order of appearance of the two monarchs, and neither side was willing to yield. Fuchai was furious about the situation, but he did not know what to do. Wang Sunluo, a counselor in front of the tent proposed to gather all the soldiers of Wu State, force Duke Ding of Jin to give up the leadership position and let Fuchai be the leader of the states.

Fuchai took Wang Sunluo's advice and thus ordered all the soldiers to hold weapons, wear armor, and go out of the camp late that night to form a battle array. The Wu army was divided into three routes: left, center, and right. Each route had 100 rows, 100 men in each row, and a total of 10,000 soldiers formed a square. The three routes formed three squares, totaling 30,000 soldiers and horses, and they were mighty. Fuchai set up his formation, personally raised his axe, and first led the central army and horses to march toward the Jin camp under the guidance of the flag with bear and tiger pattern. At night, the soldiers of the central army were all wearing white robes, white armor, holding white flags, and carrying arrows with white feathers on their waists. From a distance, they looked like white flowers blooming all over the mountains, dazzling and spectacular! The soldiers on the left were all wearing red armor and battle robes, holding high red flags, and carrying arrows with red feathers. Under the illumination of lanterns and torches, they looked like a blazing fire from afar, so majestic! The soldiers on the right were all dressed in black, like a dark cloud in the sky, full of killing intent! At daybreak, Fuchai went up to the tent and personally beat the drums in the middle of the army. At once, the three routes of army shouted, and the sound shook heaven and earth. Duke Ding of Jin woke up from his sleep, he saw the Wu army's fierce battle formation and heard the Wu army's earth-shaking shouts. He was already very frightened and hurriedly sent people to see Fuchai to express his concession. King Fuchai of Wu finally got what he wanted and became the leader of the alliance. This idiom originally describes the grand appearance of an army; it is now used to describe a large-scale action with high momentum and a fiery atmosphere.

孺子可教

Rú zǐ kě jiào

出自西汉·司马迁《史记·留侯世家》

[近义词：尊师重教、程门度雪；

反义词：朽木不雕、不堪造就]

父以足受，笑而去。良殊大惊，随目之。

父去里所，复返，曰：孺子可教矣。

A Teachable Youngster

From "Records of the Grand Historian:

House of Marquis of Liu"

by Sima Qian (145–c.86 BCE)

Zhang Liang (262–186 BCE) was a young man from Han State in the late Warring States period (475–221 BCE). Once, he failed to assassinate Qin Shi Huang (259–210 BCE) and fled to Xiapi (now Gupi town, Suining county, Xuzhou city, Jiangsu province). One morning, Zhang Liang met a white-haired old man at the Sishui Bridge. The old man deliberately kicked one of his shoes under the bridge and said to Zhang Liang in an imperative tone: "Hey, boy, go and pick up my shoe for me!" Zhang Liang saw that the man was very old, out of courtesy, he went down the bridge to pick up the shoe and handed it to him. Zhang Liang thought the man would thank him, but the old man raised one foot and said to Zhang Liang: "Hey, boy, put on my shoe for me again!" Zhang Liang was very annoyed, but then he thought: "I have already helped the old man, I might as well help him to the end!" So, he did as the old man asked. Zhang Liang put on the shoe for the old man, and the man smiled at Zhang Liang, straightened his clothes, and left without saying a word.

Zhang Liang thought that this strange old man must have some background, so he followed him quietly and walked more than a mile together. Suddenly, the old man turned around and said to Zhang Liang: "You are a teachable boy!" Then they agreed to meet at Sishui Bridge at dawn 5 days later. At dawn on the 5th day, Zhang Liang rushed to Sishui Bridge to keep the appointment. Unexpectedly, the old man had arrived before him and was waiting at the bridge head angrily. He blamed Zhang Liang and said: "Young man, why are you late? Come back in 5 days!" Five days later, Zhang Liang got up in the middle of the night and hurried to the bridge. But he found the old man had been waiting for him at the bridge head for a long time. Zhang Liang felt extremely ashamed and asked him for forgiveness. The old man patted Zhang Liang's shoulder and said: "Go home, come back in 5 days, and don't be late again!" This time, Zhang Liang was determined to arrive earlier than him. On the day of the appointment, Zhang Liang went to the bridge after midnight to wait. When it was dawn, he saw the old man walking up the bridge step by step, and he hurried forward to greet him. Seeing that Zhang Liang was very early this time, the old man took out a military book, handed it to Zhang Liang solemnly and said: "My name is Huang Shigong. This book is the *Taigong's Art of War* [also known as the *Six Secret Teachings*] that I have treasured for years, it talks about the military strategies that Jiang Ziya [1128–1015/1036 BCE] used when he assisted Zhou to destroy Shang. You should read it carefully; it will be useful in the future!" Zhang Liang took the book as an unexpected treasure. Thereafter, he had never forgotten Huang Shigong's teachings and devoted himself to study the book and finally became an outstanding strategist to assist Liu Bang (c.256–195 BCE) in founding the Han dynasty (206 BCE–220 CE).

入木三分

Rù mù sān fēn

出自唐·张怀瓘《书断·王羲之》

[近义词：力透纸背、铁画银钩；

反义词：略见一斑、走马观花]

卫夫人见，语太常王策曰："此儿必见用笔诀，近见其书，便有老成之智。"流涕曰："此子必蔽吾名！"晋帝时，祭北郊，更祝版，工人削之，入木三分。

Deeply Engraved Three-Tenths of an Inch into the Wood

From "Judgments on Calligraphers: Wang Xizhi"

by Zhang Huaiguan of the Tang Dynasty (618–907)

Often regarded as the greatest calligrapher in Chinese history, Wang Xizhi (303–361) of the Eastern Jin dynasty (317–420) combined the merits of many master calligraphers and created a unique style of his own, praised as the "Calligraphy Sage" by later generations. His most famous work is the "Preface to the Poems Composed at the Orchid Pavilion" (*Lanting Ji Xu*, written in 353). Wang Xizhi showed a talent for calligraphy at the age of 7 and had been good at writing since his childhood. When he was 12 years old, Wang Xizhi accidentally found a good book on calligraphy in his father's study and secretly took it out to read. From then on, he studied day and night and practiced calligraphy meticulously according to the methods described in the book. His calligraphy level improved rapidly. Every day after practicing calligraphy, Wang Xizhi would go to the pond in the back garden to wash his brush and inkstone. Over time, the whole pond water was stained black, which revealed how diligent Wang Xizhi practiced calligraphy.

One morning, while Wang Xizhi was walking alone at the foot of the mountain, he suddenly saw an elderly woman selling more than a dozen paper fans for 20 coins each, but no one was interested in buying them. Wang Xizhi noticed that the old woman was poor, he borrowed a pen and ink and wrote a few words on each fan. The old woman did not know at all who Wang Xizhi was. Seeing him writing on the white and clean paper fans, she complained bitterly. Wang Xizhi smiled and said: "Just say this is the handwriting of Wang Youjun, I guarantee you can sell them for 100 coins each!" The old woman took the paper fans, half-believing and half-doubting, she went to the market to sell them according to Wang Xizhi's words. When people heard this, they rushed to pay for the fans. In a short while, more than a dozen fans were sold. The old woman smiled with relief.

Legend says Wang Xizhi once wrote a "blessing plate" for the Imperial Court to offer sacrifices to the gods of heaven and earth, praying for peace and prosperity for the country, and a good harvest. After Emperor Cheng of Jin, Sima Yan (321–342) ascended the throne, he ordered the workers to change the inscription on the blessing plate. The workers spent so much time removing the characters, but they could not scrape off the original handwriting of Wang Xizhi. The workers took a closer look at the plate; they were all stunned and praised him. It turned out that every character written by Wang Xizhi was deeply engraved three-tenths of an inch into the wood, as if carved with a knife. How could they be easily scraped off? This idiom describes the vigorous and powerful strokes of calligraphy; it also refers to a deep and thorough understanding of an article or a matter.

塞翁失马

Sài wēng shī mǎ

出自西汉·刘安等《淮南子·人间训》

[近义词：因祸得福、失之东隅，收之桑榆；

反义词：福过灾生、利深祸速]

近塞上之人有善术者，马无故亡而入胡。人皆吊之，其父曰："此何遽不为福乎？"居数月，其马将胡骏马而归。人皆贺之，其父曰："此何遽不能为祸乎？"家富良马，其子好骑，堕而折其髀。人皆吊之，其父曰："此何遽不为福乎？"居一年，胡人大入塞，丁壮者引弦而战。近塞之人，死者十九。此独以跛之故，父子相保。故福之为祸，祸之为福，化不可极，深不可测也。

The Old Man at the Frontier Lost His Horse

From "Huainanzi: Lessons from the Human World"

by Liu An (179–122 BCE) *et al*.

In a place near the frontier, there lived a man who was good at predicting good fortune or misfortune of human affairs. Once, his horse crossed the border for no reason and ran to the barbarians. Everyone in the neighborhood came to condole. But his father said: "Why can't this be considered a good thing?"

A few months later, the horse returned with a barbarian horse. Everyone came to congratulate. But his father said: "Why can't this be considered a bad thing?"

As the family had a steed, the son liked to ride it. He fell off the horse and broke his thigh. Everyone came to condole again. But the father said: "Why can't this be considered a good thing?"

A year later, the barbarians crossed the border and invaded the area. The strong and abled men took up arms to go to war. Nine out of ten warriors died in the battle. Because the old man's son was lame, he was not called up to join the army. So, the father and the son both saved their lives.

Therefore, good fortune can be turned into misfortune, and misfortune can be transformed into good fortune. There is no way to reach the extreme of creation, and there is no way to explore its profoundness.

三令五申

Sān lìng wǔ shēn

出自西汉·司马迁《史记·孙子吴起列传》

[近义词：发号施令、千叮万嘱]

出宫中美女，得百八十人。孙子分为二队，以王之宠姬二人各为队长，皆令持戟。……约束既布，乃设铁钺，即三令五申之。

Warned Repeatedly Three-to-Five Times

From "Records of the Grand Historian:
Biographies of Sunzi and Wu Qi"
by Sima Qian (145–c.86 BCE)

During the Spring and Autumn period (770–476 BCE), there was a military strategist named Sun Wu (c.545–c.470/480 BCE) who wrote a famous military book, *Suzi Bingfa (The Art of War)*. The King of Wu, Helü (?–496 BCE) read and admired the book very much, so he summoned Sun Wu to the palace. As soon as they met, the king asked: "Can you use your military strategies to train the palace ladies?" Sun Wu knew that the king wanted to test his command ability, he replied without hesitation: "Of course." The king then gathered 180 palace ladies to let Sun Wu train them. Sun Wu divided these ladies into two lines and asked the king's two favorite concubines to be the leaders. He stood on the command platform and gave orders loudly: "When I say front, you look in front; when I say left, look to the left; when I say right, look to the right; when I say back, look behind." After the orders were clearly explained, Sun Wu commanded to put down a guillotine on the side and then repeated these orders to the palace ladies.

Everything was set, Sun Wu beat the drum and ordered: "Right!" Unexpectedly, the palace ladies treated Sun Wu's command as a joke, no one obeyed his order, and they all laughed. In the stands, the King of Wu and the nobles also laughed. The ladies laughed even louder when they saw this. For a moment, the entire training ground was filled with laughter. Sun Wu remained calm and said: "The order may not have been explained clearly; it is my fault." He repeated it once and then beat the drum again to issue the order: "Left!" The ladies continued to laugh, especially the king's two favorite concubines at the front who laughed so hard that they bent over and fell backward. Sun Wu was furious and shouted: "If the order was unclear, it would be the fault of the general. I have repeatedly warned you, but you didn't obey. This is the fault of the leader. According to military law, you should be beheaded!" Then he ordered the king's two favorite concubines to be beheaded in public. When the king realized that Sun Wu was going to execute his two favorite concubines, he hurriedly sent a messenger to tell Sun Wu that: "I have already known that the general is good at using troops! The general should not execute my two favorite concubines!" Sun Wu asked the messenger to reply to the king, saying that: "I have been asked to be the general. When I am in the army, I don't have to obey the king's orders!" After that, he instructed the execution of the king's two favorite concubines. Sun Wu beat the drum again to pass the order, and this time the palace ladies all behaved well and obeyed his order. From then on, Sun Wu's ability to use troops was valued by the King of Wu, who gave Sun Wu full command of the Wu army, and finally made Wu a powerful state in the Spring and Autumn period.

神机妙算

Shén jī miào suàn

[近义词：锦囊妙计、料事如神；

反义词：无计可施、束手无策]

妙算申帷幄，神谋出庙庭。

–出自唐·刘知几《仪坤庙乐章》

妙算神机，须信道，国手都无勍敌。

–宋·赵佶《念奴娇》

Divine Intelligence and Ingenious Calculation

From "Music Movement in the Yikun Temple"

by Liu Zhiji (661–721); and

"The Charm of a Maiden Singer"

by Zhao Ji (1082–1135)

In 208 CE, shortly after Cao Cao (155–220) unified the north, he led several hundred thousand troops to the south, attempting to eliminate the forces of Sun Quan (182–252) and Liu Bei (161–223) in the south to unify the country. At that time, Liu Bei had only 10,000 troops and was unable to resist Cao Cao's attack, so he sent military advisor Zhuge Liang (181–234) to persuade Sun Quan to jointly fight against Cao Cao. Sun Quan took Zhuge Liang's advice; he gave up the idea of surrendering to Cao Cao and was determined to join forces with Liu Bei to fight with Cao army to the death. Zhou Yu (175–210), the governor of Eastern Wu, was very jealous of Zhuge Liang's talent, and always wanted to find an opportunity to get rid of him. Zhuge Liang knew Zhou Yu's malicious intentions, but he had to be alert when dealing with Zhou Yu for the sake of the overall situation. Once, Zhuge Liang issued a military order, declaring that he could make 100,000 arrows within 3 days, and that if he failed to complete the task, he was willing to be beheaded.

Zhou Yu was secretly pleased, as he thought Zhuge Liang would not be able to complete the task, and he furtively ordered the arrow-making army craftsmen to deliberately delay the process so that Zhuge Liang could not complete the task on time, and so that he could remove him legitimately. Two days had passed, but Zhuge Liang looked confident as he had already figured out a way to complete the task. Between 3-5 am on the 3rd day, Zhuge Liang privately asked Lu Su (172–217) for 20 straw boats, each of which was hung with a green cloth tent and placed more than 1,000 straw men. Zhuge Liang took advantage of the heavy fog before dawn and ordered the soldiers to sail the straw boats to Cao army's water fort. When they arrived at the water fort, Zhuge Liang and Lu Su started to drink wine in the boat while ordering the soldiers to beat drums and shout on the boat, pretending to attack Cao's army. Cao Cao was indeed trapped and hurriedly ordered his army to shoot arrows. In a flash, more than 10,000 archers from Cao's army and navy shot arrows into the river. After the fog cleared, Zhuge Liang immediately ordered all the boats to withdraw quickly. At this time, the 20 straw boats were already full of arrows, far more than 100,000. Zhuge Liang asked the soldiers on the boats to shout in unison: "Thank you, Your Highness, for lending us your arrows." By the time Cao Cao realized what had happened, Zhuge Liang's straw boats had already sailed away, and Cao Cao was filled with regret. Afterwards, Lu Su told Zhou Yu the story of Zhuge Liang borrowing arrows with straw boats. Zhou Yu exclaimed: "Zhuge Liang is so smart; I'm not as smart as him!" This story is called "Borrowing Arrows with Straw Boats" in Chinese history. The idiom refers to amazing wit and wise planning; it also describes accurate prediction and good assessment of the situation and strategy.

声东击西

Shēng dōng jī xī

[近义词：出其不意、出奇制胜；反义词：无的放矢]

故用兵之道，示之以柔而迎之以刚，示之以弱而乘之以强，为之以歙而应之以张，将欲西而示之以东。–出自汉·刘安《淮南子·兵略训》

声言击东，其实击西。–唐·杜佑《通典·兵六》

Making a Feint to the East and Attacking in the West

From "Huainanzi: Military Strategy Training"

by Liu An (179–122 BCE); and

"Comprehensive Statutes: Military Strategy VI"

by Du You (735–812)

During the Chu-Han Contention (206–202 BCE), one year, the King of Han, Liu Bang (c.256–195 BCE) led his army to attack Pengcheng, the capital of Chu, but was defeated by the Chu army whose commander was Xiang Yu (232–202 BCE), and thus Liu Bang fled to Xingyang. At this time, many generals who had previously surrendered to Liu Bang saw that the situation was not good and then surrendered to Xiang Yu. Liu Bang's formerly captured general Wei Bao (?–204 BCE) also left the Han camp and returned to his fiefdom in Henan. Immediately after Wei Bao arrived in Henan, he blocked Linjin Pass on the west of the Yellow Riverbank, cutting off the route of retreat of the Han army and went to seek peace with Xiang Yu, the King of Chu. Consequently, the Han army was attacked from all sides, and the situation was very critical. So, Liu Bang sent his general Li Shiqi (?–203

BCE) to persuade Wei Bao to rejoin Liu Bang. But Wei Bao insisted on his own way and refused. Liu Bang was furious and sent his general Han Xin (231–196 BCE) to conquer Wei Bao.

After hearing this, Wei Bao ordered Bai Zhi to lead a large force to guard the Puban area on the west of the Yellow Riverbank, preventing the Han army from crossing the river. Han Xin led the Han army to the east of the Yellow Riverbank, while he saw that Puban had a terrain that was strategically located and difficult to access, and there were heavy troops guarding the opposite bank. He knew that it would be difficult to win by force. Han Xin thus planned to use the military tactic of "making a feint to the east and attacking in the west" to cross the natural barrier of the Yellow River. To confuse Bai Zhi, Han Xin ordered a small number of soldiers to set up camps on the opposite bank of Puban, and let them practice and patrol all day, making it seem like the Han army was going to forcefully cross the Yellow River from there. Secretly, Han Xin dispatched troops and generals to transfer the main force of the Han army to the mouth of the Xiayang River, preparing to sneak across the Yellow River from Xiayang and attack Wei Bao. As expected, Bai Zhi fell into Han Xin's trap and thought that the Han army was really going to cross the river from Puban. He reported it to Wei Bao, saying that Puban was well defended as solid as a rock. After Han Xin led his elite troops to Xiayang, he immediately ordered his soldiers to cut down trees and make many wooden barrels. Then they tied them together in twos and threes with rafts for crossing the Yellow River. As soon as the Han army landed, they went straight to Anyi, the old nest of Wei Bao. Wei Bao hurriedly gathered his troops to fight but could not be a match for the Han army. As a result, the Chu army was defeated miserably by the Han army, and Wei Bao himself was captured alive by Han Xin. This idiom is a tactical strategy to create an illusion for the opponent by claiming to attack in the east but attacking in the west. In military terms, it is a tactic to confuse the enemy and achieve a surprise victory.

失之东隅，收之桑榆

Shī zhī dōng yú, shōu zhī sāng yú

出自南朝·宋·范晔《后汉书·冯异列传》

[近义词：塞翁失马，焉知非福、因祸得福；

反义词：赔了夫人又折兵、人财两空]

玺书劳异曰："赤眉破平，士吏劳苦，始虽垂翅回溪，终能奋翼黾池，可谓'失之东隅，收之桑榆'。方论功赏，以答大勋。"

Lose at Sunrise and Gain at Sunset
(Lose in Hake but Gain in Herring)

From "Book of the Later Han: Biography of Feng Yi"

by Fan Ye (398–445)

Feng Yi (?–34) was a renowned general in the Eastern Han dynasty (25–220), who was proficient in military tactics. He followed Emperor Guangwu of Han, Liu Xiu (5 BCE–57 CE) in his campaigns and made great military accomplishments, thus he was highly valued by Liu Xiu. Feng Yi had good military management, yet he was modest and never took credit for himself. After each battle, when other generals would sit around in their tents to boast about their achievements, Feng Yi would sit quietly under a big tree alone, without saying a word. As such, the soldiers of the three armies admired him deeply and called him "Big Tree General." After Liu Xiu became emperor, he appointed Feng Yi as the General of the Western Expedition and ordered him to lead the Han army to join the armies of Deng Yu (2–58) and Deng Hong (?–115) to march westward to attack the Chimei (lit. "Red

Eyebrow") Army which was occupying the Guanzhong area.

At that time, the strong and powerful Chimei Army had 200,000 soldiers stationed there. Feng Yi judged the situation and suggested sending people to the Chimei Army to induce surrender and weaken the enemy's morale. Feng Yi then asked the two generals Deng Yu and Deng Hong to lead their armies to attack the Chimei Army in the east, and he would lead the Han army to attack them in the west, as confronting the enemy from both sides would ensure victory. However, Deng Yu and Deng Hong did not take Feng Yi's advice. They hastily led their armies to attack the Chimei Army but were defeated and lost 3,000 soldiers. Upon hearing the news, Feng Yi hurriedly led his troops to move and wait for the opportunity to fight. A few days later, Feng Yi set up an ambush in Mianchi, he asked his soldiers to change into the uniforms of the Chimei Army, and to hide on the roadside to lure the enemy. The Chimei Army fell into the trap. Feng Yi gave an order, and the ambushes rose up all around, killing the Chimei soldiers and making them flee in all directions. In the Mianchi Battle, Feng Yi wiped out 80,000 enemies and won a great victory. When the news of victory reached the capital, Liu Xiu immediately wrote an edict and sent it to the front to congratulate. Liu Xiu said in the letter: "The soldiers in the front fought very hard and won the battle. Although you were like defeated birds fleeing Xiban with your wings drooping at the beginning, you finally spread your wings and flew high in Mianchi. It can be said that you 'lost at sunrise and gained at sunset.'" The original meaning of this idiom is lost in the morning and gained in the evening (Dongyu refers to sunrise and morning; Sangyu refers to sunset and evening). Later, this proverb means that what is lost in one place will be compensated in another.

师出无名

Shī chū wú míng

[近义词：平白无故、兵出无名；

反义词：名正言顺、师出有名]

君王计敝邑之罪，又矜而赦之，师与有无名乎？

-出自《礼记·檀弓下》

臣闻顺德者昌，逆德者亡。兵出无名，事故不成。

-东汉·班固《汉书·高帝纪》

No Legitimate Reason to Send Troops

From "Book of Rites: Tan Gong (Part 2)"; and

"The Book of Han: Annals of Emperor Gaozu"

by Ban Gu (32–92)

In 208 BCE, Liu Bang (c.256–195 BCE) led his army to Bashang and approached the Qin capital Xianyang. The last King of Qin, Ziying (?–206 BCE), saw that the situation was hopeless, he surrendered. After Liu Bang entered Xianyang, he ordered people to seal up all the jewels and treasures in the Qin Palace and made promises that he would never do anything to harm the people and then led his army out of the city and returned to Bashang. Soon, Xiang Yu (232–202 BCE) marched to Hangu Pass in a mighty force. He heard that Liu Bang tried to win popular support in Xianyang and wanted to be king in Guanzhong, he was furious and wanted to get rid of Liu Bang. Liu Bang knew that he could not defeat Xiang Yu, so he went to see Xiang Yu in person and repeatedly stated that he dared not to be the king in Guanzhong. Seeing Liu Bang's sincere attitude, Xiang Yu gave up the idea of killing him. A few days later, Xiang Yu led his army into Xianyang, ordered to execute the King of Qin Ziying and burn the Qin Palace. The 400,000 Chu troops slaughtered the people and plundered the city, turning Xianyang into a living hell.

Soon, Xiang Yu plotted and killed Emperor Yi of Chu, Xiong Xin (?–206 BCE), and established himself as the Overlord of Western Chu in Pengcheng. Xiang Yu's brutal actions aroused strong negative emotions among the vassal kings, who accused him of excessive violence and treason. At this time, Liu Bang led his troops to Luoyang, while one of the three elders of Xincheng, Mister Dong, suggested to him: "Since ancient times, those who follow virtue have prospered, and those who go against virtue have perished. If the army has no legitimate reason to send troops, nothing can be accomplished. At present, Xiang Yu has committed atrocities and killed Emperor Yi, he is hated by the people of the whole country. You can take this opportunity to raise a righteous army and attack Xiang Yu in the name of revenge for Emperor Yi. In this way, the vassal kings will admire your virtue and obey your orders." Liu Bang took Mister Dong's sensible advice, personally held a funeral for Emperor Yi, and sent messengers to issue orders to the vassal kings, saying: "The whole country had jointly established Emperor Yi, and we, as subjects, respected him as the Son of Heaven. Now Xiang Yu has killed Emperor Yi in the south of the Yangzi River, which is a big rebellion! I thus held the funeral for Emperor Yi, and all my soldiers wore white mourning clothes to mourn the king. Now I want to raise an army of benevolence and righteousness, and I'm willing to follow the vassal kings to attack Xiang Yu who killed Emperor Yi." From then on, Liu Bang and Xiang Yu launched the Chu-Han Contention (206–202 BCE), and Liu Bang finally won the war and established the Western Han dynasty (206 BCE–23 CE). This idiom means that there is no legitimate reason to send troops to war; it can be extended to mean that there is no legitimate reason to do something.

师旷问学

Shī kuàng wèn xué

出自西汉·刘向《说苑》

[近义词：师旷喻学]

晋平公问于师旷曰："吾年七十，欲学，恐已暮矣。"师旷曰："何不炳烛乎？"平公曰："安有为人臣而戏其君乎？"师旷曰："盲臣安敢戏其君乎！臣闻之，少而好学，如日出之阳；壮而好学，如日中之光；老而好学，如炳烛之明。炳烛之明，孰与昧行乎？"平公曰："善哉！"

Shi Kuang's Question About Learning

From "Garden of Stories" by Liu Xiang (77–6 BCE)

Duke Ping of Jin (r.557–532 BCE) said to Shi Kuang (572–532 BCE): "I'm 70 years old, so I'm afraid it's too late to study." Shi Kuang asked: "Why don't you light a candle?" Duke Ping said: "How can a minister mock the monarch?" Shi Kuang said: "How dare I, a blind man, mock the monarch? I heard that when a person likes to study at a young age, it is like the rising sun; when a person likes to study in their prime, it is like the sunlight at noon; and when a person likes to study at an old age, it is like holding a candlelight. Which is better, lighting a candle or walking in the dark?" Duke Ping said: "That's a good idea!"

世外桃源

Shì wài táo yuán

出自东晋·陶渊明《桃花源记》

[近义词：洞天福地、蓬莱仙境、极乐世界；

反义词：人间地狱]

晋太元中，武陵人捕鱼为业。缘溪行，忘路之远近。忽逢桃花林，夹岸数百步，中无杂树，芳草鲜美，落英缤纷，渔人甚异之，复前行，欲穷其林。林尽水源，便得一山，山有小口，仿佛若有光。便舍船，从口入。初极狭，才通人。复行数十步，豁然开朗。土地平旷，屋舍俨然，有良田、美池、桑竹之属。阡陌交通，鸡犬相闻。其中往来种作，男女衣着，悉如外人。黄发垂髫，并怡然自乐。见渔人，乃大惊，问所从来。具答之。便要还家，设酒杀鸡作食。村中闻有此人，咸来问讯。自云先世避秦时乱，率妻子邑人来此绝境，不复出焉，遂与外人间隔。问今是何世，乃不知有汉，无论魏晋。此人一一为具言所闻，皆叹惋。余人各复延至其家，皆出酒食。停数日，辞去。此中人语云："不足为外人道也。"既出，得其船，便扶向路，处处志之。及郡下，诣太守，说如此。太守即遣人随其往，寻向所志，遂迷，不复得路。南阳刘子骥，高尚士也，闻之，欣然规往。未果，寻病终，后遂无问津者。

The Peach Spring Beyond This World

From "The Peach Blossom Spring"

by Tao Yuanming (365–427)

Tao Yuanming (365–427) was an outstanding poet in the Eastern Jin dynasty (317–420). He was open-minded, not greedy for fame, fortune, or status. In his early years, he served as the Pengze county magistrate. However, he was dissatisfied with the darkness of the officialdom. After only 81 days in office, he resigned and returned home to live a leisurely life of seclusion. "The Peach Blossom Spring" is Tao Yuanming's masterpiece, in which he tells the story:

During the Taiyuan period (376–396) of the Eastern Jin dynasty, there was a fisherman in Wuling county. One day, he went out fishing and rowed his boat down the stream. Suddenly, he saw a dense peach forest. The fisherman had never seen such a beautiful scenery before. He was very surprised and continued to row along. After a while, the boat reached the end of the forest, and a green mountain appeared in front of him. There was a narrow pass at the foot of the mountain. A ray of sunlight came through it. The fisherman tied up the boat and went ashore and walked from the mountain pass to the inside. After walking a few steps, a flat and wide field came into view. In the field, men and women in strange costumes were busy farming; on the footpath between paddy fields, the elderly and children were playing carefree. While the fisherman was fascinated by the scene, the people of Taohuayuan (lit. "Peach Blossom Spring") saw him and asked him where he came from. The fisherman told them the truth. The people warmly invited him to the village, killed chickens and set up wine to entertain him. All the villagers came to see the fisherman, asked about this and that, and told him about their own situations. It turned out that the ancestors of these people took their wives and children to hide in this unknown place to escape the wars of the Qin dynasty (221–206 BCE) and never left. The fisherman stayed in Taohuayuan for a few days and then said goodbye. Before leaving, the villagers repeatedly told him: "Don't tell anyone about us here!" The fisherman walked out of the mountain and rowed back along the same route while he carefully marked the points. Immediately after he returned home, he reported the incident to the governor, who sent people to follow the fisherman to find the Peach Blossom Spring, but they got lost and never found the beautiful place again. This idiom originally refers to an ideal state of being isolated from the real world and living a happy life. Later, it also refers to a place with a tranquil ambiance and a comfortable life.

守株待兔

Shǒu zhū dài tù

出自《韩非子·五蠹》

[近义词：刻舟求剑、墨守成规；反义词：通达权变]

宋人有耕者。田中有株，兔走触株，折颈而死。因释其耒而守株，冀复得兔。兔不可复得，而身为宋国笑。

Waiting for Rabbits to Hit the Tree Stump

From "Han Feizi: Five Moths"

Once upon a time, there was a farmer in Song State who made a living by farming. There was a tree stump in his field. One day, he was tired from farming and sat by the tree stump to rest. Suddenly, a rabbit ran over and hit the tree stump with its head and died. The farmer was very pleased, he picked up the dead rabbit, took it home, and had a delicious meal of rabbit meat. From then on, he stopped tilling and stayed in front of the tree stump all day, waiting to pick up dead rabbits. However, he never saw rabbits hitting the tree stump again, and the field became barren day by day. The people of Song State laughed at him for this. This idiom is used to refer to someone who sticks to their experience and does not know how to adapt. It is also used to satirize the mentality of hoping for something for nothing.

熟能生巧

Shú néng shēng qiǎo

出自宋·欧阳修《归田录·卖油翁》

[近义词：游刃有余、得心应手、驾轻就熟；

反义词：半路出家、半途而废、浅尝辄止]

乃取一葫芦置于地，以钱覆其口，徐以杓酌油沥之，自钱孔入，而钱不湿。因曰："我亦无他，惟手熟尔。"康肃笑而遣之。

Practice Makes Perfect

From "Return to the Countryside: The Oil Seller"
by Ouyang Xiu (1007–1072)

Chen Yaozi (posthumous name "Kangsu," 970–1034) was an archer in the Northern Song dynasty (960–1127). One day, he was performing archery at the shooting range, and it showed that his archery skill was indeed extraordinary. Of the ten arrows he shot, eight or nine hit the target. The onlookers applauded him. Chen Yaozi raised his bow and arrow, laughing loudly, feeling very proud! Among the crowd, there was a gray-haired oil seller who stood there and watched for a while. After watching, he just nodded slightly, looking like he did not care. Chen Yaozi was not pleased when he saw this, he deliberately asked the old man: "Do you know archery? What do you think of my archery skill?"

The old man replied: "Your archery skill is not bad, but there is no secret, it's just practice!" After hearing this, Chen Yaozi was even more dissatisfied, he asked the old man: "How dare you look down on my archery skill? Do you have any better skills?" The old man said humbly and sincerely: "It's not that I look down on your archery skill. Based on my many years of experience in selling oil, I know that your archery skill is also based on practice!" After saying this, the old man put a gourd for oil on the ground, took out a copper coin from his pocket, and put it on the mouth of the gourd. Then, he held up a spoon full of oil and poured it down to the hole of the coin. The poured oil slowly passed through the hole of the coin like a thread and flowed into the gourd. The oil in the spoon was all poured out, but there was not a drop of oil on the copper coin. The onlookers were stunned after watching the oil seller's amazing skill. Chen Yaozi was also impressed and nodded his head repeatedly. At this time, the old man patted Chen Yaozi on his shoulder and said calmly: "There is nothing special about me, it's just that practice makes perfect!" Then, the old man picked up the oil basket and walked away from the archery range. This idiom means that when one becomes proficient in something, they can do it with ease.

树倒猢狲散

Shù dǎo hú sūn sàn

出自北宋·庞元英《谈薮·曹咏妻》；

元末明初·陶宗仪《说郛》

[近义词：墙倒众人推、众叛亲离；

反义词：一人得道，鸡犬升天]

宋曹咏依附秦桧，官至侍郎，显赫一时。咏百端威胁，德斯卒不屈。及秦桧死，德斯遣人致书于曹咏，启封，乃《树倒猢狲散赋》一篇。

When the Tree Falls, the Monkeys Scatter

From "Tan Sou: Cao Yong's Wife"

by Pang Yuanying; and

"Commentaries on the Five Classics"

by Tao Zongyi (1329–1410)

During the Song dynasty (960–1279), Chancellor Qin Hui (1091–1155) was in power, and many people scrambled to curry favor with him. There was a man named Cao Yong who became a high-ranking official because of Qin Hui. Cao Yong's brother-in-law, Li Desi, was only a village junior officer at the time, but he did not try to please Cao Yong like others. After Qin Hui's death, those who followed him fell from power one after another, and Cao Yong was demoted to Xinzhou (now Xinxing county, Guangdong province) to be a minor official. After hearing about this, Li Desi sent Cao Yong a poetic essay, titled "When the tree falls, the monkeys scatter." This idiom is a metaphor that once the leader falls, the followers will also scatter.

水滴石穿

Shuǐ dī shí chuān

[近义词：绳锯木断、铁杵磨针、积土成山；

反义词：半途而废、浅尝辄止]

泰山之管穿石，单极之绠断干。水非石之钻，索非木之锯，渐靡使之然也。–出自东汉·班固《汉书·枚乘传》

张乖崖为崇阳令，一吏自库中出，视其鬓旁巾下有一钱，诘之，乃库中钱也。乖崖命杖之，吏勃然曰："一钱何足道，乃杖我耶？尔能杖我，不能斩我也！"乖崖援笔判云："一日一钱，千日千钱，绳锯木断，水滴石穿！"自仗剑下阶斩其首，申台府自劾，崇阳人至今传之。–南宋·罗大经《鹤林玉露》

Water Dripping Continuously Can Penetrate Through Stone

From "The Book of Han: Biography of Mei Cheng"

by Ban Gu (32–92); and

"Jade Dew from Crane Forest"

by Luo Dajing (1196–c.1252)

During the Song dynasty (960–1279), there was a man named Zhang Guaiya (Zhang Yong, 946–1015) who served as the Chongyang County magistrate. One day, when Zhang Guaiya was patrolling around the government office, he suddenly saw a petty official sneaking out of the treasury in a panic. Zhang Guaiya stopped the clerk and asked: "Hey! Why are you in such a hurry?" "Nothing." The clerk replied. Zhang Guaiya thought that the treasury was often stolen, and judged that the clerk might have embezzled, so he asked his attendants to search the clerk. As a result, a copper coin was found in the clerk's headscarf. Zhang Guaiya took the clerk back to the hall for interrogation and asked him how much money he had stolen from the treasury in total. The clerk refused to admit that he had stolen any more money, so Zhang Guaiya ordered the torture. The clerk shouted angrily: "What's the big deal about stealing a copper coin? You torture me like this; can you kill me?" Zhang Guaiya was furious that the clerk dared to contradict him. He picked up a red pen without hesitation and pronounced the verdict: "If you steal one coin a day, you can steal a thousand coins in a thousand days; over time, a rope can saw through wood, and water can drip through stone." After the verdict was made, Zhang Guaiya drew his sword from its sheath, walked into the government courtyard, and personally beheaded the petty official. This verdict had a strong deterrent effect. From then on, the theft in Chongyang County was curbed and the social atmosphere improved greatly. This idiom means that water dripping continuously can penetrate through a stone; it is a metaphor that perseverance and the accumulation of subtle forces can achieve big results.

死灰复燃

Sǐ huī fù rán

出自西汉·司马迁《史记·韩长孺列传》

[近义词：东山再起、起死回生、卷土重来；

反义词：付之一炬、石沉大海、一蹶不振]

御史大夫韩安国者，梁成安人也。...事梁孝王为中大夫。吴楚反时，孝王使安国及张羽为将，...安国持重，以故吴不能过梁。吴楚已破，安国、张羽名由此显。...其后安国坐法抵罪，蒙狱吏田甲辱安国。安国曰："死灰独不复然（燃）乎？"田甲曰："然即溺之。"居无何，梁内史缺，汉使使者拜安国为梁内史，起徒中为二千石，田甲亡走。

Extinguished Ashes Rekindled

From "Records of the Grand Historian:

Biography of Han Changru"

by Sima Qian (145–c.86 BCE)

During the reign of Emperor Jing of Han (188–141 BCE), there was a capable, resourceful, and modest minister named Han Anguo (?–127 BCE), who led troops to quell the Rebellion of the Seven States headed by Prince of Wu, Liu Bi (216–154 BCE), and who was highly appreciated by Emperor Jing and became the emperor's favorite. One year, Han Anguo was implicated in a case and was imprisoned in Meng County Prison, awaiting judgment. The jailer Tian Jia was a snobbish villain with evil intentions. Seeing that Han Anguo had lost his power, Tian Jia often humiliated him for no reason.

Han Anguo could not bear it anymore; he pointed at Tian Jia's nose and cursed: "You despicable and shameless villain! Don't think that I will never succeed again! You look at me as extinguished ashes but can't extinguished ashes be rekindled?!" Tian Jia sneered and said: "I have never heard of extinguished ashes emitting sparks. If dead ashes can be rekindled, I will urinate to put it out!" Soon, Emperor Jing's brother, Prince Xiao of Liang (2–144 BCE) appreciated Han Anguo's contributions and asked Emperor Jing to pardon Han Anguo. Emperor Jing agreed and released Han Anguo from Meng County Prison. After being released, Han Anguo became a treasurer in charge of civil affairs, an official position higher than before. Tian Jia was so scared that he ran away. When Han Anguo heard that the jailer had escaped, he ordered to find him and deliberately spread the word that if Tian Jia would not return, his entire family would be executed. Tian Jia panicked and had to bite the bullet to see Han Anguo. As soon as they met, Tian Jia kneeled and kowtowed for mercy. Seeing Tian Jia's miserable appearance, Han Anguo could not help laughing and said: "Tian Jia, now extinguished ashes are rekindled, come and urinate to put it out!" Tian Jia was so frightened that he collapsed on the floor. Han Anguo had no intention of punishing Tian Jia, he said: "Get up! People like you are not worthy of my revenge!" Tian Jia was surprised and felt even more ashamed. This idiom originally describes a person who has lost and regained power. The story tells that do not bully people in trouble as extinguished ashes can be rekindled, never give up hope.

四面楚歌

Sì miàn chǔ gē

出自西汉·司马迁《史记·项羽本纪》

[近义词：四面受敌；反义词：安然无恙]

项王军壁垓下，兵少食尽，汉军及诸侯兵围之数重。夜闻汉军四面皆楚歌，项王乃大惊，曰："汉皆已得楚乎？是何楚人之多也。"

Besieged on All Sides

From "Records of the Grand Historian: Biography of Xiang Yu"

by Sima Qian (145–c.86 BCE)

In the late Qin dynasty (221–206 BCE), the Han army led by Liu Bang (c.256–195 BCE) and the Chu army led by Xiang Yu (232–202 BCE) fought a decisive battle in the Central Plains for supremacy, both sides wanted to take over the country. In 202 BCE, Liu Bang led the Han army to surround Xiang Yu's Chu army at Gaixia (today's Lingbi county, Anhui province). The Chu army was besieged for many days and was in a very critical situation. Xiang Yu, the brave and warlike king of western Chu, led the Chu army to break out several times but failed. Late one night in his tent, Xiang Yu was looking for strategies from a military book, he suddenly heard waves of Chu folk songs coming from all directions. Xiang Yu was shocked and thought: "Has the Han army completely occupied Chu State? Otherwise, how can there be so many Chu people on the Han army's position?" In fact, the Han army did not completely occupy Chu. Liu Bang ordered the Han soldiers to sing the Chu folk songs to disperse the Chu army's morale.

    Sure enough, when the Chu soldiers heard the hometown accent coming from the Han army's position, they all thought that their hometown had been occupied by the Han army. The Chu folk songs sung by the Han soldiers aroused the Chu soldiers' homesickness, so they sang along with the Han soldiers, and many of them sang and wept at the same time. For a while, there was a cry over the Chu camp. Xiang Yu sat in the tent, watching the Chu army's morale collapse that was no longer controllable, he was in a state of despair. At this time, his beloved concubine Yu Ji danced with a sword and sang Chu songs for the king in a sad voice to comfort him. Xiang Yu listened, watched, and could not help but burst into tears. In order not to drag down the King of Chu, Yu Ji committed suicide after singing. That night, Xiang Yu led a group of 800 Jiangdong soldiers, cut a bloody path, broke through the siege, and fled south. Liu Bang hurriedly led more than 10,000 Han troops to chase him. Xiang Yu fled to the Wujiang Riverbank, with only 20 or so cavalrymen left. At this critical moment, the head of Wujiang River paddled his boat to the riverside and tried hard to persuade Xiang Yu to cross the river and return to Chu to regroup. Xiang Yu knew that the situation was hopeless, he could not face the Jiangdong people again, and he would rather die than cross the river to escape. He brandished his sword and fought a desperate battle with the pursuing Han army, killing several hundred Han soldiers by himself. In the end, Xiang Yu committed suicide on the Wujiang Riverbank. Liu Bang took over the entire country himself. This idiom refers to the Chu folk songs being heard from all directions, which is a metaphor for being surrounded by rivals in an isolated and helpless situation.

(姜)太公钓鱼，愿者上钩

(Jiāng) tài gōng diào yú, yuàn zhě shàng gōu

[近义词：心甘情愿、一个愿打，一个愿挨]

太公望吕尚者……本姓姜氏，从其封姓，故曰吕尚。吕尚盖尝穷困，年老矣，以渔钓奸（干）周西伯（周文王）。西伯将出猎……遇太公于渭之阳，与语大说（悦），曰："自吾先君太公曰：'当有圣人适周，周以兴。'子真是邪？吾太公望子久矣。"故号之曰"太公望"，载与俱归，立为师。-出自西汉·司马迁《史记·齐太公世家》

姜尚……直钩沟渭水之鱼，不用香饵之食，离水面三尺，尚自言曰："负命者上钩来！"-元·无名氏《武王伐纣平话》

Jiang Taigong Fishing, Those Who Are Willing Will Take the Bait

From "Records of the Grand Historian: The Family of Duke Tai of Qi" by Sima Qian (145–c.86 BCE); and "The Story of King Wu's Conquest of King Zhou of Shang" by Anonymity in the Yuan Dynasty (1271–1368)

At the end of the Shang dynasty (1600–1046 BCE), King Zhou of Shang (Di Xin, 1106–1046 BCE) was in power. He was a cruel monarch who took pleasure in killing people. Many court officials and common people died for no reason under his hands. Jiang Ziya (Jiang Taigong, 1128–1015/1036 BCE) was originally an advisor in the court. Seeing that Di Xin was so dissolute and unrighteous, he was unwilling to serve such a tyrant. He heard that the vassal Ji Chang (1113–1056 BCE) cared for the people and recruited talents, he resolutely gave up his official position and lived in seclusion on the Wei Riverbank under Ji Chang's jurisdiction, waiting for the opportunity.

Jiang Ziya usually fished by the Wei River. But his fishing method was different. The hook he used was straight, placed at 3 feet above the water level, without bait on it, while he kept saying: "Jiang Taigong is fishing, those who are willing will take the bait." His bizarre behavior soon reached the ears of Ji Chang, who thought this hermit was very strange and wanted to meet him, so he sent a soldier to find Jiang Ziya. When Jiang Taigong saw the soldier, he ignored him and continued fishing. While fishing, he said to himself: "Fun, fun, the fish won't bite, and the shrimps are messing around." The soldier did not know what to do, so he went back empty-handed to report. When Ji Chang heard this, he thought this man might have some background, he immediately sent an official to invite Jiang Ziya to meet him on his behalf. When Jiang Ziya saw the official, he still ignored him and continued fishing. While fishing, he said to himself: "Fun, fun, the big fish won't bite, and the small fish are messing around." The official felt embarrassed and went back to report. Ji Chang was surprised but pleased, knowing that he had found a rare talent, so he fasted for 3 days, took a shower and changed his clothes, and ordered to bring generous gifts to visit Jiang Ziya in person on the Wei Riverbank. Seeing that Ji Chang was eager to seek talents, Jiang Taigong agreed to accept the offer. After Jiang Ziya entered the court, Ji Chang appointed him as military advisor and later as military strategist. Jiang Ziya lived up to his wish and assisted King Wen and King Wu of Zhou to overthrow King Zhou of Shang and established the Zhou dynasty (1046–221 BCE). The phrase "Jiang Taigong fishing, those who are willing will take the bait" describes the willingness to do something that might result in losses or deception.

螳臂当车

Táng bì dǎng chē

[近义词：螳臂当辕、螳螂之勇、蚍蜉撼树、
自不量力；反义词：量力而行]

汝不知夫螳螂乎？怒其臂以当车辙，
不知其不胜任也，是其才之美者也。
—出自《庄子·人间世》

齐庄公出猎，有一虫举足将搏其轮。
问其御曰："此何虫也？"
对曰："此所谓螳螂者也。其为虫也，
知进而不知却，不量力而轻敌。"
庄公曰："此为人，而必为天下勇武矣！"
回车而避之。—《淮南子·人间训》

A Mantis Trying to Stop a Chariot

From "Zhuangzi: In the Human World"; and
"Huainanzi: Lessons from the Human World"

Once, Duke Zhuang of Qi (?–c.731 BCE) was out hunting in a chariot. Suddenly, a small green insect stretched out its two front legs on the road ahead, trying to block the big wheels with its small body. If the wheels ran over it, the insect would surely be crushed to pieces. Duke Zhuang of Qi quickly stopped the chariot and asked the driver: "What kind of insect is this?" The driver replied: "Your Majesty, this is a praying mantis. This little insect only knows how to move forward, but not backward. It overestimates its own abilities!" Duke Zhuang of Qi laughed and said: "Haha, if this praying mantis is a human, it must be an outstanding warrior. Let's not hurt it!" He then ordered the driver to rein in the horse and take a detour to avoid hurting the praying mantis. This incident soon spread. The Qi soldiers who heard about it were very moved and thought that Duke Zhuang of Qi respected warriors. Thereafter, many brave warriors came to join Duke Zhuang of Qi, and Qi State became increasingly powerful. People often say that a mantis trying to stop a chariot is overestimating its own abilities. However, if one looks at it from another perspective, the courage of the mantis is truly admirable. Shouldn't this kind of courage be an inspiration to us?

天衣无缝

Tiān yī wú fèng

出自前蜀·牛峤《灵怪录·郭翰》

[近义词：完美无缺、浑然一体；

反义词：千疮百孔、漏洞百出、破绽百出]

太原郭翰，盛暑乘月卧庭中，仰视空中，见有人冉冉而下，直至翰前，曰："吾天上织女也。"徐视其衣，并无缝。翰问之，曰："天衣本非针线为也。"每去辄以衣服自随。

Divine Garments Are Seamless

From "Records of Ghosts and Monsters: Guo Han"

by Niu Qiao (9th century CE)

Legend has it that in Taiyuan, there was a man named Guo Han who was sleeping in the courtyard one summer night because of the extreme heat. He looked up at the sky and saw a bright moon hanging among the floating white clouds. Suddenly, a floating cloud turned into a fairy and floated down from the sky. Guo Han thought he was dreaming, but in an instant the fairy appeared in front of him, clearly in reality. So, he hurriedly stood up and bowed to the fairy, saying: "Excuse me, where did you come from?" The fairy returned the bow and said softly: "I am the Weaver Girl from Heaven." Guo Han carefully examined the Weaver Girl's clothes, wondering what material they were made of. What surprised him most was that the clothes she wore had no seams. He was very curious and asked: "May I ask why there are no seams in the clothes you are wearing?" The Weaver Girl smiled and replied: "I am wearing heavenly clothes which are not sewn with needle or thread, so naturally there are no seams." This idiom originally refers to the clothes worn by heavenly immortals that have no seams; later it is used to describe the naturalness of poetry, or the thoroughness and perfection of things without any trace of artificiality.

铁杵磨针

Tiě chǔ mó zhēn

出自南宋·祝穆《方舆胜览》

[近义词：铁杵成针]

磨针溪，在象耳山下。世传李太白读书山中，未成，弃去。过是溪，逢老媪方磨铁杵。问之，曰："欲作针。"太白感其意，还卒业。

Grinding an Iron Pestle into a Needle

From "Exhausting Overview of All Parts of the Empire"

by Zhu Mu (1190–1256)

Mozhen (lit. "Grinding Needle") Creek is at the foot of Xianger (lit. "Elephant Ears") Mountain. Legend has it that when the celebrated poet Li Bai (701–762) was studying in the mountains, he gave up and left without completion. When he passed by this creek, he met an old woman who was grinding an iron pestle. He asked her what she was doing, the woman replied: "I want to grind it into a needle." Li Bai was moved by her spirit and went back to complete his studies. This idiom means that if one is determined to work hard, they can succeed in any task, no matter how difficult it is.

挺身而出

Tǐng shēn ér chū

[近义词：自告奋勇；反义词：退避三舍、畏缩不前]

君弘挺身出，或曰："事未可判，当按兵待变，成列而斗可也。"–出自后晋·刘昫等《旧唐书·敬君弘传》

后数日城陷；景思挺身出；使人告于邻郡；得援军数百；逐其草冠；复有其城；毫民赖是以济。–北宋·薛居正等《旧五代史·周·唐景思传》

Stand Out and Step Forward

From "Old Book of Tang: Biography of Jing Junhong"
by Liu Xu (888–947) *et al*.; and
"Old History of the Five Dynasties:
Zhou: Biography of Tang Jingsi"
by Xue Juzheng (912–981) *et al*.

Emperor Gaozu of Tang, Li Yuan (566–635), had three sons: Li Jiancheng (589–626), Li Shimin (598–649), and Li Yuanji (603–626). The second son Li Shimin made great contributions in helping his father to overthrow the Sui dynasty (581–618) and establish the Tang dynasty (618–907). The eldest son Li Jiancheng thus feared that the throne would be taken away by Li Shimin, he conspired with Li Yuanji to kill Li Shimin. When Li Shimin heard this, he immediately discussed with his confidant Fang Xuanling (579–648) and others and decided to strike first. The soldiers sent by Li Shimin ambushed at Xuanwu Gate.

When Li Jiancheng entered the court, he was shot dead, and Li Yuanji was also killed. Feng Li and Xie Shufang (601–652), the subordinates of Li Jiancheng and Li Yuanji, immediately led their troops to attack Li Shimin. They fought all the way to Xuanwu Gate, and General Jing Junhong (576–626) led his troops to defend it. The two sides fought fiercely, and arrows kept shooting into the palace. His confidants advised Jing Junhong not to rush to fight and wait to see what the situation would be like, but Jing Junhong did not listen. Jing Junhong and General Lü Shiheng (?–626) shouted, stepped forward, and commanded the soldiers to fight back. Seeing Jing Junhong leading the way, everyone fought bravely to the death. At this time, Li Shimin's reinforcements arrived and engaged in a melee with Feng Li's army. Jing Junhong was greatly encouraged, together with the reinforcements, he defeated Feng Li's army. After Li Shimin ascended the throne, he rewarded Jing Junhong and others who stood up to the danger. This idiom describes the act of volunteering to stand out from the crowd and take on the responsibility when faced with a dangerous situation.

铤而走险

Tǐng ér zǒu xiǎn

出自春秋•左丘明《左传•文公十七年》

[近义词：逼上梁山、孤注一掷；

反义词：安分守己、循规蹈矩]

铤而走险，急何能择？

Take a Risk

From "The Zuo Tradition: The 17th Year of Duke Wen"

by Zuo Qiuming (556–452 BCE)

During the Spring and Autumn period (770–476 BCE), there were more than 170 vassal states, large and small. They fought for power and supremacy, the conflicts among them were complex and fierce, and wars continued endlessly. In the middle of the era, Jin and Chu states became two leading hostile camps, both sides were evenly matched. In this situation, small states were in a dilemma, not knowing which side to turn to. To survive, they had to change their attitudes from time to time in exchange for temporary peace. In 610 BCE, Jin gathered the vassal states in Hudi to demonstrate to Chu and exert pressure on it.

The monarch of Jin State suspected that Zheng State was secretly colluding with Chu State and it had two minds, so he refused to meet with the monarch of Zheng who came to the gathering, which made the monarch of Zheng panic and embarrassed. After the monarch of Zheng returned to his state, the prince of Zheng, Guisheng (?–599 BCE), wrote a letter to the minister of Jin, Zhao Dun (656–601 BCE), stating Zheng's position. In the letter, Guisheng said: "Zheng State has always respected and been friendly with Jin State, but this still cannot satisfy Jin. Zheng State is therefore in a dilemma that fears offending both Jin and Chu. Zheng is like a deer being chased by hunters, reluctant to leave the lush forest, but once the hunters corner it, it can jump down from the most dangerous cliff. If Jin forces Zheng into a corner, Zheng will have no choice but to take the risk and seek protection from Chu. At that time, Jin must not regret it!" After reading the letter, Zhao Dun persuaded the monarch of Jin to change his attitude toward Zheng to prevent it from falling into the arms of Chu. However, in the following decades, Zheng's foreign policy changed with the situation, sometimes relying on Jin and sometimes following Chu, making Jin and Chu not to know whether to laugh or cry. This idiom refers to taking risky actions when there is no other way out.

同甘共苦

Tóng gān gòng kǔ

出自西汉·刘向《战国策·燕策一》

[近义词：同舟共济、休戚与共、有福同享；
反义词：同床异梦、离心离德、尔虞我诈]

燕王吊死问生，与百姓同其甘苦。

Share Joys and Sorrows

From "Strategies of the Warring States: Strategies of Yan I" by Liu Xiang (77–6 BCE)

In the middle of the Warring States period (475–221 BCE), the northerly located Yan State declined due to internal strife and became the weakest of the "Seven Kingdoms of the Warring States Period." In 311 BCE, Prince Zhi of Yan (c.336–279 BCE) returned to Yan State with the help of Zhao State and was made King Zhao of Yan, a monarch who wanted to make a difference but did not know where to start because there were so many things to be reestablished to revive the state. He heard that a man named Guo Wei (c.351–297 BCE) was very knowledgeable and strategic, so he brought a generous gift and went to ask for advice in person. King Zhao said sincerely: "I hope to find talented people to help me reform politics and make the state prosperous as soon as possible. Can you tell me what good methods are there?"

Guo Wei replied: "There are ways. If you sincerely invite talented people, the wise men in the world will gather in Yan State." King Zhao asked: "How can I make them know that I am sincere?" Guo Wei said: "You might as well start with me. If everyone sees that a person with little ability like me can be valued, would people with greater abilities be afraid of the long journey and not come to Yan State?" King Zhao readily agreed and immediately acknowledged Guo Wei as his teacher and built a courtyard house for him. King Zhao also erected a high platform, called the "Golden Platform," next to Yi Mountain, which was filled with gold and specially used as a fund to recruit talents. The news spread quickly, many talented people were called to Yan at that time, including Zou Yan (c.305–240 BCE) from Qi State, Ju Xin (?–242 BCE) from Zhao State, Qu Yong (Qu Yuan's father) from Wei (卫) State, and the most important person among them was Yue Yi (c.300–c.260 BCE) from Wei (魏) State, who all tried their best to make plans for Yan. King Zhao of Yan also practiced what he preached: when someone died in a commoner's family, he went to condole in person; when a child was born in a commoner's family, he went to celebrate in person – he shared the joys and sorrows with the commoners. After 28 years of hard work, Yan State became stronger, the people were prosperous, and the soldiers were willing to fight for it. The strength of Yan impressed the princes of various states, and King Zhao of Yan's long-held goal had finally been achieved.

同心同德

Tóng xīn tóng dé

出自《尚书·泰誓中》

[近义词：同心合力、同心协力；

反义词：离心离德、各怀鬼胎、各行其是]

受有亿兆夷人，离心离德。

予有乱臣十人，同心同德。

One Heart One Mind

From "The Book of Documents: The Great Oath"

The last king of the Shang dynasty (1600–1046 BCE) was named Zhòu (纣). King Zhòu of Shang (Di Xin, 1106–1046 BCE) was cruel. Legend has it that the wine he drank was enough to fill a large pool, and the strips of meat for his consumption were hung in the palace like a forest. In his eyes, the lives of ministers were not as important as grass roots, and the lives of the people were not as important as dirt. He plundered the people endlessly for his own extravagant enjoyment. To suppress the people's resistance, he invented all kinds of torture. Under this tyrant's rule, the state was in terror. While King Zhòu was committing atrocities, the people fled to a small state called Zhōu (周) in the west.

In 1027 BCE, the leader of this small state, King Wu of Zhōu (1076–1043 BCE), led 3,000 warriors and united 800 princes to attack King Zhòu, and the people in the country responded. King Wu of Zhōu read out the proclamation of the attack on King Zhòu at the oath-taking ceremony: "Because King Zhòu is licentious, immoral, and extremely evil, the emperor is furious and has ordered Zhōu State to lead a benevolent army to kill King Zhòu. Although King Zhòu has tens of thousands of people, they no longer have the same mind as him. Even though Zhōu State has only ten people, they have the same mind. If everyone has the same mind, there is no need to worry about not being able to kill the evil King Zhòu!" On the day of the decisive battle, the Zhòu army turned against their own side and revolted in anger. Seeing that the defeat was inevitable, King Zhòu set himself on fire, and the Shang dynasty finally perished. This idiom refers to the unity of thought and action.

投笔从戎

Tóu bǐ cóng róng

出自南朝·宋·范晔《后汉书·班超传》

[近义词：弃文就武、弃文从武；

反义词：弃武从文、解甲归田]

永平五年，兄固被召诣校书郎，超与母随至洛阳。家贫，常为官佣书以供养。久劳苦，尝辍业投笔叹曰："大丈夫无他志略，犹当效傅介子、张骞立功异域，以取封侯，安能久事笔砚间乎？"

Throw Away the Pen and Join the Army

From "Book of the Later Han: Biography of Ban Chao"

by Fan Ye (398–445)

In the early years of the Eastern Han dynasty (25–220), there were two brothers named Ban Gu (32–92) and Ban Chao (32–102). The elder brother Ban Gu was a prominent writer and historian who wrote excellent poems and articles and became an official at a young age. The younger brother Ban Chao had great ambitions but did not like to study classics and always hoped to make a difference in the military. At that time in Luoyang, the Ban family lived in poverty, and Ban Chao had to help supplement the family income and support his mother by copying official documents and letters in the government office.

However, Ban Chao was unwilling to spend his life in mediocrity, he longed to gallop on the battlefield and make contributions to the country. One day, after copying an official document, Ban Chao threw away his pen and said with a long sigh: "A real man should be like Fu Jiezi [?–65 BCE] who served the country and killed the enemy, and like Zhang Qian [c.164–114 BCE] who went to remote places and made great achievements. How can I always make a living between pens and inkstones?" In 73 CE, the time for Ban Chao to realize his long-cherished wish finally came. In this year, the northern Xiongnu frequently sent troops to harass the Han ethnic group, and Emperor Ming of Han (28–75) sent General Dou Gu (?–88) to lead troops to fight against the Xiongnu. Ban Chao threw away his pen and joined the army to the north. He fought bravely and showed extraordinary military talent and was appreciated and valued by Dou Gu and promoted to a general. Later, Ban Chao, under the order of the emperor, led troops to guard the Western Regions for 31 years, quelled the rebellions of Xiongnu many times, actively developed the Western Regions, promoted friendly relations and exchanges between the people of all ethnic groups in the Western Regions, and became a renowned general of the Eastern Han dynasty with outstanding merits. This idiom refers to a scholar who throws away their pen to join the army and aspires to serve the country.

推心置腹

Tuī xīn zhì fù

出自南朝·宋·范晔《后汉书·光武帝纪上》

[近义词：开诚布公、肝胆相照、

披肝沥胆、推诚相见；

反义词：钩心斗角、勾心斗角、

居心叵测、尔虞我诈]

萧王推赤心置人腹中，安得不投死！

Treat Others Sincerely

From "Book of the Later Han:
Chronicle of Emperor Guangwu (Part 1)"
by Fan Ye (398–445)

After Wang Mang (45 BCE–23 CE), the Grand Marshal of Emperor Ping of Han (9 BCE–6 CE), usurped the power of the Han dynasty (206 BCE–220 CE), peasant uprisings broke out in various places, among which the most powerful were the Chimei (lit. "Red Eyebrow") Army and the Lülin (lit. "Green Forest") Army. In 23 CE, the peasant army fought a decisive battle with Wang Mang's 420,000 troops in Kunyang (now Ye county, Henan province), among which a general named Liu Xiu (5 BCE–57 CE) was very active. In this battle, Wang Mang was defeated miserably, and almost all his troops were annihilated. Soon, the peasant army attacked the capital and killed Wang Mang. Liu Xuan (?–25 CE), a member of the Imperial Family, was revered as the Gengshi Emperor, and Liu Xiu was named King Xiao for his great merits. Liu Xiu was a very shrewd person and was not willing to let Liu Xuan become the emperor.

Liu Xiu fought against the scattered peasant army that opposed Liu Xuan in the north of the Yellow River while expanding his own power. In 24 CE, Liu Xiu defeated the Chimei Army in Weizhou and Puyang, incorporated the surrendered troops, and made the commander of the surrendered army a marquis, and other officers who led the troops also accepted their official positions. However, these surrendered officers and soldiers were very worried that they would be eliminated by Liu Xiu in the future. Liu Xiu saw their worries and took an unexpected measure. He ordered each surrendered general to return to their old units and command the troops they originally belonged to. He himself only brought a few followers to inspect the surrendered troops and did not guard against them, to show that he was confident in them. Seeing that Liu Xiu treated them as his own people, these surrendered officers and soldiers dispelled their doubts and talked to each other, saying: "King Xiao is so open-hearted, what do we have to worry about? Shouldn't we go through fire and water for him?" So, the officers and soldiers obeyed Liu Xiu very much, and Liu Xiu's ability to give people an "open-hearted" impression helped him obtain the throne. After becoming emperor, Liu Xiu did not kill meritorious officials like what the first emperor of the Han dynasty, Liu Bang (c.256–195 BCE) did, but rewarded them with fiefs, money, and privileges, and persuaded them to return to their fiefs, live a life of wealth and glory, and no longer ask about government affairs. He also sent officials to visit these retired meritorious officials from time to time, bringing them rare treasures presented to him by foreign countries. In this way, Liu Xiu not only consolidated his imperial power, but also gained a good reputation for not killing meritorious officials. This idiom means to give one's sincere heart to others, which is a metaphor for treating others sincerely.

退避三舍

Tuì bì sān shè

出自春秋·左丘明《左传·僖公二十三年》

[近义词：委曲求全、恬退隐忍；

反义词：针锋相对、锋芒毕露]

（晋公子重耳）及楚，楚子飨之，曰："公子若反晋国，则何以报不谷？"对曰："子女玉帛，则君有之；羽毛齿革，则君地生焉。其波及晋国者，君之余也。其何以报君？"曰："虽然，何以报我？"对曰："若以君之灵，得反晋国，晋楚治兵，遇于中原，其辟君三舍。

Retreat to Avoid Conflict

From "The Zuo Tradition: The 23rd Year of Duke Xi"

by Zuo Qiuming (556–452 BCE)

During the Spring and Autumn period (770–476 BCE), Duke Xian of Jin (?–651 BCE) sent people to capture Prince Chong'er (697–628 BCE) of Jin, the younger brother of Shensheng (?–655 BCE). Upon hearing the news, Chong'er fled. During his more than 10-year exile, he begged for food and suffered from cold receptions and contempt of many small states. When he stayed in Chu State, King Cheng of Chu (?–626 BCE) treated him with the courtesy of entertaining princes, and the two were very good friends. At a banquet, King Cheng of Chu jokingly asked Chong'er: "If you return to Jin and become the king in the future, how will you repay me?"

Chong'er replied: "If I can return and govern, I will be friendly with your state and let the people of both states live in peace. If Jin and Chu must go to war and the two armies must face each other, I will order the Jin army to retreat three times to repay your kindness."

Soon, Chong'er bid farewell to King Cheng of Chu and went to Qin at the invitation of Duke Mu of Qin (c.705–621 BCE). Under the escort of the Qin army, he finally returned to Jin and took power and was named Duke Wen of Jin. Under the governance of Duke Wen, Jin was very prosperous. At that time, Chu was also very powerful and often attacked other states. In 633 BCE, the Chu general Cheng Dechen (?–632 BCE) led the coalition forces of four states to attack Song State and surrounded the capital of Song. Song urgently asked Duke Wen of Jin for help. Duke Wen of Jin decided to send troops to rescue Song. After the Jin and Chu armies confronted, Duke Wen of Jin really kept his promise and ordered the Jin army to retreat three times, each time by 30 miles, for a total of 90 miles. Cheng Dechen thought that the Jin army dared not fight and became more arrogant and underestimated the enemy. As a result, they were ambushed by the Jin army and completely defeated. Duke Wen of Jin did not lead his troops to pursue and let the defeated soldiers of Chu escape. This idiom means to retreat 90 miles to avoid conflict with the other party.

完璧归赵

Wán bì guī zhào

出自西汉•司马迁《史记•廉颇蔺相如列传》

[近义词：物归原主、物归旧主；

反义词：久假不归、巧取豪夺]

赵惠文王时，得楚和氏璧。秦昭王闻之，使人遗赵王书，愿以十五城请易璧。赵王与大将军廉颇诸大臣谋：欲予秦，秦城恐不可得，徒见欺；欲勿予，即患秦兵之来。计未定，求人可使报秦者···相如曰："秦强而赵弱，不可不许。"王曰："取吾璧，不予我城，奈何？"相如曰："秦以城求璧而赵不许，曲在赵。赵予璧而秦不予赵城，曲在秦。均之二策，宁许以负秦曲。"王曰："谁可使者？"相如曰："王必无人，臣愿奉璧往使。城入赵而璧留秦；城不入，臣请完璧归赵。"赵王于是遂遣相如奉璧西入秦。

Return the Jade Disk to Zhao

From "Records of the Grand Historian: Biographies of Lian Po and Lin Xiangru" by Sima Qian (145–c.86 BCE)

Zhao State had a "Heshi Bi" (jade disk) and the King Zhaoxiang of Qin (325–251 BCE) wanted it very much. He said he was willing to exchange it for 15 cities. King Huiwen of Zhao (310–266 BCE) felt difficult to handle this situation because Qin had always been dishonest, and if Zhao was cheated and ridiculed, it would damage Zhao's image, but if Zhao would not give the jade disk to Qin, Zhao was afraid that Qin would seize the opportunity to invade. It was a dilemma.

At this time, the eunuch leader Miao Xian recommended: "I have a retainer named Lin Xiangru in my house. He is wise and brave. Let him think of a tactic." The King of Zhao had no choice but to ask him to try and said: "The King of Qin wants to exchange 15 cities for the Heshi Bi of Zhao. Will you give it or not?" Lin Xiangru said: "Qin is strong, and Zhao is weak. We cannot refuse." The King of Zhao asked again: "What if Qin accepts the Heshi Bi but does not give us the cities?" Lin Xiangru said: "Qin has made this request. If we do not agree, Zhao will be in the wrong. If Qin accepts the Heshi Bi of Zhao but does not give us the cities, then Qin will be in the wrong. In comparison, I think the latter method is better. If the King really has no one else to send, I can try. If the King of Qin gives us the cities, I will leave the Heshi Bi to Qin. If they are unwilling to hand over the cities, I will return the Heshi Bi intact to Zhao." The King of Zhao thought that Lin Xiangru was eloquent and thoughtful, so he sent him to Qin with the Heshi Bi. The King of Qin met Lin Xiangru in the palace. He looked casual and proud while sitting in the hall, so Lin Xiangru had to hold the Heshi Bi up with both hands. The King of Qin looked at it repeatedly and liked it very much. Then he passed it to the palace concubines, and everyone praised it. They cheered and congratulated the King of Qin. Lin Xiangru stood in the hall for a long while, but no one paid attention to him. The King of Qin did not propose to cede 15 cities. Lin Xiangru knew that the King of Qin was deliberately deceiving him. After thinking, he said: "There is a small defect on the jade disk, which is difficult to see without pointing out. Please let me show it to everyone."

The King of Qin did not think much about it and handed the jade disk to Lin Xiangru. Lin Xiangru took the jade and immediately ran to the pillar in the hall. He said to the King of Qin in anger: "Your Majesty wants this jade disk and sent people to ask for it from Zhao. The ministers of Zhao think that Qin is greedy and unfaithful. Qin just relies on its power to cheat Zhao about the jade disk. Everyone in Zhao is against sending the Heshi Bi. But I think that even commoners should be trustworthy and loyal when they interact with others, not to mention that Your Majesty is the ruler of a state. It is irrational to destroy the harmony between Qin and Zhao for a piece of jade that is of little use. The King of Zhao listened to me and bathed and fasted for 5 days. In the court, the letter of state and the jade disk were handed to me, and I was asked to present them to Qin. This was such a respectful etiquette! But when I came to Qin and presented the jade disk to the king, the king was casual and arrogant, and even passed the beautiful jade to the palace ladies to look at, which was an insult to Zhao. You did not say a word about ceding the 15 cities, which showed that you have no sincerity. So, I asked for the jade disk back. Now, the jade is in my hand. If you must force me, I will let my head and the jade smash on this pillar." After saying this, Lin Xiangru raised the jade disk angrily, looking at the pillar with his eyes slanting, ready to smash it at any time. The King of Qin was afraid that he would smash the jade, so he quickly apologized and asked someone to bring a map, pointing out that 15 cities from such and such a place would belong to Zhao. Lin Xiangru knew that the King of Qin was not serious, so he tried to slow the process.

Lin Xiangru said to the King of Qin: "Since the king loves the Heshi Bi, Zhao dare not refuse to offer it. However, to show respect, the King of Zhao bathed and fasted for 5 days before sending the Heshi Bi. Your Majesty should also bathe and fast for 5 days before accepting the Heshi Bi." The King of Qin had no choice but to agree. Lin Xiangru returned to the guesthouse and made careful arrangements. He had people dressed in linen clothes, disguised as ordinary people, and secretly took the Heshi Bi back to Zhao through a small road. Five days later, the King of Qin held a grand ceremony in the court to receive the Heshi Bi. Lin Xiangru calmly stepped forward and said to the King of Qin: "Qin has had more than 20 kings since Duke Mu of Qin, but I have never heard of any king who talked about trust and loyalty. I am worried that you have deceived me, so I have asked people to send the jade disk back to Zhao. Zhao is weak, and Qin is strong. If the King of Qin is sincere in exchanging 15 cities for Zhao's Heshi Bi, Zhao has no reason to refuse. If an envoy is sent, Zhao will immediately send the Heshi Bi. In the past, Meng Mingshi deceived Jin, Shang Yang deceived Wei, and Zhang Yi deceived Chu. Now, I don't want to see the king bear the bad reputation of deceiving Zhao again, so I sent the jade disk back to Zhao first. If I have deceived the king, please punish me." The King of Qin and his ministers were very angry but had no way to refute. Lin Xiangru was not afraid of death, and killing him would be useless, but that would leave Qin with a bad reputation. It would be better to release Lin Xiangru, so that Qin would appear to be magnanimous and did not defraud Zhao of the jade. Lin Xiangru returned the jade disk intact to Zhao, which not only saved Zhao's treasure, but also did not give Qin any evidence against him. Lin Xiangru's reputation also rose because of this.

万事俱备，只欠东风

Wàn shì jù bèi, zhǐ qiàn dōng fēng

出自明·罗贯中《三国演义：第四十九回》

[近义词：深谋远虑；反义词：万无一失]

孔明索纸笔，屏退左右，密书十六字曰："欲破曹公，须用火攻；万事俱备，只欠东风。"

Everything Is Ready, Only East Wind Is Missing

From "Romance of the Three Kingdoms: Chapter 49"

by Luo Guanzhong (c.1330–c.1400)

At the end of the Eastern Han dynasty (25–220), wars continued. All the states recruited soldiers to fight for the country. At that time, Cao Cao (155–220) pacified the north and planned to further unify the country, so he led an army of 800,000 to the south, ready to destroy the forces of Liu Bei (161–223) and Sun Quan (182–252) all together. Liu Bei was stationed in Fancheng, and he did not expect Cao's army to arrive suddenly, so he had to flee in a hurry and sent Zhuge Liang (181–234) to ask Sun Quan for help, hoping to unite with Sun Quan to fight against Cao Cao. Zhuge Liang met Sun Quan, analyzed the situation in the country, and persuaded Sun Quan to unite with Liu Bei.

Sun Quan hesitated and said: "I heard that Liu Bei had just suffered a defeat, why should I unite with him?" Zhuge Liang said: "Although Liu Bei had just suffered a defeat, he still had many soldiers under his command. Besides, Cao's army came from afar and was already exhausted. Their soldiers came from the north and were not used to fighting on the water. If General is willing to send tens of thousands of troops to join with Liu Bei, we can defeat Cao's army." Sun Quan totally agreed and went to discuss it with his subordinates. At this time, Cao Cao's letter of persuasion to surrender was delivered to Sun Quan, who showed the letter to his subordinates. Those ministers were frightened by Cao Cao and advocated surrendering promptly. Only Lu Su (172–217) disagreed. He advised Sun Quan not to surrender and asked him to call the captain commander Zhou Yu (175–210). As soon as Zhou Yu came back, he said to Sun Quan: "General, you occupy the Jiangdong area with elite troops and sufficient supplies. Why should you surrender to Cao Cao? Now Cao Cao is leading his troops to fight against Dongwu, which is clearly a suicide mission. Cao's army comes from the north and is not adapted to the wet climate and water in the south. What kind of war can they fight?! General, you should take this opportunity to defeat Cao's army in one go!"

Sun Quan then made up his mind to unite with Liu Bei to fight against Cao Cao. He sent Zhou Yu to lead troops to meet Liu Bei. The Sun and Liu armies went upstream to the Chibi (lit. "Red Cliffs") area and met Cao's army crossing the river. As Zhou Yu expected, Cao's army had been infected with diseases due to the climate and water, and their morale was low. Zhou Yu took the opportunity to fight Cao Cao and Cao's army was defeated. Cao Cao had to bring his navy to the north of the river to join the army and moored the warships on the north bank to train the sailors. Zhou Yu moored the warships on the south bank and confronted Cao's army across the river. Cao's soldiers were not used to living on the ship, so they tied the warships together. Zhou Yu's subordinate Huang Gai (?–215) suggested: "Cao's army is most suitable for fire attack if they tie the warships together." So, Zhou Yu found ten warships, filled them with dry firewood, poured oil on them, wrapped them with tents, put flags on them, and prepared speedboats to tie to the stern. Huang Gai first asked someone to send a letter to Cao Cao, falsely claiming that he was coming to surrender. Then, Huang Gai set off with ten warships. The warships came to the middle of the river, hoisted the sails, and moved forward quickly under the fierce east wind.

When the soldiers in Cao's army saw it, they all thought Huang Gai was coming to surrender and were not prepared to fight at all. While the warships approached Cao's army, Huang Gai ordered people to light fires at the same time. For a moment, the flames shot up into the sky. The warships quickly rushed into Cao's fleet and set all of Cao's ships on fire. The fire spread, and even Cao's camp on the shore was not spared. Cao's army was in chaos. Zhou Yu took advantage of the situation and led the elite troops to attack, and Cao's army was defeated. Cao Cao led the remaining troops to flee in a hurry. Liu Bei and Zhou Yu chased them from both land and water, and Cao's army suffered countless casualties. This was the famous Battle of Red Cliffs. After the battle, Cao Cao lost the possibility of unifying the country in a short period of time. Sun Quan and Liu Bei also began to grow stronger because of the victory of this battle and gradually formed a situation of three kingdoms. This idiom means that all preparations are done, except for the last important condition.

亡羊补牢

Wáng yáng bǔ láo

出自西汉·刘向《战国策·楚策四》

[近义词：知错就改；反义词：防患未然]

见兔而顾犬，未为晚也；亡羊而补牢，未为迟也。

Fix the Fence After the Sheep Has Rid

From "Strategies of the Warring States: Strategies of Chu IV" by Liu Xiang (77–6 BCE)

During the Warring States period (475–221 BCE), King Xiang of Chu (329–263 BCE) was addicted to pleasure, which made his minister Zhuang Xin very worried. He went to persuade the king and said: "Your Majesty, you often spend time together with four villains, Zhou Hou, Xia Hou, Yan Ling Jun, and Shou Ling Jun, who are all greedy for pleasure. If Your Majesty does not govern the state well, I am afraid that Chu will perish." King Xiang said indifferently: "I think you are old and confused! Now the state is peaceful, how can Chu perish?" Zhuang Xin said: "Of course I dare say this because I have seen the consequences of the matter. If Your Majesty continues to favor these four people, Chu will perish. If Your Majesty does not believe me, please let me retreat to Zhao for a while and see how things will develop." King Xiang agreed.

Zhuang Xin stayed in Zhao for only 5 months before Qin attacked Chu and conquered Chu's capital city, Yingdu. King Xiang fled to Chengyang. Only then did he realize Zhuang Xin's words were correct and felt very regretful. He quickly sent someone to Zhao State to invite Zhuang Xin back and said: "I should not have disobeyed your advice at the beginning. Now that things have developed to this point, please show me a way."

Zhuang Xin saw that King Xiang was indeed repentant, he told him the story: "Once there was a herdsman who raised a flock of sheep. One morning when he was grazing the sheep, he found a hole in the sheepfold. At night, a wolf got in through the hole and took away a sheep. The neighbor advised the herdsman: 'Repair the sheepfold quickly!' But the man said: 'The sheep is lost, why bother repairing the sheepfold?' The next morning, when the man went to herd his sheep, he found that the wolf had come in through the hole and took away another sheep. He regretted not listening to his neighbor and quickly patched up the hole in the sheepfold. From then on, his sheep were never lost again."

After telling the story, Zhuang Xin said to King Xiang: "Even shepherds know the principle of mending the fold after the sheep is lost, not to mention that Chu still has thousands of miles of territory left. If you are willing to reform yourself, why worry about not being able to govern the state well?" This idiom is a metaphor for finding ways to remedy a problem after it has occurred to avoid further losses in the future.

望梅止渴

Wàng méi zhǐ kě

出自南朝宋·刘义庆《世说新语·假谲》

[近义词：画饼充饥、纸上谈兵；

反义词：名副其实、实事求是]

魏武行役，失汲道，军皆渴，乃令曰："前有大梅林，饶子，甘酸可以解渴。"士卒闻之，口皆出水，乘此得及前源。

Imagining Plums to Quench Thirst

From "A New Account of the Tales of the World: False and Fraud" by Liu Yiqing (403–444)

Cao Cao (155–220) was a very talented politician and military strategist. He would often think of ways to win by surprise when leading his troops in battle. One summer, Cao Cao led his troops on a long expedition to attack Zhang Xiu (?–207) in Wancheng (southwest of Henan province). The sun was scorching that day, and the heat was oppressive, making the soldiers feel breathless. The army had not had a drop of water for a long time, and the marching speed was getting slower. Seeing this, Cao Cao ordered the troops to stop advancing and look for water everywhere. But this place was a wasteland with no rivers or ponds, and the land was so scorched that it cracked.

Cao Cao was extremely anxious. He had to think of a way to cheer up the troops and get them out of this death zone. He thought for a while and suddenly had an idea. He reined in his horse, jumped onto a small mound, and shouted to the soldiers: "There is water!

There is water!" When the soldiers heard that there was water, they immediately became energetic and looked around and asked: "Where is it? Where is it?" Cao Cao waved his whip, pointed forward, and said: "I see a large plum forest ahead. This season is when plums are ripe. We can have a big meal there." When the soldiers heard that they could eat plums, they naturally imagined the sour and sweet taste of plums, their mouths watered, and they suddenly felt less thirsty. The troops cheered up and marched forward at a faster pace. They finally walked out of the desert-like wilderness and reached a place with water. Cao Cao relied on his wit to lead his troops to overcome the difficulties and obstacles on the expedition and successfully reached the destination. This idiom refers to imagining plums to quench thirst. The fable tells people that when encountering difficulties, one should not retreat blindly but should motivate themselves with the desire for success. In this way, one will have the courage to overcome difficulties. Success often lies in the effort of persevering a little longer.

闻鸡起舞

Wén jī qǐ wǔ

出自唐·房玄龄等《晋书·卷六二·祖逖列传》

[近义词：自强不息、废寝忘食、锲而不舍；

反义词：苟且偷安、自暴自弃]

范阳祖逖，少有大志，与刘琨俱为司州主簿，同寝，中夜闻鸡鸣，蹴琨觉，曰："此非恶声也！"因起舞。

Getting up to Practice Martial Arts at Cockcrow

From "Book of Jin: Volume 62: Biography of Zu Ti"

by Fang Xuanling (579–648) *et al*.

Legend has it that Zu Ti (266–321) was a general in the Eastern Jin dynasty (317–420) who was very ambitious at a young age. Whenever he discussed current affairs with his good friend Liu Kun (270–318), he was always passionate. To better serve the country, they would usually get up as soon as they heard cockcrow at dawn and said: "This must be good sound!" Then, they would draw their swords and practice martial arts.

瓮中捉鳖

Wèng zhōng zhuō biē

出自元・康进之《李逵负荆・第四折》

[近义词：十拿九稳、稳操胜券、胜券在握；

反义词：水中捞月、海底捞月、海底捞针]

这是揉着我山儿的痒处，

管叫他瓮中捉鳖，手到拿来。

Catching Turtles in a Jar

From "Li Kui Carrying the Thorns: Chapter 4"

by Kang Jinzhi (1264–1294)

At the end of the Northern Song dynasty (960–1127), the emperor favored flatterers, and the people lived in poverty. The good men at Liangshan Lake revolted in Shandong and supported Song Jiang (?–1122) as the leader of the uprising. The rebel army was disciplined, killed the rich and helped the poor, suppressed local tyrants and evil gentry, repeatedly defeated the Imperial Army, and created a reputation. Song Jiang was well-known for his righteousness and became the head of Liangshan Lake.

At the foot of the mountain near the Liangshan Lake stronghold, there was an apricot blossom village with a small inn, whose owner was an old man called Wang Lin, who had an 18-year-old daughter named Mantang Jiao. Mantang Jiao was beautiful, charming, had not been betrothed, and depended on her father for a living. Although the father and daughter were not rich, they were living a peaceful life. Li Kui was a frequent visitor to this tavern. One day, Li Kui entered the inn and saw Wang Lin filling his glass with a sad face, so he asked Wang Lin what was bothering him.

Wang Lin knew that Li Kui was a warm-hearted chivalrous man, so he stammered out the reason. As it happened that just before Li Kui arrived, two men came to the tavern, one called himself "Song Jiang" and the other called himself "Lu Zhishen." The two people forcibly took the old man's daughter and said that they would take her to the mountain to be Song Jiang's wife. Wang Lin had no choice but to watch them ride away with his daughter. When Wang Lin finished speaking, the impatient Li Kui had already exploded with anger. He rode on a fast horse and went straight to Liangshan to find Song Jiang. Song Jiang and the others explained to Li Kui, but Li Kui refused to listen and cut down the apricot yellow flag in anger. Song Jiang was furious and signed a military order with Li Kui. He brought Lu Zhishen and Li Kui to Wang Lin's tavern to confront him. Wang Lin carefully identified them and repeated the characteristics of the two people who took his daughter away. Only then did everyone realize that the two people were imposters. Everyone returned to Liangshan, and Song Jiang questioned Li Kui in the main hall. Wang Lin then followed to Liangshan and said to Song Jiang: "The two thieves who took my daughter away the other day came to my tavern again. I have made them drunk. Please go and catch them." Song Jiang asked Li Kui to make meritorious service for his mistake. Li Kui bowed to Song Jiang and said: "This is a matter of catching turtles in a jar. Please rest assured, brother, I will catch the two thieves and ask you to deal with them." Li Kui deeply regretted his previous reckless behavior and asked for forgiveness. He also worked with Yan Qing to capture the criminals to make up for his mistake. This idiom means that the thing that one wants to capture is already within their reach, and that they can obtain it with ease and certainty.

卧薪尝胆

Wò xīn cháng dǎn

[近义词：发愤图强、奋发图强、励精图治；

反义词：胸无大志、妄自菲薄、自甘堕落]

越王勾践反国，乃苦身焦思，置胆于坐，坐卧即仰胆，饮食亦尝胆也。–出自西汉·司马迁《史记·越王勾践世家》

仆受遗以来，卧薪尝胆。悼日月之逾迈，而叹功名之不立。–北宋·苏轼《拟孙权答曹操》

力役未息，兵革方殷，朕所以尝胆卧薪，废食辍寝，虽居亿兆之上，不以九五为尊，渐冀承平，永安遐迩，内则禀太后之慈训，外则仗多士之忠勋。–北宋·薛居正等《旧五代史·汉书·隐帝纪》

Sleeping on Straw and Tasting Gall

From "Records of the Grand Historian: The Family of Gou Jian, King of Yue" by Sima Qian (145–c.86 BCE); "Imitating Sun Quan's Reply to Cao Cao" by Su Shi (1037–1101); and "Old History of the Five Dynasties: Book of Han: Chronicle of Emperor Yin" by Xue Juzheng (912–981) *et al*.

In 496 BCE, Wu and Yue states fought each other. Wu's army won a great victory and conquered the capital of Yue, Kuaiji. King Goujian (?–464 BCE) of Yue and his wife used themselves as collateral to seek peace with King Fuchai (?–473 BCE) of Wu. To achieve supremacy and show his magnanimity, Fuchai decided not to kill Goujian but took him back to Wu as a stableman. Every time Fuchai went out in a carriage, Goujian would always lead his horse. The people of Wu followed behind, pointed at Goujian and said: "Look, our king's new groom!" Goujian felt humiliated but pretended not to hear. Goujian lived in a stone stable for 3 years, feeding horses and sweeping horse manure all day long. He served Fuchai carefully, tried his best to pretend to be docile, and never showed any resentment on his face. Seeing Goujian's loyalty, Fuchai felt sorry for him and said to Goujian: "You treat me well, I will let you go back to your country." After Goujian was released and returned to Yue, he vowed to take revenge. He feared that the comfortable life in the palace would wear down his ambition, so he ordered the soft mattress to be removed and replaced with hard firewood to sleep on. He also hung a bitter gall above the dining table, so that he could always taste it before eating.

After 10 years of hard work, Yue became increasingly stronger, surpassing Wu. While King Goujian of Yue was sleeping on straw and tasting gall, working hard to become greater, King Fuchai of Wu was militaristic and indulged in sensual pleasures. In 482 BCE, Fuchai ignored the advice of his ministers and sent troops to attack Qi, which caused complaints from the country. Goujian took the opportunity to send troops to attack Wu and invaded Wu's capital Gusu (today's Suzhou). Fuchai hurriedly sent people to ask for peace. Goujian estimated that his troops could not destroy Wu for a while, so he agreed to the conditions for peace. A few years later, Goujian led his army to attack Wu again, sweeping through Wu's army and annihilating it. Fuchai was forced into a desperate situation and committed suicide with his sword. This idiom originally refers to King Goujian of Yue who slept on firewood and straw and often licked bitter gall to remind himself of the suffering he had endured after his defeat in battle. Later, it is used to describe a person who works hard to motivate themselves and strive to become better.

乌合之众

Wū hé zhī zhòng

[近义词：蜂营蚁队、一盘散沙；反义词：坚甲利兵]

今东帝无尺寸之柄，驱乌合之众，

跨马陷敌，所向辄平。

–出自《东观汉记·公孙述传》

归发突骑以轥乌合之众，如摧枯折腐耳。

–南朝·宋·范晔《后汉书·耿弇传》

A Motley Crowd

From "Dongguan Hanji: Biography of Gongsun Shu";
and "Book of the Later Han: Biography of Geng Yan"
by Fan Ye (398–445)

In the late Western Han dynasty (206 BCE–23 CE), politics became increasingly corrupt, and society was in turmoil. Under such circumstances, Wang Mang (45 BCE–23 CE) seized the throne and established the Xin dynasty (9–23 CE), but he was unable to save the situation, and the new dynasty was short-lived. In the late Xin dynasty, various peasant uprisings broke out, among which the Lülin (lit. "Green Forest") Army overthrew the Xin dynasty and supported Liu Xuan (?–25 CE), an Imperial Family member of the Western Han dynasty, as the emperor, known in history as the Gengshi Emperor.

After the Gengshi Emperor ascended the throne, many local people rushed to join him, and Geng Yan (3–58 CE) was one of them. Geng Yan learned riding and shooting since childhood, he loved *The Art of War* and hoped to achieve something by following Liu Xuan. On his way to Liu Xuan, a man named Wang Lang pretended to be Liu Ziyu, the son of Emperor Cheng of Han, and proclaimed himself "emperor" in Handan. Geng Yan's men decided to go to Wang Lang instead and urged Geng Yan to go with them. But Geng Yan said: "This man is not the real Liu Ziyu. His army is just a motley crowd, not worth mentioning at all. When I arrive in Chang'an [today's Xi'an] and explain the situation to the emperor, the court will send troops to deal with them. If you choose to go to him now, I think you will destroy yourselves soon." The people accompanying him did not listen to Geng Yan's advice and left anyway. Geng Yan did not go to Chang'an because of the road blockage, he went to see Liu Xiu (5 BCE–57 CE), who was then the Grand Marshal of Gengshi. Liu Xiu valued Geng Yan very much and allowed him to lead troops to break through Handan, killed Wang Lang and others, and Geng Yan was named a Lieutenant-General. This idiom originally refers to a group of people who are mixed like crows, which is a metaphor for people without any organization or discipline.

下笔成章

Xià bǐ chéng zhāng

出自三国·魏·曹植《王仲宣诔》

[近义词：落笔成章、下笔如有神、文思敏捷、出口成章；反义词：江郎才尽]

文若春华，思若涌泉，发言可咏，下笔成篇。

One Can Write an Article Readily and Quickly

From "Elegy for Wang Zhongxuan"

by Cao Zhi (192–232)

Cao Zhi (192–232) was the third son of Cao Cao (155–220) and Lady Bian (c.160–230). He was intelligent and studious since childhood. When he was over 10 years old, he had already read hundreds of thousands of poems and essays, and could write articles quickly and well, with fresh and fluent language. Everyone who knew him was amazed at his quick wit. Cao Cao himself was an outstanding writer and was very impressed by Cao Zhi's talent. Once, he deliberately asked Cao Zhi: "I have read all your articles. They are well written. Did you ask someone to help you write them?" Cao Zhi quickly knelt and said: "Father, I can speak eloquently and write articulately. Why do I need help from others? If you don't believe me, please test me in person."

Soon, the Bronze Sparrow Tower built by Cao Cao in Yexia was completed. Cao Cao wanted to test the literary talent of his sons, so he asked them all to go up to the tower for a tour and then asked each of them to write a poem on the topic of "Bronze Sparrow

Tower" on the spot. Cao Zhi picked up the pen and started writing. His thoughts flowed like clouds and his words flowed like spring water. After a while, he handed it to Cao Cao. Cao Cao was full of praise after reading it, and he loved Cao Zhi even more and wanted to make Cao Zhi the crown prince to inherit his career. Although Cao Zhi was very talented in literature, he was arrogant and enjoyed alcohol, and was not as stable, mature, or shrewd as his elder brother Cao Pi (187–226). After a long period of observation, Cao Cao finally felt that Cao Zhi was not as capable as Cao Pi in politics and decided to make Cao Pi the heir. Later, Cao Pi became Emperor Wen of Wei. After Cao Pi ascended the throne, Cao Zhi was repeatedly suspected and excluded by Cao Pi. He lived in fear and loneliness until he was 41 years old and died of depression. His works such as the "Song of the White Horse," "Farewell to Brothers Ying Rong and Ying Yu," "Song to the Prince of White Horse," and "Ode to the Goddess of the Luo River," were all famous works widely circulated at the time and in later generations.

相煎太急

Xiāng jiān tài jí

出自南朝宋·刘义庆《世说新语·文学》；

曹植《七步诗》

文帝（曹丕）尝令东阿王（曹植）七步中作诗，不成者行大法，应声便为诗曰：

　　煮豆持作羹，漉菽以为汁。

　　萁在釜下燃，豆在釜中泣。

　　本是同根生，相煎何太急。

帝深有惭色。

Too Hasty to Fight

From "A New Account of the Tales of the World: Literature" by Liu Yiqing (403–444); and "Seven-Step Poem" by Cao Zhi (192–232)

Cao Cao (155–220) and Lady Bian's (c.160–230) eldest son, Cao Ang (177–197), died when he followed his father to fight in battle. The second son Cao Pi (187–226) and the third son Cao Zhi (192–232) stayed by Cao Cao's side and participated in military and political activities. Cao Pi was an outstanding talent with both civil and military skills. He was not only good at riding and archery, but also proficient in literature, and composed famous poems such as "A Song from Yan," and wrote China's first theoretical work dedicated to literature, *Classics and Essays*.

Cao Zhi was intelligent and studious since childhood, and his intelligence was far higher than that of ordinary people. At the age of 10, he could recite poems and essays of more than 100,000 words. At the age of 19, he wrote the famous poem "Bronze Sparrow Terrace" which impressed Cao Cao and his followers. His poems surpassed that of his elder brother Cao Pi in both quality and quantity, especially the "Ode to the Goddess of the Luo River" and "A Yellow Sparrow in the Wild Fields," which were famous pieces even after his passing. In 216 CE, Cao Cao was promoted to King of Wei and intended to make Cao Zhi the crown prince. Cao Zhi himself also made friends with Cao Cao's important advisers, hoping that they could help him obtain the right to inherit the throne. At the same time, Cao Pi, relying on his actual status as the eldest son, his achievements in politics and military affairs, and his good relations with most civil and military officials, also worked hard to be appointed as the crown prince. As a result, a serious conflict of interest arose between the two brothers. Cao Cao initially wanted to make Cao Zhi the crown prince, but after a period of observation, Cao Cao found that Cao Zhi was too willful in his behavior, indulged in life, and could not restrain himself. So, he temporarily put the matter of establishing a crown prince on hold.

In 220 CE, Cao Cao died of illness. Cao Pi, as the actual eldest son, obtained the right to inherit the throne. Cao Pi was worried that Cao Zhi would compete with him for power, so he wanted to kill Cao Zhi. One day, Cao Pi sent troops to arrest Cao Zhi, on the pretext that he did not pay respect to the monarch according to the etiquette after he inherited the throne. He also announced in public that Cao Zhi had to write a poem in the short time of seven steps. If he could not finish it on time, he would be executed. As soon as Cao Pi finished the mandate, Cao Zhi immediately recited the following poem:

> Burning bean pods when cooking beans,
>
> The beans are crying in the pot.
>
> We were born from the same roots,
>
> Why are we so hasty to fight?

After hearing the poem that Cao Zhi blurted out, Cao Pi felt ashamed. He turned his anger into joy, and exempted Cao Zhi from the "death penalty."

先发制人

Xiān fā zhì rén

[近义词：先声夺人、先下手为强；

反义词：后发制人]

秦二世元年七月，陈涉等起大泽中。其九月，会稽守通谓梁曰："江西皆反，此亦天亡秦之时也。吾闻先即制人，后则为人所制。吾欲发兵，使公及桓楚将。"–出自西汉·司马迁《史记·项羽本纪》

秦二世元年，陈胜起。九月，会稽假守通素贤梁，乃召与计事。梁曰："方今江西皆反秦，此亦天亡秦时也。先发制人，后发制于人。"–东汉·班固《汉书·项籍传》

A Preemptive Strike

From "Records of the Grand Historian:
Biography of Xiang Yu"
by Sima Qian (145–c.86 BCE); and
"The Book of Han: Biography of Xiang Ji"
by Ban Gu (32–92)

In 209 BCE, toward the end of the Qin dynasty (221–206 BCE), Chen Sheng (?–208 BCE) and Wu Guang (?–208 BCE) launched a peasant uprising in Daze township, which later swept across the country, and the Qin dynasty's rule was on the verge of collapse. Some nobles and local officials also took the opportunity to revolt against Qin, Yin Tong (?–209

BCE), the governor of Kuaiji, was one of them. However, Yin Tong felt that he was too weak to do so, thus he invited Xiang Liang (?–208 BCE), a prestigious social figure in Wuzhong, to discuss the matter.

Yin Tong said: "Now both sides of the middle reaches of the Yangzi River have revolted against the tyranny of Qin dynasty. This is heaven's will, and the opportunity cannot be missed. I heard that if you act first, you can subdue the other party, but if you act later, you will be subdued by the other party. I want to announce the uprising as soon as possible and ask you and Huan Chu to lead the troops. What do you think?" Yin Tong did not expect that Xiang Liang's ambitions would be greater than his. Xiang Liang thought that Yin Tong was incompetent and would never become a great man, so how could he be his subordinate? Nonetheless, Xiang Liang concealed his intentions and said calmly: "Very good. But Huan Chu fled to another place, only my nephew Xiang Yu knew his whereabouts. Let me bring him here to discuss it together." Yin Tong agreed. After a while, Xiang Liang brought Xiang Yu (232–202 BCE) in. After entering the house, Xiang Liang winked at Xiang Yu, who immediately drew his sword and killed Yin Tong. The uncle and nephew took out Yin Tong's official seal and ordered the bailiffs in the prefecture to surrender. Those who disobeyed the order were immediately killed by Xiang Yu. The rest of them saw that Xiang Yu was brave and unstoppable; they all surrendered. Xiang Liang announced that he would succeed the governor of Kuaiji, recruited soldiers from the counties under the prefecture, and took on many Jiangdong young men. He organized an army of more than 8,000 people, read out the anti-Qin declaration, crossed the river and marched westward to conquer the country. This team was full of vigor and fighting spirit and became the backbone of Xiang Yu's hegemony. Yin Tong wanted to have "a preemptive strike," but he ended up losing his head and life.

项庄舞剑，意在沛公

Xiàng zhuāng wǔ jiàn, yì zài pèi gōng

出自西汉·司马迁《史记·项羽本纪》

[近义词：醉翁之意不在酒；

反义词：光明磊落、光明正大]

今者项庄拔剑舞，其意常在沛公也。

Xiang Zhuang Dances with a Sword, Aiming at Pei Gong

From "Records of the Grand Historian:
Biography of Xiang Yu"
by Sima Qian (145–c.86 BCE)

In 209 BCE, Chen Sheng (?–208 BCE) and Wu Guang (?–208 BCE) launched the peasant uprising in Daze township, and anti-Qin forces surged all over the country. In the struggles with the Qin court, several relatively large military forces were formed, among them, one was led by Xiang Yu (232–202 BCE) and another by Liu Bang (c.256–195 BCE). In 206 BCE, while Xiang Yu's army was fighting a decisive battle with the main force of the Qin army in Julu, Liu Bang took advantage of the situation and attacked Qin capital, Xianyang, and overthrew the Qin dynasty (221–206 BCE). Xiang Yu was very angry because he thought that he fought the battle, but Liu Bang took the credit. Xiang Yu thus ordered his troops to Xianyang to settle accounts with Liu Bang. Xiang Yu's army soon reached Hongmen (lit. "Swan Goose Gate") in Xinfeng county, which was only 20 km away from where Liu Bang was stationed. Xiang Yu's military advisor Fan Zeng (c.277–205 BCE) advocated to take immediate actions to eliminate Liu Bang.

Liu Bang's spy also informed Xiang Yu that Liu Bang had the ambition to become king. Xiang Yu was furious and decided to attack Liu Bang the next day. Xiang Yu's uncle Xiang Bo (?–192 BCE) was a good friend of Zhang Liang (262–186 BCE), who was a subordinate of Liu Bang. Xiang Bo was worried that Zhang Liang's life would be in danger if a fight broke out the next day, so he rushed to Liu Bang's camp overnight and told Zhang Liang to flee quickly. Zhang Liang reported this to Liu Bang. Liu Bang knew that his army was not as strong as that of Xiang Yu, so he decided to take a compromise strategy temporarily and go to Hongmen in person the next day. Early the next morning, Liu Bang, accompanied by his adviser Zhang Liang, warrior Fan Kuai (242–189 BCE), and more than a hundred followers, rushed to Hongmen. Liu Bang pretended to be terrified and said to Xiang Yu: "At the beginning, you fought the Qin army in Hebei, and I fought in Henan. I didn't expect to be able to enter Guanzhong and break through Xianyang first. Since I entered the pass, I have not dared to move anything. I have only counted the household registration of officials and civilians, sealed up the Qin's treasury, and looked forward to the king's arrival. I sent troops to guard the pass only to maintain order and prevent thieves. I have no intention of confronting King Xiang. I heard that some villains spread rumors and slandered me in front of the king, please don't believe them."

Xiang Yu was a rough man. Seeing Liu Bang so humble, his anger soon disappeared. He immediately changed his tone and asked people to set up a banquet to entertain Liu Bang. At the feast, Xiang Yu raised his glass to persuade Liu Bang to drink, and his attitude became increasingly friendly. Fan Zeng winked at Xiang Yu several times and raised the jade ring he was wearing as a hint, urging Xiang Yu to kill Liu Bang. However, Xiang Yu felt that Liu Bang was sincere and was reluctant to kill him. Fan Zeng was anxious and called Xiang Yu's cousin Xiang Zhuang and said: "King Xiang is too soft-hearted. You go in and pretend to toast to cheer him up and kill Liu Bang while dancing with your sword. Otherwise, you and I will both become Liu Bang's captives in the future!" Xiang Zhuang entered the tent with a sword, and after toasting, he drew out his long sword and danced in the banquet. The cold and shining sword edge was getting closer to Liu Bang. Xiang Bo saw that Xiang Zhuang came with ill intentions, he quickly stood up, drew out his long sword and dealt with Xiang Zhuang, secretly protecting Liu Bang, so that Xiang Zhuang could not do anything. Zhang Liang saw that the situation was critical, he left the table quickly and called Fan Kuai who was waiting outside the tent and said: "Xiang Zhuang is dancing with a sword inside, it seems that he wants to kill Pei Gong!" Fan Kuai jumped up anxiously, knocked down the guards at the door, and rushed into the tent.

After Xiang Yu learned that Fan Kuai was Liu Bang's driver, he gave Fan Kuai wine and meat. Fan Kuai took the opportunity to rebuke Xiang Yu for listening to villains and wanting to kill people who made positive contributions. Xiang Yu had nothing to say and offered Fan Kuai a seat. Fan Kuai seized the chance to sit next to Liu Bang. Xiang Zhuang saw that he could not do anything, he put away his sword. Liu Bang was relieved and pretended to go to the lavatory and slipped out. Zhang Liang and Fan Kuai followed closely and advised him to leave Hongmen immediately. Liu Bang said: "How can I leave without saying goodbye to Xiang Yu?" Fan Kuai said: "People who do great things don't have to be so particular about small details. Now they are the sharp knife and the chopping board. If we don't do it well, we will become fish meat. Why say goodbye!" Liu Bang left a pair of white jade disks and two jade cups for Xiang Yu and Fan Zeng. He then rushed back to the camp under the escort of Fan Kuai and others. Zhang Liang estimated that Liu Bang had arrived safely at the military camp, he then went into the tent to say farewell to Xiang Yu. Fan Zeng was furious and sighed to the sky: "In the future, the one who will compete with King Xiang will be Liu Bang. Let's all wait to be his captives!" After the Hongmen Banquet, the struggle between Liu Bang and Xiang Yu for the throne became increasingly intense. In the end, Xiang Yu was defeated by Liu Bang.

笑容可掬：空城计

Xiào róng kě jū: Kōng chéng jì

出自明·罗贯中《三国演义·第九十五回》

[近义词：眉开眼笑、喜形于色；

反义词：愁眉苦脸、咬牙切齿]

果见孔明坐于城楼之上，笑容可掬，焚香操琴。

Smiling Face: The Empty Fort Strategy

From "Romance of the Three Kingdoms: Chapter 95"

by Luo Guanzhong (c.1330–c.1400)

In 228 CE, during the Three Kingdoms period (220–280), Zhuge Liang (181–234) launched a war against Cao Wei (220–266) in the north. From a strategic point of view, the timing of this northern expedition was not ripe. After the Shu army was severely damaged by the Wei army in Jieting (now southeast of Zhuanglang, Gansu province), the situation was very critical for Zhuge Liang. To reverse the defeat, and based on both sides, Zhuge Liang made a strategic decision to retreat. When the Shu army retreated to Xicheng ("West city," now Ankang, Shaanxi province), the Wei army commander Sima Yi (179–251) led 150,000 troops to pursue and kill. Sima Yi was very proud and wanted to "catch turtles in a jar."

Zhuge Liang was indeed in a dangerous situation: he had no generals, but only 2,500 soldiers. If he wanted to fight, he could not beat the Wei army; if he wanted to defend, he could not persist for an hour; if he wanted to run, he had nowhere to escape. The attendants and officials were all dismayed. Zhuge Liang climbed up the tower and saw dust all over the northeast. The Wei army had already rushed toward Xicheng. At this desperate moment, Zhuge Liang frowned and came up with a plan. He ordered the soldiers to put away all the military flags on the fortress and open the four gates widely; inside and outside each gate, 20 soldiers must pretend to be commoners to clean the streets, and they must not be panic; all officers should stay at their posts and be calm, otherwise they would be executed immediately. Zhuge Liang himself took two young male servants and sat on the tower, playing the guqin leisurely. Sima Yi arrived at the foot of the fortress and looked around. He saw Zhuge Liang sitting on the tower, holding a feather fan and a long scarf, burning incense and playing the guqin, smiling, as if nothing had happened. Sima Yi knew that Zhuge Liang had always been cautious in deploying troops and never took risks. Now, the fortress gates were wide open. Wasn't this clearly a trick to lure the Wei army into a trap? The more he thought about it, the more he suspected that there was an ambush in the city, so he hurriedly ordered his troops to withdraw. Zhuge Liang was full of stratagems, and he turned the danger into safety. This is the famous "Empty Fort Strategy."

挟天子以令诸侯

Xié tiān zǐ yǐ lìng zhū hóu

[近义词：挟天子而令天下]

据九鼎，按图籍，挟天子以令天下，
天下莫敢不听，此王业也。
–出自西汉·刘向《战国策·秦策一》

今操已拥百万之众，挟天子以令诸侯，
此诚不可与争锋。
–西晋·陈寿《三国志·蜀书·诸葛亮传》

Hold the Emperor Hostage to Order the Princes

From "Strategies of the Warring States: Qin Strategy I" by Liu Xiang (77–6 BCE); and "Records of the Three Kingdoms: Records of Shu: Biography of Zhuge Liang" by Chen Shou (233–297)

During the Warring States period (475–221 BCE), the increasingly powerful Qin State sought to expand its territory. In 318 BCE, Qin generals Sima Cuo and Zhang Yi (?–309 BCE) argued in front of King Huiwen of Qin (356–311 BCE) about how to enlarge the land. Sima Cuo advocated sending troops to attack Shu State, while Zhang Yi suggested attacking Han State. King Huiwen said: "Stop arguing, each of you should give your reasons!" Zhang Yi said: "Han State has a close relationship with Wei and Chu states. If Qin sends troops to Yiyang, it can occupy the dangerous pass to the east. It can defend when retreating and occupy Wei and Chu when advancing. Even if it can fight all the way to the capital of Zhou, it will not be a problem. At that time, Qin can find an excuse to attack the emperor of Zhou, and Zhou knows that it is not a match for Qin, so it will hand over their Nine Tripod Cauldrons and treasures. Once Qin has the Nine Tripod Cauldrons symbolizing national power, and the household registrations of the people in the country, it can hold the emperor hostage to order the princes, and no one in the country will dare to resist. This is the way to achieve the kingship. If Qin attacks Shu, that area is desolate and remote. Qin will not only waste its lives and wealth but also gain no fame or fortune. It is far from the kingship that Qin pursues!"

Sima Cuo said: "That's not the case. I heard that to make a country rich, we must try to expand the territory; to make the army strong, we must benefit the people; to achieve the kingship, we must be kind and righteous to the states. If these three things are met, the kingship will naturally succeed. With Qin's military strength, attacking Shu ruled by a tyrant is as easy as a wolf chasing a flock of sheep. Qin can expand its territory, obtain wealth, and replenish its military supplies from Shu without causing many casualties. In this way, the states will not think that Qin is cruel, and the princes will not think that Qin is greedy. Most people will also think that Qin is doing this to stop violence and chaos, and it can be said that Qin will gain both fame and fortune. If we attack Han and hijack the Zhou emperor as Zhang Yi advocated, we will have a bad reputation. What good will it do? If other states unite in the name of rescuing the Zhou emperor and jointly deal with Qin, our situation will be dangerous. Therefore, it is still beneficial to attack Shu." Finally, King Huiwen of Qin decided to adopt Sima Cuo's proposal to attack Shu to enlarge Qin's land. This idiom means to hold the emperor hostage to order the princes. In modern Chinese, it generally refers to issuing orders in the name of authority.

胸有成竹

Xiōng yǒu chéng zhú

[近义词：成竹在胸、心中有数、胜券在握；

反义词：不知所措、心中无数、束手无策]

竹之始生，一寸之萌耳，而节叶具焉。自蜩腹蛇蚹，以至于剑拔十寻者，生而有之也。今画者乃节节而为之，叶叶而累之，岂复有竹乎？故画竹必先得成竹于胸中，执笔熟视，乃见其所欲画者，急起从之，振笔直遂，以追其所见，如兔起鹘落，少纵则逝矣。与可之教予如此，予不能然也，而心识其所以然。–出自北宋·苏轼《文与可画筼筜谷偃竹记》

与可画竹时，胸中有成竹。–北宋·晁补之《赠文潜甥杨克一学文与可画竹求诗》

Have a Carefully Considered and Formed Idea

From "A Record of Wen Yuke Painting the Bamboo Grove of Yundang Valley" by Su Shi (1037–1101); and "A Gift to My Nephew Yang Keyi Who Learned from Wen Yuke to Draw Bamboos and Seek Poems"

by Zhao Buzhi (1053–1110)

During the Northern Song dynasty (960–1127), there was a renowned painter named Wen Yuke (Wen Tong, 1018–1079), who was most celebrated for his ink bamboo paintings with dark black leaves on the front and light ink on the back, which were elegant and graceful, and highly praised by his contemporaries. Even the great writer Su Shi (1037–1101) once revealed: "I learned my black bamboo paintings from Wen Yuke."

Wen Yuke was very serious about his artistic creations. To paint bamboo well, he planted many bamboos in front of his window and carefully observed the shape and growth of bamboo branches and leaves every day, to understand the changes in bamboo's shape in different seasons and weather conditions. After many years of planting and observing, he not only knew bamboo's characteristics, but also formed various bamboo outlines in his mind. Before he painted each piece, he had countless lifelike bamboo images in his memory, to the point where they were ready to come out. When he suspended his wrist over the scroll and painted with his brush, he could freely and skillfully paint the bamboos standing tall among the dead trees and strange rocks with form, spirit, and different styles. Zhao Buzhi (1053–1110), an artist colleague of Wen Yuke, once commented on his black bamboo art: "When Yuke paints bamboo, he already has a carefully considered and formed bamboo in his head." That is why Wen Yuke's bamboo paintings are so perfect because he had mentally conceived the bamboo images and had a certainty of success. Many later bamboo painters learned from Wen Yuke, and this school is called the "Huzhou Bamboo School." The famous painting "Ink Bamboos" preserved from the Song dynasty (960–1279) is said to be the work of Wen Yuke.

悬梁刺股

Xuán liáng cì gǔ

出自《太平御览》卷三六三

引西汉·刘向《战国策·秦策一》和东汉·班固《汉书》

孙敬好学，晨夕不休。及至眠睡疲寝，以绳系头，悬屋梁。苏秦读书欲睡，引锥自刺其股，血流至足。

Tying from the Beam and Pricking the Thigh

From the "Imperial Readings of the Taiping Era: Volume 363"; Citing "Strategies of the Warring States: Qin Strategy I" by Liu Xiang (77–6 BCE); and "The Book of Han" by Ban Gu (32–92)

Sun Jing of the Han dynasty (206 BCE–220 CE) was very studious and studied day and night without stopping. To prevent from falling asleep while reading, he tied a rope from the beam to his hair. If he was too tired and sleepy, the rope would pull up his hair and he would wake up to continue studying. Su Qin (382–284 BCE) was also very diligent and often studied until late at night. To prevent him from falling asleep, he prepared an awl. When he was sleepy, he would use the awl to prick his thigh so that the sudden pain would wake him up, then he would continue reading.

揠苗助长

Yà miáo zhù zhǎng

出自《孟子·公孙丑上》

[近义词：拔苗助长、欲速不达；

反义词：顺其自然、循序渐进、放任自流]

宋人有闵其苗之不长而揠之者，芒芒然归，谓其人曰："今日病矣！予助苗长矣！"其子趋而往视之，苗则槁矣。天下之不助苗长者寡矣。以为无益而舍之者，不耘苗者也；助之长者，揠苗者也。非徒无益，而又害之。

Pulling up the Seedlings to Help Them Grow

From "Mengzi: Gongsun Chou (Part 1)"

There was a man in Song State who was dissatisfied with his rice seedlings which he felt they did not grow fast enough. He went to pulled them up one by one and returned home and said: "I am really exhausted today! But I finally made the rice seedlings grow tall suddenly!" His son ran to the field to see that all the rice seedlings had died. There are very few people in the world who do not make this mistake of pulling up the seedlings to help them grow. Those who think that it is useless to maintain crops and do not weed them are lazy people; and those who think that they can help the crops grow by pulling up the seedlings are against the development of things. This fable tells that "Haste makes waste," everything should be done according to the natural laws, violating the laws of nature will eventually lead to failure.

言过其实

Yán guò qí shí

出自汉·应劭《风俗通义·正失》；

西晋·陈寿《三国志·蜀书·马良传》

[近义词：夸大其辞、夸夸其谈；

反义词：名副其实、言必有据]

凡此十余事，皆俗人所妄传，言过其实。

Exaggeration

From "Customs and Meanings: Correcting Mistakes"

by Ying Shao (140–206); and

"Records of the Three Kingdoms:

Records of Shu: Biography of Ma Liang"

by Chen Shou (233–297)

Ma Su (190–228) was a younger brother of Ma Liang (187–222), a palace official of Shu Han State. Initially, Ma Su followed Liu Bei (161–223) to conquer Shu, during which time it revealed that his talent and knowledge were beyond the average person. Ma Su had read many military books and liked to discuss military strategies. When Zhuge Liang (181–234) was on the southern expedition, Ma Su suggested a strategy of psychological attack, which was adopted by Zhuge Liang, and thus he gained Zhuge Liang's appreciation. However, when Liu Bei was alive, he saw that Ma Su had the problem of being unrealistic and boastful. Before his death, Liu Bei specifically told Zhuge Liang: "Ma Su likes to exaggerate. He must not be entrusted with important tasks. I hope the Grand Chancellor will be cautious in employing him in the future."

Zhuge Liang did not pay enough attention to Liu Bei's advice; he still appointed Ma Su as a military officer and often talked about military affairs with him. This time, he sent Ma Su as the vanguard, responsible for defending Jieting, a military stronghold. Before leaving, Zhuge Liang repeatedly warned Ma Su: "Although Jieting is small, it is the throat to Hanzhong and is of great importance. If it is lost, our army will be defeated. Remember, when you get there, you must set up camp near the mountain and water!" After arriving at Jieting, Ma Su took his army to a mountain far away from water source and set up camp without authorization. Deputy General Wang Ping objected: "There is no water source or food supply on Jieting mountain. If the Wei army cuts off our water source and blocks our food supply, we will lose. Besides, you must obey the Grand Chancellor's orders." Ma Su said angrily: "The Grand Chancellor always asks me for advice when he uses troops. How can you, Wang Ping, a rough man, understand the art of war?" Then Ma Su said: "I am the chief general, and you are the deputy general. I will take full responsibility for anything that happens. I am willing to be dismissed and beheaded." When Emperor Ming of Wei, Cao Rui (204–239), learned that Ma Su's army had set up camp on Jieting mountain, he immediately sent Zhang He (?–231) to lead troops to fight against them. Zhang He arrived at Jieting and was overjoyed after observing the Shu army. He immediately sent troops to cut off the water supply, block the food supply, and set fire to the mountain. The Shu army panicked and was defeated without fighting. Ma Su's loss of Jieting directly led to the Shu army having to retreat to Hanzhong. Later, Zhuge Liang had no choice but to execute Ma Su with tears. This idiom refers to exaggeration that is inconsistent with the actual situation.

掩耳盗铃

Yǎn ěr dào líng

出自战国·吕不韦《吕氏春秋·自知》

[近义词：自欺欺人；反义词：开诚布公]

范氏之亡也，百姓有得钟者，欲负而走，则钟大不可负。以锤毁之，钟况然有音。恐人闻之而夺己也，遽掩其耳。

Covering One's Ears and Stealing the Bell

From "Master Lü's Spring and Autumn Annals: Self-Knowledge" by Lü Buwei (291–235 BCE)

During the Spring and Autumn period (770–476 BCE), there was a greedy and foolish man who was unwilling to work hard but kept peeping at other people's property. He loved everything he saw and always wanted to get his hands on it. One day, he heard that Zhi Bo (506–453 BCE) of Jin State had destroyed the Fan family, so he hurried to the Fan's house, hoping to find some valuables in the chaos. Unexpectedly, all the treasures in the Fan's house were looted. He really regretted that he had made this trip in vain. Suddenly, he saw a bright light in the firewood pile in the yard, he walked over and pulled apart the firewood. It turned out to be a big bell. He examined it and concluded that the big bell was made of high-quality brass. He was overjoyed.

    He was desperate to carry the bell home, but it was too big and heavy, impossible to even move it, let along carrying it. Seeing that he could not take possession of the thing that was about to be in his hands, he was very anxious. At this moment, he saw a big hammer in the corner of the courtyard wall. He immediately had an idea and said to himself: "Heaven really helps me!" He hastily swung the hammer and smashed it hard at the bell, hoping to break it into several pieces and then put them back in a sack. However, the loud noise from the bell startled him, and the "buzzing" sound echoed over the yard for a long time, almost deafening his ears. He was afraid that others would come and steal the bell after hearing the sound, so he quickly covered his ears with his hands and then could no longer hear it. He thought that if he could not hear it, others would not hear it either, so he boldly smashed the bell. Every time he hit it, he had to cover his ears with both hands and only let go of his hands after the bell rang and then hit it again. He repeated this, and the loud sound of the bell could be heard from far away. People rushed to the scene after hearing the bell and caught the thief. This fable tells that anything that exists objectively will not change according to people's subjective will, just like the sound of a bell. If one touches it, it will make a sound regardless of whether they cover their ears or not. This idiom describes self-deceiving and trying to cover up something that cannot be covered up.

偃旗息鼓

Yǎn qí xī gǔ

出自西晋·陈寿《三国志·蜀书·赵云传》

裴松之注引《云别传》

[近义词：销声匿迹；反义词：大张旗鼓、重整旗鼓]

云入营，更大开门，偃旗息鼓，公军疑云有伏兵，引去。

Lay Down the Flags and Stop the Drums

From "Records of the Three Kingdoms: Records of Shu: Biography of Zhao Yun" by Chen Shou (233–297); "Annotated Records of the Three Kingdoms" by Pei Songzhi (372–451)

During the Three Kingdoms period (220–280), Wei and Shu states fought for Hanzhong. Liu Bei (161–223) and Zhuge Liang (181–234) led troops to attack Cao Cao (155–220). Since Cao Cao suffered a heavy defeat in the battle of Dingjun Mountain, he decided to gather food and grass to fight with Shu. He led 400,000 troops to the Han River and ordered his general Zhang He (?–231) to transport food and grass from Micang Mountain to the North Mountain Stronghold of Han River for storage. Before Zhang He arrived, the troops did not move. Liu Bei and Zhuge Liang analyzed the situation. Zhuge Liang said: "Cao Cao's food and grass are not yet available, so he dares not rashly advance. It is better to take the opportunity to send troops deep into Cao's camp to burn their existing food and grass and dampen their spirit."

Liu Bei nodded in agreement and sent veteran Huang Zhong (148–220) and general Zhao Yun (?–229) to lead the troops. Huang Zhong insisted on leading the charge, so Zhao Yun had to agree to take charge. At dawn the next day, Huang Zhong led his troops to secretly cross the Han River and came to the foot of the North Mountain. Just as he was about to set fire to the grass, Wei general Zhang He arrived. The two armies met and started a fierce battle. Zhao Yun saw that Huang Zhong had not returned within the agreed time, and knew that he was in trouble, so he hurriedly led dozens of cavalries to check. Unexpectedly, they ran into Cao Cao's army on the way, and the two sides exchanged fire. Zhao Yun had to lead his soldiers to break out of the encirclement and retreat to the camp because of the large number of Cao's troops. After Zhao Yun returned to the camp, deputy general Zhang Yi advocated closing the camp gate to resist Cao's army. But Zhao Yun ordered the camp gate to be opened wide and said: "When I fought at Changbanpo, I was alone and not afraid of Cao Cao's million army; now I have soldiers and generals, what should I be afraid of?!" After that, he ordered to lay down the flags and stop the drums, and he rode alone with a gun and stood at the camp gate, ready to meet the enemy.

At dusk, Cao's army arrived. Cao Cao saw that Zhao Yun standing alone at the camp gate fearlessly, and the camp was quiet, he suspected that there were many ambushes and immediately turned around and retreated. Zhao Yun took advantage of the situation and swung his spear. The ambushed soldiers rushed out. The drums sounded, the shouts shook the sky, and the swords rained down on Cao's army. At this time, the sky was dark, and Cao's army could not figure out how many troops the Shu army had. They panicked and fled. The joined forces of Zhao Yun and Huang Zhong chased the remaining enemies, frightening Zhang He to abandon his camp and flee. Cao Cao also left the food and grass in the North Mountain Stronghold and hurried south. Zhao Yun took Cao's camp, and Huang Zhong seized the food and grass in the North Mountain Stronghold. The two won a decisive battle. The original meaning of the idiom is to lay down the military flags, stop beating the drums, and march secretly without exposing the target. Later, it is used to refer to a truce or a silent cessation of activities.

杨布打狗

Yáng bù dǎ gǒu

出自列御寇《列子·说符》

杨朱之弟曰布，衣素衣而出。天雨，解素衣，衣缁衣而反。其狗不知，迎而吠之。杨布怒，将扑之。杨朱曰："子无扑矣，子亦犹是也。向者使汝狗白而往黑而来，岂能无怪哉？"

Yang Bu Hit the Dog

From "Liezi: On Symbols"

by Lie Yukou (450–375 BCE)

Yang Zhu's younger brother Yang Bu was wearing a white shirt when he went out in the morning to his friend's house. It rained heavily on the way, so Yang Bu took off his white shirt and changed into a black shirt before returning home in the evening. His dog at home did not recognize Yang Bu, so it came up to him and barked. Yang Bu was very angry and was about to hit the dog. At this time, his brother Yang Zhu came out and said: "Don't hit the dog. If it were you, you would be like it. If your dog was white when it left and turned black when it came back, how could you not feel strange about it?" This fable suggests that one should put themselves in other people's shoes to better understand them, do not rush to blame others.

叶公好龙

Yè gōng hào lóng

出自西汉·刘向《新序·杂事五》

叶公子高好龙，钩以写龙，凿以写龙，屋室雕文以写龙。于是天龙闻而下之，窥头于牖，施尾于堂。叶公见之，弃而还走，失其魂魄，五色无主。是叶公非好龙也，好夫似龙而非龙者也。

Duke Ye Liked Dragons

From "New Order: Miscellaneous Matters V"

by Liu Xiang (77–6 BCE)

Duke Ye Zigao liked dragons. He had dragons engraved or carved on his belt hooks, wine vessels, and inside and outside his house. When a heavenly dragon heard about this, it came to Duke Ye's house, putting its head on the windowsill and stretching its tail into the hall. When Duke Ye saw the real dragon, he was terrified as if he had lost his soul and ran away immediately. Thus, Duke Ye did not truly like real dragons, but things that looked like dragons.

夜郎自大

Yè láng zì dà

[近义词：自高自大、妄自尊大、不可一世；

反义词：虚怀若谷、妄自菲薄]

滇王与汉使者言曰："汉孰与我大？"及夜郎侯亦然。以道不通，故各以为一州主，不知汉广大。–出自西汉·司马迁《史记·西南夷列传》

滇王与汉使言："汉孰与我大？"及夜郎侯亦然。各自以一州王，不知汉广大。–东汉·班固《汉书·西南夷传》

Yelang Thought Highly of Itself

From "Records of the Grand Historian:
Treatise on the Southwestern Yi People"
by Sima Qian (145–c.86 BCE); and
"The Book of Han:
Treatise on the Southwestern Yi People"
by Ban Gu (32–92)

During the Han dynasty (206 BCE–220 CE), there was a small state called Yelang in southwestern China. Although it was an independent state, it had a small territory, few people, and even less products. However, because Yelang was the largest state in the neighboring area, the king of Yelang, who had never left the state, thought that Yelang was the largest country in the world. One day, when the king of Yelang was inspecting the border with his subordinates, he pointed to the front and asked: "Which country is the largest here?" To please the king, his subordinates said: "Of course, Yelang is the largest!"

As they walked, the king of Yelang looked up at the mountain in front and asked: "Is there any mountain higher than this in the world?" The subordinates replied: "There is no mountain higher than this in the world." Later, they came to the river, and the king said again: "I think this is the longest river in the world." The subordinates still answered in unison: "Your Majesty, you are absolutely right!" From then on, the king believed that Yelang was the largest country in the world. Once, the Han dynasty sent an envoy to Yelang. On the way, he first passed through Yelang's neighboring state, Dian. The king of Dian asked the envoy: "Which is bigger, the Han or my country?" The envoy was shocked when he heard it. He did not expect that this small state would be so ignorant that it could be compared with the Han. But the envoy did not expect that when he later arrived at Yelang, the proud king who did not know that the state he ruled was only about the size of a county in the Han, also asked him: "Which is bigger, the Han or my country?" This fable implies that the more knowledgeable people are, the humbler they become; and the more ignorant people are, the more arrogant they can be. The idiom warns people that if they hide in a small world and keep themselves closed, and do not learn about new things or accept new experiences from others, they can never move forward.

一不做，二不休

Yī bú zuò, èr bù xiū

出自唐·赵元一《奉天录·卷四》

[近义词：破釜沉舟；反义词：半途而废、优柔寡断]

光晟临死而言曰：

"传语后人，第一莫作，第二莫休。"

Either Don't Do It, Or Don't Give up Halfway

From "Fengtian Records: Volume 4"

by Zhao Yuanyi of the Tang Dynasty (618–907)

During the reign of Emperor Dezong of Tang (742–805), Lulong Circuit's military governor Zhu Ci (742–784) was dismissed from his post due to his brother's rebellion and lived in seclusion in Chang'an (now Xi'an). Soon, an army mutinied in Chang'an, and Emperor Dezong fled in a hurry to Fengtian (now Qian County, Shaanxi province). The rebels established Zhu Ci as the emperor, and Zhu Ci self-proclaimed emperor of the Qin dynasty, appointed Zhang Guangsheng (?–784) as his deputy general, and led his troops to attack Fengtian. The defenders resisted stubbornly, and Zhang Guangsheng besieged Fengtian for a long time but failed to conquer it.

Emperor Dezong of Tang summoned Li Sheng (727–793) and others to rescue Fengtian, thus Zhu Ci had to retreat to Chang'an with Zhang Guangsheng. Li Sheng led his troops to approach Chang'an. Zhang Guangsheng selected elite troops to confront Li Sheng at Jiuqu. Seeing Zhu Ci's hopeless situation, Zhang Guangsheng secretly contacted Li

Sheng, who welcomed his surrender. Zhang Guangsheng then led his troops to surrender, and Li Sheng promised to petition the emperor on his behalf to reduce his sentence and appoint him. Zhang Guangsheng hence thanked Li Sheng repeatedly and attended a banquet with him. Huazhou Circuit's military governor Yuan Guang (727–793) cursed Zhang Guangsheng and said: "I will never sit at the same table with the rebel!" Everyone left in a bad mood. Li Sheng had to put Zhang Guangsheng under house arrest and wait for the court's order. Soon, Emperor Dezong issued an imperial decree: "Zhang Guangsheng's crime is unforgivable, and he should be executed." Li Sheng had to command Zhang Guangsheng to be executed. Before his death, Zhang Guangsheng said: "Pass on a message to future generations: Either don't do it, or don't give up halfway."

一鼓作气

Yì gǔ zuò qì

出自春秋·左丘明《左传·庄公十年》

[近义词：趁热打铁、一气呵成；

反义词：偃旗息鼓、一败涂地]

公与之（曹刿）乘，战于长勺。公将鼓之。刿曰："未可。"齐人三鼓。刿曰："可矣。"齐师败绩。公将驰之。刿曰："未可。"下视其辙，登轼而望之，曰："可矣。"遂逐齐师。既克，公问其故。对曰："夫战，勇气也。一鼓作气，再而衰，三而竭。彼竭我盈，故克之。夫大国，难测也，惧有伏焉。吾视其辙乱，望其旗靡，故逐之。"

Finishing Work in One Go

From "The Zuo Tradition:

The 10th Year of Duke Zhuang"

by Zuo Qiuming (556–452 BCE)

In the Spring and Autumn period (770–476 BCE), wars were fought frequently among the states. In 684 BCE, the powerful Qi State sent troops to attack the weak Lu State. Duke Zhuang of Lu (706–662 BCE) personally led his army to the battlefield. When they arrived at Changshao, the two armies set up their positions for a big fight. The Qi army took the lead and beat the war drums to challenge the Lu army. Duke Zhuang of Lu was about to fight, but Cao Gui, who had volunteered to accompany him, said: "Your Majesty, the time is not right yet. We fight later." Seeing that the Lu army did not move, the Qi army beat the war drums again, waved flags, and shouted. Duke Zhuang of Lu wanted to fight again, but Cao Gui still asked him to hold his troops. Seeing that the Lu army did not come out, the Qi army beat the war drums again to challenge the Lu army. But Cao Gui still asked Duke Zhuang of Lu to order the troops to hold on. The Qi army had attempted to attack three times, but the Lu army did not respond. The Qi army's morale dropped greatly as they were tired of waiting. They thought that the Lu army would not fight again, so they sat down to rest and the Qi army began to loosen up. At this time, Cao Gui made a prompt decision and said to Duke Zhuang of Lu: "It's time to fight!" As the drums sounded like raindrops, the Lu army fought bravely after a long preparation. The Qi army did not expect this, the soldiers immediately abandoned their armors and fled everywhere.

After the victory of the battle, Duke Zhuang of Lu asked Cao Gui: "Why did we have to wait until the Qi army beat the drums three times before we could attack?" Cao Gui replied: "When two armies fight, morale is usually the key to victory. The first beating of the war drums can lift the soldiers, and their courage is at its peak; the second beating of the war drums will cause the morale to drop a little; and when the third beating of the war drums occurs, the morale will begin to wane. When the Qi army beat the drums for the third time, they were already showing signs of lack of energy, while the Lu army just beat the drums for the first time, which was when they were in high spirits and full of courage, and thus we were able to defeat them. Besides, Qi is a big state after all, and big states may behave unexpectedly in war. Although they showed they were defeated, they may have retreated to advance. I saw that the traces of their wheels were disordered, and their flags were down, so I concluded that they were indeed defeated, that's why I asked you to give the order to pursue." After hearing this, Duke Zhuang of Lu suddenly realized what was going on and secretly praised Cao Gui for his military intelligence. The original meaning of this idiom is that morale is at its highest when the first drumbeat of a battle is sounded. It is a metaphor for taking advantage of the time when one is full of energy to muster up the motivation and finish work in one go.

一箭双雕

Yí jiàn shuāng diāo

出自唐·李延寿《北史·长孙晟传》

[近义词：一石二鸟、一举两得；

反义词：一无所得、徒劳无功]

尝有二雕飞而争肉，因以箭两只与晟，请射取之。晟驰往，遇雕相攫，遂一发双贯焉。

One Arrow Hit Two Vultures

From "History of the Northern Dynasties:
Biography of Zhangsun Sheng"
by Li Yanshou (?–687)

Zhangsun Sheng (c.552–609) was a military commander in Luoyang during the Northern Zhou dynasty (557–589). He was intelligent and studious, proficient in military tactics, and highly skilled in martial arts, especially archery. During the reign of Emperor Xuan of Northern Zhou (559–580), Ishbara Khagan (Ashina Helu, c.540–587), the leader of the Turkic Khaganate in the northwest, came to the Northern Zhou regime to propose marriage. Emperor Xuan agreed to let his daughter marry him and sent Zhangsun Sheng to lead a group of people to escort the princess to the Turkic region. The Khagan respected Zhangsun Sheng very much and let him live in the Turkic region for a year and often went out hunting with him. Over time, Zhangsun Sheng became well-known far and wide.

The Turkic Khaganate praised Zhangsun Sheng's fast horse-riding posture as "lightning," and the sound of his brave and fierce arrows as "thunderbolt." Once, Zhangsun Sheng went out hunting with the Khagan as usual, and suddenly found two large vultures in the sky, fighting for a piece of meat while flying. The Khagan wanted to show Zhangsun Sheng's archery skill to his followers, so he took out two arrows from his quiver, handed them to Zhangsun Sheng and said: "General, please shoot down these two vultures." Zhangsun Sheng took the two arrows, urged his horse, and galloped forward. At this time, the two vultures were fighting hard. Zhangsun Sheng put on an arrow, drew his bow, and took advantage of the moment when they were tightly entangled, and shot the arrow, which penetrated both vultures at once. Suddenly, all the people present cheered and praised: "General, you shot two vultures with one arrow, you are really a sharpshooter! We admire you so much!" The Khagan was very pleased and immediately ordered his junior family members and subordinates to take Zhangsun Sheng as their teacher and learn the art of archery from him respectfully. This idiom refers to the superb archery skill of taking one arrow to hit two vultures. Later, it is used to describe doing one thing to achieve two goals.

一鸣惊人

Yì míng jīng rén

[近义词：一举成名、一步登天；

反义词：身败名裂、默默无闻]

楚庄王莅政三年，无令发，无政为也。右司马御座而与王隐曰："有鸟正南方之阜，三年不翅，不飞不鸣，嘿然无声，此为何名？"王曰："三年不翅，将以长羽翼；不飞不鸣，将以观民则。虽无飞，飞必冲天；虽无鸣，鸣必惊人。子释之，不谷知之矣。"处半年，乃自听政。所废者十，所起者九，诛人臣五，举处士六，而邦大治。举兵诛齐，败之徐州，胜于河雍，合诸侯于宋，遂霸天下。庄干不为小害善，故有大名；不蚤见示，故有大功。故曰："大器晚成，大音希声。" –出自战国·韩非《韩非子·喻老》

淳于髡者，齐之赘婿也。长不满七尺，滑稽多辩，数使诸侯，未尝屈辱。齐威王之时喜隐，好为淫乐长夜之饮，沉湎不治，委政卿大夫。百官荒乱，诸侯并侵，国且危亡，在于旦暮，左右莫敢谏。淳于髡说之以隐曰："国中有大鸟，止王之庭，三年不蜚又不鸣，王知此鸟何也？"王曰："此鸟不飞则已，一飞冲天；不鸣则已，一鸣惊人。"于是乃朝诸县令长七十二人，赏一人，诛一人，奋兵而出。诸侯振惊，皆还齐侵地。威行三十六年。–西汉·司马迁《史记·滑稽列传》

A Loud Sound That Surprised People

From "Han Feizi: Illustrations of Laozi's Teachings"

by Han Fei (c.280–233 BCE); and

"Records of the Grand Historian:

Biographies of Humorists"

by Sima Qian (145–c.86 BCE)

In 613 BCE, King Zhuang of Chu (?–591 BCE) ascended the throne and became the king. Jin State took the opportunity to pull several states that had always been affiliated with Chu State and signed an alliance. The ministers of Chu were very dissatisfied and asked King Zhuang of Chu to send troops to fight for supremacy, but the king refused to act. He hunted during the day and drank wine and listened to music at night but did not care about national affairs and spent 3 years in such a cowardly manner. He knew that the ministers were very dissatisfied with him, so he issued an order: "Whoever dare to advise the king would be sentenced to death." There was a minister named Wu Ju who could not stand it and decided to see King Zhuang of Chu. The king was having fun. When he heard Wu Ju wanted to see him, he asked Wu Ju: "What are you doing here?" Wu Ju said: "Someone asked me to guess a riddle, but I cannot answer it. Your Majesty is a man of many talents, so please guess it." When the king heard it was a riddle, he was very interested and said: "Tell me about it." Wu Ju said: "On the mountain of Chu State, there is a big bird with colorful feathers and a majestic look, but it has been staying still for 3 years, neither flying nor singing, what kind of bird is this?"

King Zhuang of Chu knew whom Wu Ju was referring to and said: "This is not an ordinary bird. If this bird flies, it will soar into the sky; and if it sings, it will be amazing. Go ahead, I understand." After a while, another minister Su Cong saw that King Zhuang of Chu had not made any move, he went to persuade the king again. King Zhuang of Chu asked him: "Don't you know the ban I issued?" Su Cong said: "I know. But if the king can listen to my advice, I am willing to violate the ban and commit a capital crime." King Zhuang of Chu said: "You are all sincere for the good of the country, how could I not understand?" After this, King Zhuang of Chu was determined to reform politics. He transferred a group of flatterers and promoted Wu Ju and Su Cong who dared to give advice to help him deal with state affairs. At the same time, he made weapons and trained soldiers. That year, he conquered many tribes in the south. In the 6th year, he defeated Song State. In the 8th year, he defeated the Rong tribe of Luhun and fought all the way to the vicinity of Zhou capital Luoyi. Thereafter, he dominated the country. The original meaning of this idiom is to surprise people with a loud sound, which is a metaphor for making amazing achievements suddenly without prior outstanding performance.

一诺千金

Yí nuò qiān jīn

出自西汉·司马迁《史记·季布栾布列传》

[近义词：言而有信；反义词：背信弃义、言而无信]

得黄金百斤，不如得季布一诺。

A Promise Is Worth One Thousand Ounces of Gold

From "Records of the Grand Historian:
Biographies of Ji Bu and Luan Bu"
by Sima Qian (145–c.86 BCE)

Ji Bu (220 BCE–?), a Chu man in the late Qin dynasty (221–206 BCE), was always righteous, willing to help others, trustworthy, and enjoyed an excellent reputation in his hometown of Chu. He had served as a general in Xiang Yu's (232–202 BCE) army and had beaten Liu Bang's (c.256–195 BCE) Han army many times. Later, Xiang Yu was besieged and committed suicide. Liu Bang conquered the country, established the Han dynasty (206 BCE–220 CE), and became the emperor. Liu Bang then issued an order to offer a reward for the capture of Ji Bu. However, due to Ji Bu's high prestige, no one reported him for greed. Instead, a man named Zhou helped Ji Bu disguise himself and secretly escorted Ji Bu to a Zhu family in Lu State. Zhu knew that the visitor was Ji Bu wanted by Liu Bang, so he tried to protect him and asked his son to treat him well. Then, he made a special trip to Luoyang and found his good friend Xiahou Ying (?–172 BCE), who had been named "Marquis of Ruyin" by Liu Bang, and asked him to rescue Ji Bu.

Xiahou Ying was very close to Liu Bang since a young age. Later, he joined Liu

Bang's army, fought in various places, and made great contributions to Liu Bang's establishment of the Han dynasty. Xiahou Ying sympathized with Ji Bu's unfortunate situation and interceded for Ji Bu in front of Liu Bang, which finally made Liu Bang pardon Ji Bu and appointed him as a minister. Soon after, Ji Bu was appointed governor of Hedong. Then, there was a man named Cao Qiusheng in Chu, who was eloquent and made friends with the powerful to raise his own value and take the opportunity to make some more benefits. Ji Bu hated this kind of person and did not want to talk to him. But Cao Qiusheng kept pestering Ji Bu and said to him: "You are my fellow countryman, and the friendship between fellow countrymen is more precious than anything else. We have a saying in Chu, 'A hundred ounces of gold is not as good as a promise from Ji Bu.' How did you get such a high reputation? Your virtue of keeping your word has spread far and wide, and this is all the result of my publicity for you! I have spread your fame all over the country, isn't this friendship important? But I heard that you didn't even want to see me." Ji Bu could not resist the compliment and immediately changed his attitude and said: "No, no, I have been waiting for you." He treated Cao Qiusheng as a guest of honor for several months and gave him a generous gift when he left. From then on, Cao Qiusheng also worked harder to promote Ji Bu, making Ji Bu's reputation of "a promise worth a thousand ounces of gold" bigger and wider. This idiom signifies a promise of immense value, often equivalent to a substantial amount of gold, highlighting their honesty and trustworthiness, and a strong commitment of great reliability.

一去不复返

Yí qù bú fù fǎn

[近义词：荆轲刺秦王、石沉大海；

反义词：东山再起、卷土重来]

风萧萧兮易水寒，壮士一去兮不复还。–出自西汉·司马迁《史记·刺客列传》

又前而为歌曰："风萧萧兮易水寒，壮士一去兮不复还。"复为慷慨羽。–西汉·刘向《战国策·燕策三》

黄鹤一去不复还，白云千载空悠悠。–唐·崔颢《黄鹤楼》

Gone Forever

From "Records of the Grand Historian:
Biographies of Assassins"
by Sima Qian (145–c.86 BCE);
"Strategies of the Warring States: Strategies of Yan III"
by Liu Xiang (77–6 BCE); and
"Yellow Crane Tower" by Cui Hao (c.704–c.754)

In the late Warring States period (475–221 BCE), the King of Qin (Ying Zheng, 259–210 BCE) was very ambitious and determined to seize other states and took part of Yan State. Crown Prince Dan (?–226 BCE) of Yan hated the King of Qin very much and wanted revenge, but he could only place his hope on assassins. Later, he found a very capable warrior named Jing Ke (?–227 BCE). Prince Dan treated Jing Ke like a distinguished guest, and Jing Ke was very grateful to him. In 227 BCE, the Qin army destroyed Zhao State, captured the King of Zhao, and marched northward, approaching Yan State. Prince Dan was very worried, so he went to see Jing Ke and asked him to disguise himself as a messenger to assassinate the King of Qin. Jing Ke said: "If we want to get close to the King of Qin, we must first make him believe that we are going to ask for peace with him. I heard that the King of Qin has long been eager to get the most fertile land of Yan State, Du Kang. If I can present the map of Du Kang to the King of Qin, he may be willing to see me." Prince Dan said: "Okay, I'll ask someone to send you the map."

At that time, there was a Qin general named Fan Yuqi (?–227 BCE), who had offended the King of Qin and fled to Yan for refuge, and was hosted by Prince Dan. Jing Ke knew that Fan Yuqi had a grudge against the King of Qin, so he went to see him and said: "I have an idea that can help Yan get rid of the disaster and avenge the general, but I just can't say it out." Fan Yuqi asked what the idea was. Jing Ke said: "I've decided to assassinate, but I'm afraid that I will not be able to see the King of Qin. I know that the King of Qin is looking for you. If I take your head to present to him, he will meet me." Fan Yuqi said: "Okay, you can take it." After saying that, he drew his sword and cut his own throat. Jing Ke took the map and Fan Yuqi's head and set off with his assistant Qin Wuyang (240–227 BCE). Prince Dan knew that Jing Ke was determined to die this time, so he and the officials wore white clothes and white hats and escorted them to the Yi River like a funeral procession. At this moment, Jing Ke sang a sad song:

> The wind is whistling,
>
> The Yi River is cold.
>
> The warrior has left,
>
> He never returned.

After singing the song, Jing Ke jumped on the carriage and left without even looking back. Unfortunately, Jing Ke's carefully planned assassination failed, and he was killed by the

King of Qin's sword.

一衣带水

Yī yī dài shuǐ

出自唐·李大师、李延寿《南史·陈本纪》

[近义词：一水之隔、近在咫尺、近在眉睫；
反义词：天各一方、天涯海角、万水千山]

隋文帝谓仆射高颎曰：
"我为百姓父母，岂可限一衣带水不拯之乎？"

A River as Narrow as a Belt

From "History of the Southern Dynasties:
Annals of Chen"
by Li Dashi (570–628) and Li Yanshou (?–687)

In 581 CE, Emperor Wen of Sui, Yang Jian (541–604), seized the Northern Zhou regime and established the Sui dynasty (581–618). He ruled the land well, won the hearts of the people, and the territory became increasingly powerful. At this time, the southern part of the country was the Chen regime, whose emperor, Chen Houzhu (Chen Shubao, 553–604), was a man with no idea about how to manage state affairs but only knew how to listen to music, watch dances, drink wine, and enjoy himself. He built three luxurious pavilions for his eight concubines and often held banquets with his imperial writers all night. Chen Houzhu was extremely extravagant and very cruel in plundering the people, and the people were starving to death.

A minister, Fu Zai (531–585), submitted a memorial to Chen Houzhu and said: "Now it has reached a point where the heaven is angry, and the people are resentful. If it continues, I am afraid the Chen regime will be over." After reading the memorial, Emperor Chen Houzhu became furious and sent someone to tell Fu Zai: "Do you know your faults? If you are willing to correct them, I will forgive you." Fu Zai said: "My heart is the same as my appearance. If my appearance can be changed, then my heart can be changed." Emperor Chen Houzhu thus killed Fu Zai. However, the development of the situation was unfortunately predicted by Fu Zai. In 588, Emperor Wen of Sui was determined to attack the Chen regime and unify all of China. He said to his ministers: "The people in Jiangnan [south of the lower reaches of the Yangzi River] have been harmed by Chen Shubao [Emperor Chen Houzhu]. How can I not save them just because of the narrow Yangzi River that is like a belt?" He personally issued an edict to attack the Chen regime and announced 20 crimes of Emperor Chen Houzhu. Then he appointed his son, Prince of Jin, Yang Guang, as the commander-in-chief, leading an army of 500,000 soldiers and marching toward Jiangnan in eight routes.

Emperor Chen Houzhu thought that the natural barrier of the Yangzi River would prevent the Sui army from defeating him, and that there were still peace and prosperity. It was not until the first month of the following year, when the two Sui armies crossed Zhenjiang and Caishi respectively, and approached Jiankang (today's Nanjing), that Emperor Chen Houzhu panicked. At that time, there were still more than 100,000 people in Jiankang city, which could have resisted for a while. But Chen Houzhu's favorite ministers Jiang Zong and Kong Fan did not know how to command, and the city was in chaos. Chen Houzhu was so anxious that he cried and was at a loss. The Sui army successfully attacked Jiankang city, and the Chen army soldiers surrendered one after another. The last emperor of the Chen regime, who was hiding in the Rouge Well, was also dragged out by the Sui army and became a prisoner. The Chen regime, which was separated from the Sui only by a river as narrow as a belt, perished from then on. This idiom originally refers to two places of geographical proximity that are separated only by a narrow river. Later, it is used to describe that although there are rivers, lakes, and seas separating two places, they are still connected like a belt.

一字千金

Yí zì qiān jīn

出自西汉·司马迁《史记·吕不韦列传》

[近义词：一字千钧、一字一珠、一字连城、字字珠玑；反义词：一文不值]

吕不韦乃使其客人人著所闻，集论以为八览、六论、十二纪，二十余万言，以为备天地万物古今之事，号曰《吕氏春秋》。布咸阳市门，悬千金其上，延诸侯游士宾客，有能增损一字者，予千金。

One Word Is Worth a Thousand Gold Coins

From "Records of the Grand Historian:

Biography of Lü Buwei"

by Sima Qian (145–c.86 BCE)

King Xiaowen of Qin (302–250 BCE) had a son named Yiren (281–247 BCE), who was once a hostage in Zhao State. A wealthy merchant from Yangzhai, Lü Buwei (292–235 BCE), thought of many ways and spent much money, not only to have rescued Yiren back to Qin State, but also have made him the Crown Prince. After King Xiaowen died, Yiren ascended the throne and became King Zhuangxiang of Qin. Lü Buwei became Chancellor and was given the title of "Marquis Wenxin." However, King Zhuangxiang died of illness after only 3 years in office. His son, Ying Zheng, inherited the throne and became the legendary Qin Shi Huang (King of Qin, 259–210 BCE). Ying Zheng respected Lü Buwei as "Zhongfu" (meaning "Father's eldest younger brother").

At that time, among the "Seven Kingdoms of the Warring States Period," Wei had Lord Xinling (?–243 BCE), Chu had Lord Chunshen (?–238 BCE), Zhao had Lord Pingyuan (308–251 BCE), and Qi had Lord Mengchang (?–279), who were all well-known and powerful noblemen, and who kept a few thousand learned guests at home. Lü Buwei followed the example of others, recruited scholars, gave them generous salaries, and had 3,000 retainers. Among them, there were people from all walks of life and with all kinds of experiences. Lü Buwei asked them to write with their own strengths, and then edited their works into a masterpiece, which was divided into "Eight Views," "Six Essays," and "Twelve Annals," with more than 200,000 words in 26 volumes and 160 chapters. The content includes everything from ancient times to the moment in time. Lü Buwei was very proud of this book and named it "Master Lü's Spring and Autumn Annals." He also ordered the book to be hung on the gate of the capital Xianyang and announced: "Anyone who can point out the mistakes, delete a word or add a word, will be rewarded with a thousand gold coins." Gold was placed next to it to show his sincerity. But no one dared to try this fortune of "one word worth a thousand gold coins." Lü Buwei was a powerful chancellor at the time, and *Master Lü's Spring and Autumn Annals* was his pride. Who would have the courage to point out its shortcomings? The original meaning of this idiom is to reward a thousand gold coins for changing one word. Later it is used to praise the exquisiteness and high value of poetry and prose.

以羊易牛

Yǐ yáng yì niú

出自《孟子·梁惠王上》

王坐于堂上，有牵牛而过堂下者，王见之，曰："牛何之？"对曰："将以衅钟。"王曰："舍之！吾不忍其觳觫，若无罪而就死地。"对曰："然则废衅钟与？"曰："何可废也？以羊易之！"

Use a Sheep to Replace the Ox

From "Mengzi: King Hui of Liang (Part 1)"

In ancient China, on certain days in temples, people held a sacrificial ceremony called "Xin Zhong," which was to slaughter animals and painted bells with their blood to show piety to the gods and seek their protection. During the sacrificial ceremony, either an ox or a sheep would be killed, and then the head of the ox or sheep was placed on a large wooden plate on the altar for offering sacrifices to the gods, and people would stand in front of the altar to pray. One day, a man came to the capital of Qi State. He walked past the palace hall with an ox. At this time, King Xuan of Qi (c.350–301 BCE) happened to see it at the gate of the hall, and he ordered people to stop the man who was leading the ox and asked: "Where are you going to take the ox?"

The man replied: "I will take it away and kill it to sacrifice to the bell." After hearing this, King Xuan of Qi looked at the ox and said: "This ox has done nothing wrong, it should not die in vain. I can't bear to see it trembling with fear. Let it go!" The man who was leading the ox said: "Your Majesty, you are so kind. Then, would you please abolish the ritual of 'Xin Zhong'?" King Xuan of Qi became serious and said: "How can this ritual be abolished? What about this, use a sheep to replace the ox!" Mengzi heard this and told King Xuan of Qi that because he used a sheep to replace an ox, people would think he was stingy and mean. King Xuan of Qi said: "I just felt sympathy when I saw the ox was afraid." Mengzi said: "Then what about the sheep? Why don't you feel sympathy?" The king was speechless. The king's sympathy was obviously aroused by what he saw, which was emotional rather than rational. He sympathized with the seen ox rather than the unseen sheep. The sheep was truly made a "scapegoat"! Oxen are living creatures, so are sheep. There is no distinction between high and low in life, and there is no difference between sheep and oxen in essence. Using a sheep to replace an ox was a false benevolence or righteousness, deceiving oneself and others, but it did not solve the actual problem.

以逸待劳

Yǐ yì dài láo

出自春秋·孙武《孙子兵法·军争篇》；

孙膑《三十六计·第四计》

以近待远，以佚待劳，以饱待饥，此治力者也。

Waiting for the Enemy to Tire out

From "The Art of War: The Military Battle"
by Sun Wu (c.545–c.470/496 BCE); and
"Thirty-Six Stratagems: Stratagem IV"
by Sun Bin (?–316 BCE)

This idiom suggests that in a battlefield, do not attack first, but wait for the right moment when the enemy tires out before you strike. This strategy requires you to be calm, clearly estimate all the conditions, pay attention to changes at any time and anywhere. When the time is not right, you must be as steady as a rock, but when the opportunity comes, you must be unstoppable. It emphasizes that putting the enemy in a difficult situation does not necessarily require offensive methods, and waiting for the right moment does not mean passively waiting for opportunities but giving full play to subjective initiative to mobilize the enemy, lead the enemy by the nose, make the enemy run around, constantly consume its energy, and wait until the enemy's spirit is exhausted before destroying it.

异军突起

Yì jūn tū qǐ

出自西汉·司马迁《史记·项羽本纪》

[近义词：别树一帜、独树一帜、别开生面]

少年欲立婴便为王，异军苍头特起。

A New Army Suddenly Emerged

From "Records of the Grand Historian:
Biography of Xiang Yu"
by Sima Qian (145–c.86 BCE)

Chen Ying (?–183 BCE) was originally a minor official in Dongyang county, Zhejiang province. In the last years of the Qin dynasty (221–206 BCE), people all over the country could not bear Qin's brutal rule anymore and rebelled. The people of Dongyang county also raised an anti-Qin banner and killed the county magistrate. But they had no leader, so they thought of Chen Ying, who was fair and honest, and unanimously nominated him as the leader. Chen Ying had a high prestige. Within a few dozen days, more than 20,000 people came to him. The soldiers of the rebel army wrapped their heads with blue cloth headscarves to show that they were a new and different army. To expand their own power and enhance their anti-Qin strength, they discussed privately and wanted to make Chen Ying the king, but Chen Ying refused.

Chen Ying's mother said to him earnestly: "Since I married into the Chen family, I have never heard of any distinguished figures among your ancestors. If you become a king, it will be a bad omen, and you must not do it! You'd better submit to others. If you fail, others will not blame you; if you win, you will be considered a meritorious official and can be made a marquis." Chen Ying obeyed his mother's sensible words. At this time, Xiang Liang (?–208 BCE) and his nephew Xiang Yu (232–202 BCE) had already raised an army in Kuaiji. Xiang Liang was a descendant of a prominent family and had a strong appeal. His troops quickly captured Guangling, and then crossed the Huai River, with frequent reports of victory along the way. Uprising troops from all over the country joined Xiang Liang, and Liu Bang (c.256–195 BCE) also joined him in the battle. Therefore, Chen Ying said to everyone: "I, Chen Ying, have limited ability and I am afraid that I will fail everyone's expectations. I heard that Xiang Liang and his ancestors have been generals for generations and are very famous in Chu. Raising an army to fight against Qin is a big deal and they are the only ones who can do it. Let's do it together with them!" The Dongyang uprising army thought Chen Ying's idea was a good one, so they followed him and joined Xiang Liang. Xiang Liang's troops suddenly increased by 60,000 to 70,000, which was a mighty and unstoppable force, and the Qin dynasty's brutal rule became shaky.

因势利导

Yīn shì lì dǎo

出自西汉·司马迁《史记·孙子列传》

善战者因其势而利导之。

Following the Trend to Guide People

From "Records of the Grand Historian:
Biography of Sunzi"
by Sima Qian (145–c.86 BCE)

During the Warring States period (475–221 BCE), Pang Juan (385–342 BCE) was a general of Wei State. He was highly appreciated by King Hui of Wei (400–319 BCE) for his successive victories. However, Pang Juan knew that Sun Bin (382–316 BCE) from Qi State was better than him. Sun Bin was a descendant of Sun Wu (c.545–c.470 BCE), and only he had mastered all the strategies in his ancestral book, *The Art of War*. Pang Juan thus tricked Sun Bin to Wei, and in front of King Hui of Wei, he falsely accused Sun Bin of having a secret communication with Qi State, which led to Sun Bin being punished and having his kneecaps gouged out, and he could no longer stand or walk. Fortunately, an envoy from Qi who was visiting Wei at the time secretly rescued Sun Bin and brought him back to Qi. With the recommendation of General Tian Ji, Sun Bin became a military advisor.

In 342 BCE, King Hui of Wei sent Pang Juan to attack Han State, so Han asked for help from Qi. Tian Ji and Sun Bin were ordered to help Han. Sun Bin did not go directly to rescue Han but went to attack Wei instead. Pang Juan received the emergency document and hurriedly withdrew his troops back to his state. But at this time, the troops of Qi had already entered Wei and were waiting for the right time to attack! Tian Ji asked Sun Bin for advice on how to fight against the Wei army. Sun Bin said: "The Wei army has always looked down on the Qi army. We should take advantage of its weakness, adapt to the situation, and take measures that are beneficial to us to eliminate it. On the first day, we will leave 100,000 soldiers' cooking stoves; on the second day, we will leave 50,000 soldiers' cooking stoves; and on the third day, we will only keep 30,000 soldiers' cooking stoves, so that the Wei army will mistakenly think that our soldiers are running away every day and our strength is getting weaker day by day, so that they will relax their vigilance, and then we will attack them." Tian Ji agreed with the military advisor's strategy very much and acted accordingly.

  Pang Juan was fooled. He led the Wei army to chase the Qi army triumphantly all the way to Maling. At this time, it was already dark, and the terrain of Maling was dangerous, with steep cliffs on both sides and only a small path in the middle. The Wei army could only move forward in the dark. Suddenly, a soldier in front came to report: "The mountain road is blocked by wood." Pang Juan looked and saw that the trees on the roadsides had indeed been cut down, leaving only the largest tree standing there, with a line of large characters faintly visible on the trunk. Pang Juan asked the soldiers to bring torches, and the eight large characters were clearly visible that read: "Pang Juan Must Be Dead Under This Tree." Pang Juan was shocked and hurriedly ordered to retreat, but it was too late. The Qi army, which had been ambushed in the ravines on both sides, fired thousands of arrows at the same time, and the Wei army was immediately in chaos, with countless casualties. Pang Juan knew that he had no way out, so he sighed and drew his sword to commit suicide. From then on, Sun Bin's good reputation of "Following the Trend to Guide People" spread throughout the vassal states, and the military strategy he wrote has been passed down to this day.

游刃有余

Yóu rèn yǒu yú

出自战国·庄周《庄子·养生主》

[近义词：庖丁解牛、挥洒自如、炉火纯青；

反义词：捉襟见肘、力不胜任]

彼节者有间，而刀刃者无厚。

以无厚入有间，恢恢乎，其于游刃必有余地矣。

Doing a Job with Skill and Ease

From "Zhuangzi: Health Master"

During the Warring States period (475–221 BCE), there was a well-known chef in Wei State named Cook Ding (Pao Ding), who was particularly good at slaughtering oxen. When an ox came into his hands, he would coordinate his hands, feet, shoulders, and knees with the scalpel, and the movements were as rhythmic as music. In a short while, the ox was slaughtered, fast and efficient. The reputation of Cook Ding gradually spread. King Hui of Wei (400–319 BCE) was skeptical and went to the kitchen to see for himself. He saw that Cook Ding could easily separate the bones and meat of the ox with his knife, and his movements were very neat. The king was amazed and asked: "Why are you so skilled?"

Cook Ding smiled and said: "Actually, there is nothing special about it. I just figured out the body structure of the ox. When I first learned how to slaughter an ox, I saw a whole ox and had no idea where to start. After 3 years of learning, I knew which bones and meat were on the ox, so I knew what to do when I cut. I just had to cut along the gap between the bones and the meat." King Hui of Wei looked at the sharp knife in Cook Ding's hand and asked: "You must be using a new knife, right?" Cook Ding shook his head and said: "No, I've used this knife for 19 years." The king was very surprised and said in disbelief: "No? I heard that butchers must change knives frequently." Cook Ding replied: "Yes, beginners who are learning to slaughter ox must change their knives every month because their blades often touch bones. Experienced butchers can change their knives once a year because their blades are only used to cut meat. I have used this knife for 19 years and have slaughtered thousands of oxen. Why is it still like new? Because I can do it with ease! The gap between meat and bones is always wider than the blade. If you aim at the gap and insert the blade, isn't it more than enough? How can the blade be blunted?" When the king heard this, he let out a long "Oh," as he gained much inspiration from the words of the chef. This idiom tells people that only by repeated practice, exploring the internal laws of things, and mastering skills proficiently can one do things with ease.

有志者事竟成

Yǒu zhì zhě shì jìng chéng

出自南朝·宋·范晔《后汉书·耿弇传》

[近义词：有志竟成；反义词：胸无大志]

将军前在南阳，建此大策，
常以为落落难合，有志者事竟成也。

Where There Is a Will, There Is a Way

From "Book of the Later Han: Biography of Geng Yan"
by Fan Ye (398–445)

Geng Yan (3–58 CE) was a founding hero of the Eastern Han dynasty (25–220), and was very loyal to Emperor Guangwu of Han, Liu Xiu (5 BCE–57 CE). Soon after establishing the regime, he suggested to the emperor to eliminate all forces and unify the country. However, Liu Xiu was skeptical about whether Geng Yan's plan could be successfully implemented. Geng Yan volunteered to lead the army to attack Zhang Bu (?–32), who occupied Shandong province. At that time, Zhang Bu's power was still relatively strong. His younger brother Zhang Lan led 20,000 soldiers and stationed in Xi'an County, Shandong. Zhang Bu himself had another troop of more than 10,000 soldiers defending in Linzi, 20 km away from Xi'an County. Geng Yan carefully analyzed the situation and thought that although Xi'an County was small, the fortification and the soldiers were strong; while Linzi was large, the fortification and the soldiers were weaker. So, he decided to make a feint attack on Xi'an County but real attack on Linzi.

Zhang Lan was very scared when he saw Geng Yan coming to attack Xi'an County and urged his soldiers to guard strictly. One night, Geng Yan suddenly concentrated his forces and launched a fierce attack on Linzi. The defenders were caught off guard and panicked. In just half a day, they surrendered, and Zhang Lan fled. Geng Yan conquered two places. Zhang Bu was very angry at losing two counties in a row and personally led an army of 200,000 to attack Geng Yan. The two sides fought a bloody battle outside Linzi. The Eastern Han army suffered heavy casualties, and Geng Yan was also wounded by an arrow. Liu Xiu was very worried about Geng Yan, so he personally led a troop to reinforce him. Before the reinforcements arrived, a general suggested to Geng Yan that he should temporarily cease fighting and wait until the reinforcements arrive before launching an attack. But Geng Yan believed that he could not leave the difficulties to others. He endured the arrow wound and fought Zhang Bu desperately, killing countless enemy soldiers from morning to night. When Liu Xiu arrived at Geng Yan's camp, Zhang Bu had already been defeated and fled. Liu Xiu praised Geng Yan in front of all the generals and said: "When General Geng was in Nanyang, he once proposed an important strategy to unify the country. However, at that time, people always thought that it was difficult to do. Now, this suggestion has finally become a reality. It is true that 'where there is a will, there is a way'!"

愚公移山

Yú gōng yí shān

出自列御寇《列子·汤问》

太行、王屋二山，方七百里，高万仞，本在冀州之南，河阳之北。北山愚公者，年且九十，面山而居。惩山北之塞，出入之迂也。聚室而谋曰："吾与汝毕力平险，指通豫南，达于汉阴，可乎？"杂然相许。其妻献疑曰："以君之力，曾不能损魁父之丘，如太行、王屋何？且焉置土石？"杂曰："投诸渤海之尾，隐土之北。"遂率子孙荷担者三夫，叩石垦壤，箕畚运于渤海之尾。邻人京城氏之孀妻有遗男，始龀，跳往助之。寒暑易节，始一反焉。

河曲智叟笑而止之曰："甚矣，汝之不惠！以残年余力，曾不能毁山之一毛，其如土石何？"北山愚公长息曰："汝心之固，固不可彻，曾不若孀妻弱子。虽我之死，有子存焉；子又生孙，孙又生子；子又有子，子又有孙；子子孙孙无穷匮也，而山不加增，何苦而不平？"河曲智叟亡以应。操蛇之神闻之，惧其不已也，告之于帝。帝感其诚，命夸娥氏二子负二山，一厝朔东，一厝雍南。自此，冀之南，汉之阴，无陇断焉。

The Foolish Old Man Removes the Mountains

From "Liezi: Tang's Questions"

by Lie Yukou (450–375 BCE)

Legend has it that in ancient times, there were two mountains in the south of Jizhou and the north of Heyang, one was called Taixing Mountain (today's Taihang Mountain) and the other called Wangwu Mountain. They were majestic, with a radius of 700 miles and a height of tens of thousands of feet. To the north of these two mountains, there lived an old man who was almost 90 years old. Everyone called him "Yugong" (lit. "Foolish Old Man"). Every time Yugong went out, he was blocked by the two mountains and had to go around and take many detours, which was very inconvenient. So Yugong determined to flatten the two mountains. One day, he gathered all his family members and said: "Let's move Taixing and Wangwu Mountains and build a road directly to Yuzhou and Han River. Yes?" Everyone agreed. Only his wife raised a question and asked: "Taixing and Wangwu Mountains are very big and high, there must be loads of soil and stones dug out. Where should we deliver them?" Before Yugong spoke, his children and grandchildren answered in unison: "Just transport them to the Bohai Sea." Yugong nodded in agreement, and his wife smiled with relief. At dawn the next day, Yugong's family set off in a mighty manner. They carried hoes, shoulder poles, baskets, dustpans, and drove donkeys carrying food and water jars, and started to work when arriving at the foot of the mountain.

Yugong was still strong and took the lead; his children and grandchildren followed him closely; some dug, some scooped, some carried, and some lifted, all working enthusiastically. The story of Yugong moving the mountains touched everyone near and far. A little boy from a neighbor's family, only seven or eight years old, also came to help, carrying soil to the Bohai Sea in a small bamboo basket. An old man from Hequ named "Zhisou" (lit. "Clever but Short-Sighted") passed by the site one day. Seeing that Yugong and his team were working hard, he walked up to Yugong and sneered: "You are so foolish! How much energy do you have with your remaining years? I'm afraid you can't even move a tree on the mountain. How can you expect to move the two mountains?" Yugong sighed and said: "Your thoughts are too stubborn to be enlightened!" Then he pulled the little boy from the neighbor's house, touched his shoulder, and said to Zhisou: "You are not as good as a child. Yes, I'm old and may not live long. But I still have sons and grandsons, and my grandsons will have sons and grandsons, there is no end. Whereas these two mountains will not grow higher. If we dig every day, they will be lower every day. Our descendants will keep digging. Can't we flatten these two mountains?" Zhisou had nothing to say and left.

    The mountain god heard all the words that Yugong said to Zhisou and was afraid that Yugong and his family would continue digging endlessly, so the mountain god quickly reported it to the Lord of Heaven. The Lord of Heaven was deeply touched by Yugong's determination and perseverance. One night, he sent two gods to the earth quietly to move Taixing Mountain and Wangwu Mountain, one was relocated to the east of Shuofang, and the other in the south of Yongzhou. From then on, a road leading directly to Yuzhou and Han River appeared in front of Yugong's house, and there were no more mountains blocking the way. Whenever people took this road without any obstacles, they would always think of the scene of Yugong leading his family to move the mountains, and they composed a jingle to praise Yugong:

> Yugong came to move the mountains,
> While his ambitions soared to the sky.
> The mountain god made way for him,
> And Yugong's reputation had spread.

鱼目混珠

Yú mù hùn zhū

出自汉·魏伯阳《参同契·卷上》

[近义词：鱼龙混杂、滥竽充数、

以假乱真、冒名顶替；

反义词：货真价实、黑白分明、

泾渭分明、是非分明]

鱼目岂为珠，蓬蒿不成槚。

Pass off the Fisheye as Pearl

From "Kinship of the Three: Volume 1"

by Wei Boyang (151–221)

In ancient times, there was a man named Manyuan, who had a pearl that was big and round, and it shone with a soft light. Obviously, it was a priceless treasure, he cherished it very much, put it in a box, and locked it carefully. Manyuan had a neighbor named Shouliang, who saw that others always talked about Manyuan's pearl with envy, so he was very jealous. He also wanted to get a pearl himself one day. Once, he went to the market to buy vegetables and suddenly found a fisheye on the ground. The fisheye was big and round. Shouliang thought it was a pearl, so he quickly picked it up and hid it in his arms and went home cheerfully.

He carefully wrapped the fisheye with a piece of red cloth, put it in a box, locked it in the chest, and then went out to show it off. He said proudly: "What's so rare about

Manyuan's pearl? I have one now!" When the neighbors heard that Shouliang also had a pearl, they all asked him to take it out to let everyone see it. But Shouliang waved his hand and walked away, his posture showed he was very proud of it.

After a while, a rich man in the village got sick. The doctor diagnosed him and prescribed a medicine that must be made of powdered pearls to cure him. The rich man knew that Manyuan and Shouliang each had a pearl, so he sent someone to negotiate with them and promised to buy them at a high price. Manyuan and Shouliang were both tempted. They went home to take out their treasured pearls and handed them to the person sent by the rich man. When the neighbors heard about this, they gathered around to watch curiously. Immediately, they could tell the real thing: Manyuan's pearl was shining and dazzling, while Shouliang's 'pearl' was dull. The neighbors laughed and ridiculed Shouliang and said: "You are using a fisheye to pretend to be a pearl!" This idiom refers to passing off fake things as real ones, or inferior things as good ones.

鹬蚌相争，渔翁得利

Yù bàng xiāng zhēng, yú wēng dé lì

出自西汉·刘向《战国策·燕策二》

赵且伐燕，苏代为燕谓惠王曰："今者臣来，过易水。蚌方出曝，而鹬啄其肉，蚌合而箝其喙。鹬曰：'今日不雨，明日不雨，即有死蚌！'蚌亦谓鹬曰：'今日不出，明日不出，即有死鹬！'两者不肯相舍，渔者得而并禽之。"

When the Snipe and the Clam Fight, the Fisherman Wins

From "Strategies of the Warring States: Strategies of Yan II" by Liu Xiang (77–6 BCE)

When Zhao State was about to go to war with Yan State, Su Dai persuaded King Huiwen of Zhao (310–266 BCE) on behalf of Yan and said: "I came here today and passed by the Yi River. I saw a clam coming out of the water to bask in the sun. A snipe flew over to peck at its flesh, and the clam immediately closed its mouth and clamped the snipe's beak. The snipe said: 'If it doesn't rain today or tomorrow, you will die of thirst!' The clam also said to the snipe: 'If you don't retrieve your mouth today or tomorrow, you will starve to death!' Neither of them would give up, so a fisherman caught them both."

约法三章

Yuē fǎ sān zhāng

出自西汉·司马迁《史记·高祖本纪》

[近义词：明文规定；反义词：胡作非为、为所欲为]

与父老约，法三章耳；

杀人者死，伤人及盗抵罪。

余悉除去秦法。

Agreement on the Three Rules of Law

From "Records of the Grand Historian: Annals of Emperor Gaozu"

by Sima Qian (145–c.86 BCE)

Qin II, Ying Huhai (230–207 BCE), was an incompetent emperor, who not only trusted a treacherous minister but also killed many loyal ones. Life was hard for the commoners at the time, so everywhere people rose up to resist Qin's tyranny. There were two men in the army of King Huai of Chu (328–296 BCE) who later influenced Chinese history: Liu Bang (c.256–195 BCE), and Xiang Yu (232–202 BCE). One day, King Huai of Chu said to them: "Whoever enters Guanzhong first can be king." Thus, Liu Bang and Xiang Yu led their troops to the west and north, respectively. Liu Bang encountered little resistance and won several battles. In 207 BCE, Liu Bang again led his troops to enter Qinchuan from the Central Plains and arrived at Xianyang, the capital of the Qin dynasty (221–206 BCE). The King of Qin, Ziying (?–206 BCE), surrendered, offered the imperial seal, and the Qin dynasty officially perished.

After Liu Bang entered the city, he protected or sealed up the important palaces and treasures of the Qin dynasty without doing any harm and withdrew 100,000 troops to Bashang outside the city. To win the hearts of the people, Liu Bang summoned the elders and the outstanding of the counties in Guanzhong and solemnly announced to them: "The harsh laws of the Qin dynasty have caused all of you suffering. Now I have made an agreement with you all that no matter who you are, you must abide by the Three Rules of Law: (1) Those who kill people must be executed; (2) Those who injure people must be punished; and (3) Those who steal must be convicted! In addition, all the complicated and harsh laws of the Qin dynasty are abolished! Officials at all levels should stick to their posts and perform their duties according to their original positions." The seniors and the outstanding all expressed their support for this law. Next, Liu Bang sent people to various counties and villages to publicize the Three Rules of Law, making them known to everyone. The locals were very happy and offered cattle, sheep, wine, and food to convey greetings to Liu Bang's soldiers, but Liu Bang refused to accept them. Because of his resolute implementation of the Three Rules of Law, Liu Bang gained the trust and support of the people and finally won the country and established the Western Han dynasty (206 BCE–23 CE).

运筹帷幄

Yùn chóu wéi wò

出自西汉·司马迁《史记·高祖本纪》

[近义词：握筹布画、运筹决策]

高祖曰："公知其一，未知其二。夫运筹策帷帐之中，决胜于千里之外，吾不如子房。镇国家，抚百姓，给馈饷，不绝粮道，吾不如萧何。连百万之军，战必胜，攻必取，吾不如韩信。此三者，皆人杰也，吾能用之，此吾所以取天下也。项羽有一范增而不能用，此其所以为我擒也。"

Strategize in the Military Tent

From "Records of the Grand Historian:
Annals of Emperor Gaozu"
by Sima Qian (145–c.86 BCE)

Zhang Liang (262–186 BCE) was a founding hero of the Western Han dynasty (206 BCE–23 CE). He was originally from Han State, and his father and grandfather both had served as grand chancellors of Han. After Han was destroyed by Qin, Zhang Liang was determined to revenge. He sold his property and went out to make friends with heroes. Later, he met a warrior and followed him to assassinate Qin Shi Huang (259–210 BCE). Zhang Liang specially cast a large iron hammer weighing 60 kg for this purpose. Unfortunately, the assassination attempt failed, and Zhang Liang was wanted, so he fled to Xiapi (today's Pi County, Jiangsu province). He hid his identity in Xiapi, studied military tactics, while waiting for the opportunity.

Xiapi was very close to Liu Bang's (c.256–195 BCE) hometown Pei County. After Liu Bang started his army, Zhang Liang joined it. However, Zhang Liang was in poor health and had never led troops in battle. Nevertheless, he was resourceful and gave Liu Bang many good strategies. Therefore, Zhang Liang, Xiao He (257–193 BCE), and Han Xin (231–196 BCE) were called the "Three Heroes of the Early Han Dynasty" and became Liu Bang's main counselors. In 202 BCE, after Liu Bang defeated Xiang Yu (232–202 BCE) and gained control of the country, he officially became the emperor, named Emperor Gaozu of Han, and held a grand banquet in Luoyang to celebrate it. During the banquet, he said to his ministers: "We are gathered here today, please do not be shy about what you say. Tell me, how did I gain control of the country? How did Xiang Yu lose it?" Minister Wang Ling (?–181 BCE) and others said: "The emperor gave titles and rewards to his soldiers, so everyone was willing to serve the emperor; Xiang Yu was jealous of others' talents, won a battle, but forgot their contributions, so he lost the country."

Emperor Gaozu of Han smiled and said: "You just know one thing but not the other. You should know that success or failure depends on whether you employ people properly. In terms of planning and winning battles thousands of miles away, I am not as good as Zhang Liang; in terms of guarding the country, comforting the people, supplying military pay, and ensuring food supply, I am not as good as Xiao He; in terms of leading the army, winning every battle and conquering every city, I am not as good as Han Xin. These three are all outstanding people of our time. I can use their strengths, which is the fundamental reason why I have won the country. Xiang Yu had a counselor Fan Zeng [c.277–205 BCE] who was not appointed. How could he win the country?" Everyone admired the insight of Emperor Gaozu of Han. A year later, Zhang Liang was named "Hero." This idiom means that if one can make a good strategic deployment in the early stage, they can succeed without going into the battle.

凿壁偷光

Záo bì tōu guāng

出自刘歆《西京杂记·卷二》

匡衡字稚圭，勤学而无烛，邻人有烛而不逮，衡乃穿壁引其光，以书映之而读之。邑人大姓文不识，家富多书，衡乃为其佣作，而不求偿。主人怪而问之，衡曰：愿得主人书，遍读之。主人感叹，资给以书，遂成大学。

Borrowing Light from Cutting a Hole in the Wall

From "Miscellaneous Records of Western Capital: Volume 2" by Liu Xin (46 BCE–23 CE)

Kuang Heng was diligent and studious, but there were no candles in his house. His neighbor had candles; however, the candlelight could not reach his room. Kuang Heng then cut a hole in the wall to let the light shine on the book he read. There was a rich man in the town called Wen Bushi who had a large collection of books. Kuang Heng volunteered as a servant in his house without asking for pay. The host was very surprised and asked him why, Kuang Heng said: "I hope to read all your books." The host was deeply impressed and lent him all the books they had. Kuang Heng thus became a great scholar afterwards.

朝三暮四

Zhāo sān mù sì

出自《庄子·齐物论》

[近义词：朝秦暮楚、见异思迁、

反复无常、朝令夕改；

反义词：矢志不移、始终不渝、

坚定不移、一如既往]

狙公赋芋，曰："朝三而暮四。"众狙皆怒。曰："然则朝四而暮三。"众狙皆悦。名实未亏而喜怒为用，亦因是也。

Three in the Morning and Four in the Evening

From "Zhuangzi: The Theory of Equality"

During the Warring States period (475–221 BCE), there was an old man in Song State who loved monkeys and kept a large group of them at home. The monkeys followed him around all day, played with him, and were like his children. Therefore, the neighbors called him "Ju Gong" (in ancient Chinese, Ju refers to monkeys). Ju Gong was very good at understanding the monkeys' psyche, and the monkeys also understood Ju Gong's words. They lived together in harmony and happiness. Ju Gong was not well off, and the food supplies were not much. The monkeys always ate voraciously, and each one had a bigger appetite than the other. Ju Gong was very worried.

Ju Gong had to reduce the food supplies for the monkeys, but he was afraid that the monkeys would be upset. So, he enticed them and said: "From now on, I will give you chestnuts every day, three in the morning and four in the evening. Is it enough?" When the monkeys heard that they could only eat three chestnuts in the morning, they were all angry, screamed and jumped up and down. Some tried to grab Ju Gong's fingers, some tried to pull Ju Gong's beard, some tried to tickle Ju Gong, and some hid Ju Gong's shoes, making Ju Gong not to know whether to laugh or cry. Ju Gong pondered for a while and suddenly had an idea. He said to the monkeys with a pleasant tongue: "Okay, okay, stop fighting. Let's change it to four in the morning and three in the evening. Is that okay?" After saying that, he patted a little monkey on the head affectionately. When the monkeys heard that there was one more chestnut in the morning, they were very pleased and shook their heads and tails, showing their happy looks. At the call of the old monkey, all the monkeys bowed down and kowtowed to thank Ju Gong. Ju Gong looked at this scene, stroked his long beard, and smiled. This idiom originally refers to a monkey breeder who fed monkeys with chestnuts and used a trick to deceive the monkeys. Later, it describes the changeable and unpredictable nature of things.

郑人买履

Zhèng rén mǎi lǚ

出自《韩非子·外储说左上》

郑人有欲买履者,先自度其足,而置之其坐。至之市,而忘操之。已得履,乃曰:"吾忘持度。"反归取之。及反,市罢,遂不得履。人曰:"何不试之以足?"曰:"宁信度,无自信也。"

A Zheng Man Buying Shoes

From "Han Feizi: On External Storage (Example 1)"

There was a man in Zheng State who wanted to buy a pair of shoes. He first measured his feet to find the right shoe size, then placed it on his seat. When he went to the market, he forgot to bring the measure. After finding the shoes, he said: "I forgot to bring the measure." So, he went back home to get the measure. When he returned, the market was closed, and he did not get his shoes. Someone asked him: "Why didn't you try them on with your feet?" He replied: "I'd rather trust the measure than my own feet."

指鹿为马

Zhǐ lù wéi mǎ

出自西汉·司马迁《史记·秦二世纪》

[近义词：张冠李戴、颠倒黑白；

反义词：循名责实、实事求是]

赵高欲为乱，恐群臣不听，乃先设验，持鹿献于二世（秦二世皇帝胡亥），曰："马也。"二世笑曰："丞相误邪？谓鹿为马。"问左右，左右或默，或言马以阿顺赵高。或言鹿者，高因阴中诸言鹿者以法。后群臣皆畏高。

Calling a Deer a Horse

From "Records of the Grand Historian: Annals of Qin II Emperor"

by Sima Qian (145–c.86 BCE)

After Qin Shi Huang's (259–210 BCE) death, his close aide, eunuch Zhao Gao (258–207 BCE), wanted to take the opportunity to usurp the power of the court. Therefore, he concealed the news of emperor's death and forged an imperial decree to make Qin Shi Huang's eldest son Fusu (241–210 BCE) commit suicide and make Qin Shi Huang's second son Huhai (230–207 BCE) the crown prince. Then he announced the national mourning. After that, Zhao Gao helped Huhai become the Emperor Qin II, and he became the Grand Chancellor and mastered the military and political power of the Qin dynasty (221–206 BCE). Zhao Gao's ambition increasingly grew, and he gradually had the evil idea of usurping the throne.

However, Zhao Gao still had concerns about whether the officials in the court would obey him. He thought about it day and night and finally produced a wicked idea. One day during court session, Zhao Gao brought a deer and said to Emperor Qin II: "I present this horse to the emperor." Qin II said with a smile: "Are you kidding me, Grand Chancellor? It's obviously a deer, how can you say it's a horse?" Zhao Gao said seriously: "Who dares to joke with the emperor! This is obviously a horse. If the emperor does not believe it, you can ask the officials in the court to see if I'm right." Qin II really doubted his own eyes. He scanned around with an inquiring look, and then asked: "Do you think it is a deer or a horse?" Those upright ministers who did not want to speak against their conscience or confuse right and wrong, but were afraid of offending Zhao Gao and causing disaster, simply kept silent. Zhao Gao's confidants and those ministers who were trying to curry favor with him said: "The Grand Chancellor is right; this is a horse!" Only a few ministers who were not afraid of Zhao Gao dared to say bluntly: "This is a deer, not a horse!" Zhao Gao believed that those who told the truth were unwilling to submit to his command, so he secretly wrote down their names and tried every means to frame and punish them. One by one, they were charged with various crimes, expelled from the court, or killed.

纸上谈兵

Zhǐ shàng tán bīng

出自西汉·司马迁《史记·廉颇蔺相如列传》

[近义词：坐而论道、高谈阔论、言之无物；
反义词：言之有物、躬行实践、脚踏实地]

赵括自少时学兵法，言兵事，以天下莫能当。尝与其父奢言兵事，奢不能难，然不谓善。括母问奢其故，奢曰："兵，死地也，而括易言之。使赵不将括即已；若必将之，破赵军者必括也！"及括将行，其母上书言于王曰："括不可使将。"王曰："何以？"对曰："始妾事其父，时为将，身所奉饭耳进食者以十数，所友者以百数；大王及宗室所赏赐者尽以予军吏士大夫，受命之日，不问家事。今括一旦为将，东向而朝，军吏无敢仰视之者，王所赐金帛，归藏于家，而日视便利田宅可买者买之。王以为何如其父？父子异心，愿王勿遣。"王曰："母置之，吾已决矣。"括母因曰："王终遣之，即如有不称，妾得无随坐乎？"王许诺。赵括既代廉颇，悉更约束，易置军吏。秦将白起闻之，纵奇兵，佯败走，而绝其粮道，分断其军为二，士卒离心。四十余日，军饿，赵括出锐卒自搏战，秦军射杀赵括。括军败，数十万之众遂降秦，秦悉坑之。

Discussing Military Strategy on Paper

From "Records of the Grand Historian:
Biographies of Lian Po and Lin Xiangru"
by Sima Qian (145–c.86 BCE)

During the Warring States period (475–221 BCE), Zhao State had a well-known general named Zhao She. He had a son called Zhao Kuo (290–260 BCE) who was familiar with various military books since childhood and often talked eloquently with his father about how to use troops. Zhao Kuo was proud of himself and thought he was invincible. However, Zhao She was worried about his son and said: "War is a matter of life and death, but Zhao Kuo made it sound very simple. In future, it will be fine if Zhao State does not employ Zhao Kuo as a general, otherwise it will be defeated!" Before his death, Zhao She called Zhao Kuo to his bedside and said: "You're not the right person to be a general, so don't force yourself to do it." He also told his wife: "If the King of Zhao wants to make Zhao Kuo a general in the future, you must refuse, otherwise it will be a loss of the army and a disgrace to the state!" In 259 BCE, Qin sent troops to attack Zhao. The Zhao army, commanded by Lian Po (327–243 BCE), resisted in Changping (today's Gaoping county, Shanxi province). Although Lian Po was old, he had much combat experience. Seeing that the Qin army was stronger, he adopted a defending but not fighting strategy, no matter how the Qin army provoked him. Fearing the situation would be difficult to deal with if it continued, Qin sent spies to Zhao to spread rumors that Lian Po was old and timid; the person the Qin army feared most was Zhao Kuo, and no other generals could do it.

King Xiaocheng of Zhao (?–245 BCE) believed the rumors and removed Lian Po and appointed Zhao Kuo as the general. Lin Xiangru was ill at the time and was very anxious when he heard about this. He said: "Zhao Kuo has only read some military books and has no actual combat experience. How can he be sent to command the army?" Zhao

Kuo's mother also went to meet King Zhao in the palace and said that her son could not be the general. However, King Zhao had made up his mind and would not listen to anyone's objection. Zhao Kuo finally became the chief general of the Zhao army and arrived at Changping in a majestic manner. He removed Lian Po's strategy of protracted warfare and replaced many generals. Then, he led his army to break out of the Zhao camp to attack. Qin general Bai Qi (332–257 BCE) was very pleased and set a trap to lure Zhao Kuo. When the two armies faced each other, the Qin army pretended to be defeated. Zhao Kuo led his troops to chase them but was surrounded by the Qin army. Then, the Qin army cut off the Zhao army's food supply. More than a month later, the Zhao army ran out of food. Zhao Kuo was forced to break out and was shot to death by the Qin army. More than 400,000 Zhao troops were also destroyed. This idiom originally refers to reading military books but not being able to use them flexibly. Later, it describes empty talks about theory but not being able to solve practical problems.

智者千虑，必有一失

Zhì zhě qiān lǜ, bì yǒu yì shī

出自春秋·晏婴《晏子春秋·杂下》

[近义词：智者千虑，或有一失；

反义词：愚者千虑，必有一得]

圣人千虑，必有一失；愚人千虑，必有一得。

Even the Wisest Will Make Mistakes

From "Annals of Master Yan: Miscellaneous (Part 2)"

by Yan Ying (578–500 BCE)

Duke Jing of Qi (?–490 BCE) had a grand chancellor named Yan Ying (578–500 BCE), who was intelligent, fair, and honest. He killed arrogant warriors, improved relations with neighboring states, and stopped the extravagance of Duke Jing. In the 32nd year of Duke Jing (516 BCE), a comet appeared. Duke Jing thought it was a sign of impending disaster and planned to pray for relief. Yan Ying said: "If you are the only one praying to heaven for relief, while tens of thousands of people are complaining, to whom the heaven will listen? Instead of praying, it is better to reduce the burden on the people and their suffering." Duke Jing believed him, and Qi State became stronger.

Duke Jing considered that Yan Ying had made great contributions, and after seeing that he lived in poverty, Duke Jing wanted to reward him with a thousand gold coins. Yan Ying declined the reward three times. Duke Jing said unhappily: "You are too stubborn. In the past, a famous grand chancellor in our state, Guan Zhong [725–645 BCE], was given reward by Duke Huan of Qi [?–643 BC], and he did not refuse it. Why did you refuse it?" Yan Ying said: "A reward of a thousand gold coins should be given to someone for their meritorious service. I have not done any meritorious service, so I do not deserve the reward. As the proverb says: 'Even the wisest will make mistakes, and even the foolish will get it right once.' I am certainly not as good as Guan Zhong. I may be a fool, but I may be more correct than Guan Zhong in refusing the reward!" He eventually declined the reward and lived a humble life. This idiom suggests that no matter who you are, no matter how smart you are, you will always have to think more. There will be contradictions between thinking and doing, but if you understand the relationship between them, you will be tranquil and self-reliant, and it will not add to your worries or regrets.

紫气东来

Zǐ qì dōng lái

出自西汉 • 刘向《列仙传》

[近义词：万紫千红]

老子西游，关令尹喜望见有紫气浮关，而老子果乘青牛而过也。

Purple Air Coming from the East

From "Biographies of Immortals"

by Liu Xiang (77–6 BCE)

Laozi (c.571–471 BCE) was very knowledgeable and wise, and served as a librarian in the Zhou dynasty (1046–221 BCE). When he was about 70 years old, wars between states often broke out. Laozi predicted that there would be bigger wars coming, so he resigned from his post, rode a green ox, left Luoyang, headed west, and passed through Hangu Pass to find a secluded place. Legend has it that before Laozi passed through Hangu Pass, the commander of the pass, Yinxi, saw purple air coming from the east, and knew that there would be a sage passing through it. As expected, Laozi came, riding a green ox. So, purple air coming from the east was a great scene when Laozi arrived, and the story has been passed down through the ages. Ancient Chinese believed that purple was related to being an official, and many official uniforms were in purple. This idiom is often used for an auspicious sign on a Chinese scholar's house gate.

自相矛盾

Zì xiāng máo dùn

出自《韩非子·难一》

[近义词：首尾乖互、鬻矛誉盾；

反义词：天衣无缝、自圆其说、无懈可击]

楚人有鬻盾与矛者，誉之曰："吾盾之坚，物莫能陷也。"又誉其矛曰："吾矛之利，于物无不陷也。"或曰："以子之矛陷子之盾，何如？"其人弗能应也。众皆笑之。夫不可陷之盾与无不陷之矛，不可同世而立。

Self-Contradiction

From "Han Feizi: Difficulties (Part 1)"

There was a man from Chu State who sold both spears and shields. One day, he came to the market and shouted: "Selling spears! Selling shields!" Soon, a group of people gathered around to watch it. He raised a shield and said: "Look at this shield, it is made of fine materials with great craftsmanship, and it is extremely strong. No matter how sharp the object is, it can't pierce it!" He put down the shield and picked up a spear and said: "Look at this spear, it has been hammered and forged, and it is extremely sharp. No matter how strong the object is, it can pierce it with one poke!" An intelligent man among the bystanders immediately asked: "What will happen if you use your spear to pierce your shield?" The seller was speechless. This idiom refers to actions and words that are inconsistent or contradictory.

坐山观虎斗

Zuò shān guān hǔ dòu

出自西汉·刘向《战国策·秦策二》

[近义词：隔岸观火、作壁上观、

坐收渔利、鹬蚌相争，渔翁得利]

有两虎诤人而斗者，管庄子将刺之。管与止之，曰："虎者，戾虫；人者，甘饵也。今两虎争人而斗，小者必死，大者必伤。子待伤虎而刺之，则是一举而兼两虎也。无刺一虎之劳，而有刺两虎之名。"

Sit on the Mountain and Watch the Tigers Fight

From "Strategies of the Warring States: Strategies of Qin II" by Liu Xiang (77–6 BCE)

During the Warring States period (475–221 BCE), Han and Wei states attacked each other for a whole year without stopping. King Huiwen of Qin (356–311 BCE) wanted to take the opportunity to send troops, so he summoned his ministers to discuss the matter. Some ministers advocated sending troops, while others did not, leaving King Huiwen at a loss. A guest official from Chu named Chen Zhen happened to return to Qin at this time, and King Huiwen of Qin asked him for his opinion. Chen Zhen did not answer King Huiwen's question directly but told a story vividly. This story is recorded in the *Postscript to the Spring and Autumn Annals*:

"During the Spring and Autumn period (770–476 BCE), there was a man from Lu State named Bian Zhuangzi who was very brave and dared to fight with tigers. One day, two tigers appeared on the mountain, and he hurriedly ran up the mountain with his sword. A waiter at the mountain inn asked him what he was doing on the mountain, he said he was going to stab those two tigers to death! The waiter grabbed his hand and dissuaded him: 'At this moment, the two tigers are fighting over a cow. The result of their fierce fight is that the weaker one will be killed, and the stronger one will also be injured. At that time, it will be easier for you to go up the mountain to deal with the remaining tiger! Moreover, you can also win the reputation of stabbing two tigers to death.' Bian Zhuangzi took the waiter's advice, and later he got the two tigers without much effort."

King Huiwen of Qin listened to the story with great interest and immediately understood Chen Zhen's intention. He decided to postpone the dispatch of troops, allowing Han and Wei to fight. After a while, Han was indeed defeated, and Wei was seriously damaged. King Huiwen of Qin then dispatched his troops with confidence and won the victory. This phrase suggests that in various conflicts, if the opposing parties are stalemated, both sides will suffer losses, and the third party will reap the benefits. It also indicates that when dealing with difficult situations, one should strike at the best time, which can often achieve twice the result with half the effort.

www.ingramcontent.com/pod-product-compliance
Lightning Source LLC
Chambersburg PA
CBHW081352070526
44583CB00020B/2536